Histories of War

Histories of War

Jeremy Black

Pen & Sword
MILITARY

First published in Great Britain in 2024 by
Pen & Sword Military
An imprint of Pen & Sword Books Limited
Yorkshire – Philadelphia

Copyright © Jeremy Black 2024

ISBN 978 1 03610 148 0

The right of Jeremy Black to be identified as
Author of this Work has been asserted by him in accordance
with the Copyright, Designs and Patents Act 1988.

A CIP catalogue record for this book is
available from the British Library

All rights reserved. No part of this book may be reproduced or
transmitted in any form or by any means, electronic or mechanical
including photocopying, recording or by any information storage and
retrieval system, without permission from the Publisher in writing.

Typeset by Mac Style
Printed in the UK by CPI Group (UK) Ltd, Croydon, CR0 4YY.

Pen & Sword Books Limited incorporates the imprints of After
the Battle, Atlas, Archaeology, Aviation, Discovery, Family History,
Fiction, History, Maritime, Military, Military Classics, Politics,
Select, Transport, True Crime, Air World, Frontline Publishing, Leo
Cooper, Remember When, Seaforth Publishing, The Praetorian Press,
Wharncliffe Local History, Wharncliffe Transport, Wharncliffe True
Crime and White Owl.

For a complete list of Pen & Sword titles please contact

PEN & SWORD BOOKS LIMITED
47 Church Street, Barnsley, South Yorkshire, S70 2AS, England
E-mail: enquiries@pen-and-sword.co.uk
Website: www.pen-and-sword.co.uk
or
PEN AND SWORD BOOKS
1950 Lawrence Rd, Havertown, PA 19083, USA
E-mail: uspen-and-sword@casematepublishers.com
Website: www.penandswordbooks.com

For
George Garnett

Contents

Preface		viii
Acknowledgements		x
List of Abbreviations		xi
Chapter 1	Issues	1
Chapter 2	Mediums	25
Chapter 3	Official Views	45
Chapter 4	The Popular Buzz	55
Chapter 5	Refighting The Last War?	60
Chapter 6	Prior to the Last Half-Millennium, –1500	69
Chapter 7	Toward the Modern? 1500–1770	87
Chapter 8	Revolution and Technology, 1770–1914	109
Chapter 9	Writing the World Wars	136
Chapter 10	Engaging with a Changing Present, 1945–2023	154
Chapter 11	Confronting the Future	174
Chapter 12	Conclusions	191
Notes		196
Index		207

Preface

'Vietnam,' 'Iraq,' 'Ukraine,' the abbreviations of combat resonate, and with equivalents across countries. Offering apparent lessons, often themselves contested with great bitterness, these lessons become the building blocks not only of military studies but of history as a whole. As with so much in offering historical accounts, easy to do, but real people lost their lives to enable others to affirm lessons; and others will also die as a result. For the discussion of past wars is not only central to military history but also to the present preparation for future conflict.

Complementing my *The Geographies of War* (2022), this book will use this urgent situation to throw light across the subject. It addresses the fundamental point that, in confronting the challenge of the future, we are inevitably, incessantly and strongly influenced by the past. It is not only a data set, but also a space for the framing of attitudes and assumptions, indeed the provider of examples as well as concepts and vocabulary. This process involves choice.

In 2022, celebrating the 350th anniversary of the birth of Peter the Great (r. 1697–1725), Vladimir Putin affirmed a clear link across the centuries. Peter was inaccurately presented as having 'reclaimed' true Russian territory, and 'it is now our own destiny to reclaim and fortify. Almost nothing has changed. It can be surprising when you start to understand this.' In practice, the comparison is a false one in terms of context, goals, means and success, but what is striking is this sense of continuity.

In practice, the range of histories of war that were, and are, available for exposition is a very wide one. Historians choose to write military history in particular ways, to include and to omit, and to do so for specific reasons. Usually, however, the method followed is to consider only individual states for limited periods, and only certain of the possible consequences. Indeed, it is usual in practice to then use that consideration as the perspective for analysis. This is unfortunate. It is necessary to range widely if light is to be thrown on war, history, and the broad currents of social understanding that helped frame the response to conflict.

It is important to note that history does not have a fixed meaning and therefore method. This is true not only of contrasts between cultures, but also within them. Thus, in eighteenth-century Britain, history was a term deployed to suggest truth, as in the accuracy about behaviour shown in novels, rather than being restricted simply to factual accounts as is at least the theory today. The use of history in this fashion in the eighteenth century, a use found across the past, in part reflected the extent to which writers as a whole sought a voice with which they could influence their readers, a voice with authority. History to many contemporaries meant narrative, but was also employed to suggest particularly authentic information.

As an example of overlaps, the fact of battle could also be covered in fiction. For example, George II's victory at Dettingen in 1743 played a role in Tobias Smollett's novel *Roderick Random* which appeared five years later. Smollett, who had served in the British navy, also included a vivid passage in *Roderick Random* describing an engagement with a French warship:

'the head of the officer of the marines, who stood near me, being shot off, bounced from the deck athwart my face, leaving me well nigh blinded with brains …a drummer … received a great shot in his belly, which tore out his entrails, and he fell flat on my breast.'[1]

And so also for other formats for depicting the past. Thus, the audience at Drury Lane on 1 January 1785 saw *The Repulse of the Spaniards before the Rock of Gibraltar*, an episode from four years earlier.

This study is designed to clarify issues and ask questions. The emphasis is contextual, global and non-linear. Conflict is too protean and universal to fix as a phenomenon, and then to chart and explain accordingly, the approach so generally taken in histories of war. Instead, in clarification and questioning, we can glimpse, at times grasp, the complexities that help pose risk to the practitioner and obstacles for the commentator. War is too important to be left to the ease of facile analysis, and, whether as participants or observers, of past, present and future, we owe a duty of understanding to those who risked, fought and suffered in our past.

Acknowledgements

Life provides the learning experiences for thought, and so also with my work and this book. I have benefited during many years working on this subject from meeting military practitioners and authors, and from speaking across the world. This is not my first attempt at military history. Each time I try to survey the field anew, I cannot expect readers to be familiar with all or any of my earlier works, but I hope some will be tempted to locate this book as part of a larger whole, both of my work and, more significantly, with reference to that of others. For this book, I found a 2018 Exeter workshop on 'the Analogy Trap? Thucydides, History and Theory in the Age of Trump,' a 2023 invitation to speak to the Foreign Policy Research Institute on the Future of War, 2022, 2023 and 2024 presentations for the Indonesian Military Academy, and a 2023 addresses to the annual conferences at the World War Two museums at Gdańsk and New Orleans particularly helpful. Listening and reading have been of value throughout, and form the basis for this acknowledgement. I have profited greatly from the comments of Kathryn Barbier, Ian Beckett, Pete Brown, Kevin Farrell, Bill Gibson, Stephen Morillo, Thomas Otte, Kaushik Roy and Ken Swope on earlier drafts of this book. They are not responsible for the views expressed, nor for errors that remain. With thanks also to Harriet Fielding for excellent desk-editing. It is a great pleasure to dedicate this book to George Garnett, a school and university contemporary, distinguished academic, and very wise friend.

List of Abbreviations

BL   London, British Library, Department of Manuscripts
EHR   *English Historical Review*
JMH   *Journal of Military History*
NA   London, National Archives

Chapter 1

Issues

'The large increase in the number of rifles in the Mullah's possession and the consequent discard of the spear ... whereas in the past the training of troops in Somaliland could, in the main, be carried out with a view to meeting one form of savage warfare, namely the Dervish rush in bush country, troops must now be trained to readily adapt themselves to a more varied form of fighting which will, in some degree, resemble hill warfare in India.'[1]

The last was a reference to the North-West Frontier of British India, which is now that of Pakistan. This British intelligence report of 1919 addressed what appeared to be an intractable situation in what was then part of modern Somalia, but which the British claimed as British Somaliland. The British noted that the past, in the shape of the background to existing training systems, had to be adaptable. Indeed it had to be fed by the new past of learning from more recent experience. Transferring skills acquired elsewhere, a key military requirement, in this case from World War One (1914–18), the British succeeded in doing so in British Somaliland, applying decisive force in 1920, including a successful surprise air attack on the Mullah's base, to end this resistance. However, disease may also have played an important role.

Thereafter, British Somaliland was secure until rapidly conquered by Italian forces in 1940 soon after Italy entered the war. This was one of the many campaigns of World War Two that tend to be ignored and subsumed into the more general narrative of what was, in practice, a highly complex struggle. In large part, the rapid fall soon after of Italian East Africa, which included the speedy recapture of British Somaliland, was highly consequential, although even that struggle tends to be a forgotten war. And that despite the scale of the conflict there. Moreover, the consequences had the British failed would have been serious as many troops would have been required to contain the possibilities had the Italians retained control, and the British position in the Middle East and the western Indian Ocean would have been endangered had their forces not been available and had Britain's strategic depth been lessened. However, the selection of topics for recollection is one shot through with issues of choice including, in this case, the total irrelevance of the Italo-British War in East Africa to the public history of the successor states in the region.

Success today, and in the future, are the prime concerns, indeed commitments, both of the military and of those who comment on war. These are in theory and practice different concerns to much military history. Instead, there is a vast engagement with the latter subject for a number of purposes and across a sphere that reaches from novels to stamps, plays to statues, scholarship to juvenilia, sermons to television, as well as much else. In tone, the range of military history is from the popular to the more judicious, and the partisan to the impartial, not that there is any clear correspondence. Instead, there can be a degree of impartiality in the more popular, not least in 'face of battle' accounts that aim to provide both sides of the story.[2]

In practice, as this book seeks to show, there are many, repeated and often unintentional overlaps between military and public discussion in categories, forums, approaches, intentions and tones. In other words, the culture of the military is not differentiated from a wider military culture. Both are suffused with social values and concerns, and thus draw on popular culture(s) as a whole. This situation can be seen across the range of military concerns, throughout time, and in all states whatever their formal constitution.

Yet, there are also major contrasts in military history between the practical and the popular. In particular, this is so in the case of strategy, most of the writing on which deals with theory that is intended of value for the military, and is unrelated to popular discussion. The discussion of strategy also presents a distinctive history. with respect to the West, notably in America. Much of this writing is a meditation on the work of Carl von Clausewitz, and, related to that, often a search for alternatives, including, sometimes, the author of whatever is the piece in question. This work has its interest, notably for military politics and intellectual thought, and its value as a source and means of reflection and/or particular expositions. Nevertheless, the extent to which strategic theory offers much as a guidance to what choices are made by commanders and how they are implemented is problematic. Indeed, as so often with theory, the argument for such influence rests more on assertion than on hard evidence.

The historical significance of these claims varies. That commanders, in the modern age of staff colleges, were lectured to about strategic issues and read theorists does not establish that they were influenced by them, although that is not a point adequately, or at all, discussed by theorists. Instead, there could have been 'confirmation bias,' in some form or other, both in terms of commanders finding support for what they wanted to do anyway, and because they could believe it appropriate to cite theorists. Such 'confirmation bias', we might even say 'conformation bias,' is also found with commentators, including historians.

Moreover, theorists could seek to argue for their personal influence, as with Basil Liddell Hart and his claims with regard both to German *blitzkrieg* in 1939–41 and to Israeli methods in 1956 and 1967 in defeating much larger Arab armies. That, however, did not establish such influence, and indeed there has been considerable scepticism about Liddell Hart's claims.[3] This point about the questionable nature of supposed influence is more generally apparent. In the case of Liddell Hart and his more thoughtful contemporary, J.F.C. Fuller, both men also wrote military history both of their particular lifetime and more generally across history. So also with some commanders, notably Field Marshal Montgomery, while it was common for commanders in both world wars to provide justification memoirs that were presented as a form of history.

A key instance of modern military thought and historical commentary, indeed possibly its inherent characteristic, is the argument that capability and effectiveness intrinsically require the active understanding and embrace of change. This argument, however, can be seen as inherently problematic, both in terms of the value based on change and with respect to the processes involved in implementing this appreciation.

The emphasis on change plays a central role in the teleological, indeed Whiggish, assumptions about improvement with time, state control and industrialisation, that are so important to military history. Indeed, much of the writing is concerned with the search for dynamism, indeed a magic bullet, in the shape of major change, and one that other states, indeed civilisations, do not match. Linked to this, comes the questionable assumptions of the existence of a paradigm offered by a supposed model power, for example Spain in late sixteenth century Western Europe, setting the pattern for other states, or as a related point, a clear and readily apparent hierarchy in military capability, and of an obvious tasking model for the military. In short, the history of war operates across an isotropic (uniform) surface, with the variant apparently set by technological or other developments that can be understood as of universal significance.

These are in practice convenient but lazy approaches that avoid the real problem of assessing the nature of circumstances. The latter include, of course, change, which is generally far from revolutionary, however the latter is defined and asserted. Far from being a free-floating variable, let alone one determining the other elements of warfare and, as it were, defining them, the processes, possibilities and status summarised as change were interactive and in large part dependent on these other elements. This was notably so due to the role of perception in helping determine the understanding, impact, and response to change.

Aside from change, the analysis of war itself in part reflects its definition and classification. More particularly, there is the degree to which, first, war can exist without armed conflict, as in war on want, cancer, et al, and, secondly, the relationship between such armed conflict and what can be seen as illegal activity that may or may not be regarded as war. For example, 'wars on drugs' involve fighting but that is usually treated as a form of law enforcement. On the other hand, rebellions or revolts entailed warfare, even if the authorities wished to treat them without accepting combatant practices, as, very differently, with slave rebellions[4] or terrorist campaigns, such as those of the Provisional IRA in Northern Ireland. The definition of terrorism itself has been very affected by political contexts and pressures.[5]

Alongside this issue comes the rhetoric of war as when Donald Trump was indicted in 2023 on the charge of misusing intelligence documents. Andy Brigs, a Republican congressman, tweeted on 9 June 'We have now reached a war phase' and another, Clay Higgins, used the rhetoric of military operations, describing the indictment as 'a perimeter probe from the oppressors.'

These circumstances provide specific tasks and particular requirements, thus ensuring that change to meet one set may not work well for another. The American military of 1963 was configured for conflict with the Soviet Union, but not for the requirements of war in Vietnam, while the American preparedness for conventional operations that helped lead to the rapid defeat of Iraq in 1991 and, again, 2003, did not translate to the necessary capability in counter insurgency operations thereafter. However, as so often when discussing explanations of change, it is easier to assert a cause-and-effect than to demonstrate one. Indeed, in these particular cases, stressing deficiencies in American doctrine may lead to an underrating of the significance of the strength of the opposition, contextual issues, and poor strategy. Each played a major role in the serious difficulties encountered in Vietnam, Iraq and Afghanistan. So also with mismatches for other militaries, indeed possibly inevitably so.

Aside from the difficulties in evaluating change, there is, separately, the problem with assuming timeless characteristics, both individual and collective, in conflict. To do so entails underplaying the changing nature of war. The latter is the case both in terms of the phenomenon itself and with reference to explanations of it.

Theory and its influence in the age of staff colleges is one matter, but how about the prior situation? What were the relevant texts or non-textual histories then? Then theory as a defined topic may well have been limited in scope and content, and not least because there was scant use of a vocabulary that approximates to what would later be codified as war or seen as strategy, a point that is even clearer on the global scale. At the same time, as a caveat to this discussion, and that even for recent times, there is no 'Ur'[6] or fundamental state of, or for, strategy, or indeed war, and thus no one description of either. In an important element of both classification and analysis, that is so whether or not we are considering theory or practice. Instead, there are significant variations, with a variety of factors, contexts and spheres (the words all have differing connotations) at play, some overlapping, including chronological, cultural, religious, political, ideological and service, elements or axes.

Vocabulary in this and other respects evades precision and invites qualification, which is an aspect of what should be seen as the inherently subjective nature of military commentary; although most writers do not accept that. Thus, for example, they write of the Western way of war while knowing little or anything about most of the West and, instead, assuming that it is somehow defined by a paradigm power, always the one that is the subject-specialism of the author in question. This is a common fault that is far from restricted to military historians. So also with the very different tendency to marginalise or at least underplay naval affairs in many general histories of war.

Indeed, there are many problems in theorising military history, some of them systemic to the conceptualisation and methodology. Illustrating the difficulty of fitting the development of a military technology into a pattern of historical exposition, and the extent to which the latter could take precedence, David Hume, a leading British historian and philosopher, as well as a former diplomat, reflected in 1778 on artillery and the conundrums it apparently posed:

> 'improvements have been continually making on this furious engine, which, though it seemed contrived for the destruction of mankind, and the overthrow of empires, has in the issue rendered battles less bloody, and has given greater stability to civil societies. Nations, by its means, have been brought more to a level: conquests have become less frequent and rapid: success in war has been reduced nearly to be a matter of calculation: And any nation, overmatched by its enemies, either yields to their demands, or secures itself by alliances against their violence and invasion.'[7]

In the event, Hume was to be proven totally incorrect. This is more generally a pattern in predictions about the military future. That failure is significant as a view of the past is generally deployed to support an interpretation for the future, and this view is commonly both partial and misleading.

Variations in the meaning, applicability, and usage of categories do not prevent discussion in terms of war, strategy, theory and capability. However, these variations underline how difficult it is to argue with reference to precise categories and classifications. Indeed, readers will notice contrasts in content, categorisation and tone in what I write here and more generally. That deliberate approach reflects the correct situation. It is clearly framed by the specific elements of particular military cultures. These are crucial, not the idea of an axiomatic *a priori* set of determining definitions of for example war or strategy that somehow operate in a diachronic fashion across history, enabling ready comparisons across time.

The pursuit of such definitions has been one of the major mistakes of part of the literature on war, and, more specifically, of strategic theory. It is more generally symptomatic of a fascination with categories and philosophy, and philosophy of a certain type. In contrast, an acceptance of the porosity of conceptual and practical usage, and, even more, categorisation in the past is more appropriate. Thus, for example, rather than a consistent separation and contrast between the military and policing, as suggested by prominent Anglo-American commentators, there is considerable overlap in practice and indeed discussion.

One aspect of engagement with both the laws on war and classic strategic theory is to argue that they tend to do violence to the past by seeking to reduce it to precisions and even quasi-mathematical prediction, including proscriptive rules, whether legal or axiomatic. In contrast, the study of military activity and strategic practice represents an engagement with the realities of the past in their range, variety, contexts and conceptual imprecision. It is the very extent of the latter that makes war and strategy workable as concepts, for, if any human phenomenon is handled in too precise a fashion, it becomes of limited value and applicability. This can be seen for example in attempts to establish clear distinctions between war and control, strategy and policy or between strategic and operational dimensions. So also with employing such a pattern of classification-markers in order to differentiate periods of time, such as ancient, medieval and modern and variants thereof; or types of military activity, as with supposed essentials of medieval warfare or naval strategy or insurgency strategy, and so on.

This point can be taken further to consider the looseness of theory and the extent to which in reality it was understood and/or applied in terms of particular circumstances. As a result, practice created theory, just as perception produced history. That axiom, however, is too pat for this author who emphasises, instead, the contingent, conjunctural and indeterminate. Yet, there is also a critical point here about the supposed direction of influence from theory to practice, one analogous to other systems of belief and thought. Theory, instead, might have been better understood in terms of the application of example, such that the direction of influence is really from practice to theory. The crucial relevant dataset is not the writings of those seen, notably by themselves, as theorists, but rather the past and the differing ways in which it was perceived and presented. Thus examples from history were repeatedly deployed. For example, Alfred von Schlieffen, Chief of the German General Staff from 1891 to 1906, employed Hannibal's crushing victory over the Romans at Cannae in 216 BCE, on which he had published a study, to conceptualise his strategy prior to World War One, and notably the possibility of delivering a rapid and total victory over France. In the event, the German offensive in 1914 was not to deliver this victory, but that of 1914 over the Russian invaders of East Prussia was to be renamed Tannenberg in order to draw on the resonance of what the Germans presented as a heroic defeat there in 1410 at the hands of a Polish-Lithuanian force. The Germans presented the 1914 battle as a justified revenge.[8] Again, there is the frequent modern use as mental props of episodes such as 'Munich' or 'Suez,' 'Vietnam' or 'Iraq'; with the usage itself in practice contestable. Both this usage and the controversies are instructive aspects of the histories of war.

In June 2023, Vladimir Putin, the Russian leader, responded to the rebellion he faced from the Wagner group, by emphasising history, beginning with his characterisation of the Ukraine war:

> 'Russia today is leading the most difficult war for its future, repelling the aggression of neo-Nazis and their handlers.... We fight for ... the right to remain Russia, a state with 1,000 years of history... actions splitting our unity ... a strike in the back of our country and our people. Exactly this strike was dealt in 1917 when the country was in World War One, but its victory was stolen. Intrigues, and arguments behind the army's back turned out to be the greatest catastrophe, destruction of the army and the state, loss of huge territories, and resulting in a tragedy and a civil war. Russians were killing Russians, brothers killing brothers. But the beneficiaries were various political chevaliers of fortune and foreign powers who divided the country, and tore it into parts.
>
> We will not let this happen.'

In another historical reference, in the speech Putin made reference to *smuta*, meaning strife, a term used to describe the anarchic Time of Troubles after the death of Ivan IV, the Terrible, in 1584.

So also with the Serb determination to control Kosovo, a determination linked to an obsession with the battles there in 1389 and, to a lesser extent, 1448 against the Turks and the legends built around the former, legends in which martyrdom, religion and nationalism played a key role. It was deployed for example in the world wars and in a victimisation narrative employed in the 1990s.[9]

In these and other cases, established memories and readings were shaped into military history and, more particularly, what has been termed, for the purpose of analysis, strategic culture. This shaping, and the supposed contents of individual national strategic cultures, represents a major form of military history. It is one in which strategic questions, and analyses lend themselves to particular circumstances. The role of history is explained and institutionalised within individual militaries, and often in a contradictory fashion to that of the other combatants.

This contradiction underlines the fragility of theory as a method and guide. All too often strategic theory, as well as the synoptic type of long-range military history, operates as a literature that might apparently serve for intellectual disquisition, and therefore offer impartial rationality, but in practice often with a failure to accept its partial and partisan character. So also with the risk that vacuous generalities can preside. Theory frequently pushes against the plausible, as with the thesis of a military revolution that lasts for a quarter-millennium (1550–1800), an analysis that pushes against the understanding of revolution as rapid and abrupt change.

If readings of the past are the most potent aspect of theory, these readings are in practice moulded by the exigencies of military need and strategic practice. Key determinants include whether the power in question is the aggressor or the recipient of attack, and, domestically, whether the perspective is insurrectionary or counter-insurrectionary. However, these categories are open to political, and therefore partisan, contention, as well as to conceptual and methodological questions. For example, despite Clausewitz's assessment of popular resistance to Napoleon, much of the literature of strategic theory follows a classic pattern of focusing on international conflict. However, that approach underplays the role of insurgencies. This role was also readily apparent in the conventional military theory of revolutionary states and movements, including in the Soviet Union in the 1920s and, more clearly, Communist China and Cuba.

Whatever the military task, there are the strategic problems of prioritisation, and the related issues of allocation, both of resources and of precedence in time-sequences of planning and execution. The nature as well as content of planning is a key element of strategic practice and should be one for military history.

Returning to a useful concept, albeit at the risk of giving it too much agency, the role of the past is encoded in strategic culture. This concept can spread to include much of a state's international commitment and social politics, but also needs to encompass the establishment of the parameters, precepts and practices that guide such factors as recruitment, discipline, and attitudes toward casualties. This, however, was not a fixed, somehow automatic and mechanistic, process of optimalisation for efficiency and thesis accordingly, nor what can be seen as a 'rational' activity to that end, if, what is, rational is considered in terms of more recent understandings of science.

Indeed, counterweighting what can be presented as a 'rational' pursuit of best practice, there was (and is) the need to adapt the latter in terms of existing social and cultural norms, as well as the reality of perceiving best practice in that fashion. As an aspect of this, the totemic character of conflict was to be seen in the widespread determination to hold onto the legacy of the past, of its honour and power. This has been seen across the cultures, from antiquity to the current day, with military units eager to list past battle honours on their standards and other markers. Alongside a fascination with the possibilities of technological change, this is a pattern that continues to the present and one that influences contention over the past, notably battle descriptions.

Owning the past could be a major theme. Giovanni Panini's painting *Alexander the Great at the Tomb of Achilles* (c. 1718–19) depicted the episode in which Alexander, who apparently believed he was descended from Achilles, the Greek hero of the Trojan War, allegedly ordered that the tomb of Achilles in Troad be opened so that he could pay tribute to the great warrior of the past, and thus assert his linkage and acquire his magic. So also with Timur's (d.1405) attempts to claim a descent from the Mongol leader Chinggis Khan (d. 1227), and thus gain the legitimacy and prestige that were offered in Central Asia. Timur also tried to legitimise his rule with the aid of Sufi sheikhs. Babur (r. 1526–30), the founder of the Mughal Empire, used both the Chinggisid and Timurid legacies.

There was a wider meaning in the popularity of images of Alexander's exploits as they came to validate Europeans' sense of their destiny in the world, as in Napoleon's approach to his conquest of Egypt in 1798 or Marzio di Colantonio's painting *Alexander the Great in His Conquest of Asia* (c. 1620). This was an aspect of the *traditio imperii*, the inheritance of Classical imperial power, that was so important in Christendom. Charlemagne had an after-echo comparable to Alexander, although more as a ruler than specifically as a warrior.[10] Modern counterparts can be considered, as in the subsequent Patton cult.

This process of transferring glory and almost a 'military magic' from the past was more generally significant, for example in China when non-Chinese dynasties were established. Indeed, however much it looked to the future in technology, war was often in the shadow of images of the past, and the military very willingly so, not least in discussing ideas of leadership. The incorporation of victory was important, being seen for example in naming, as after the crucial victory over Hannibal, the Carthaginian general, at Zama in 202 BCE, with Scipio, the victorious Roman general, thereafter called Africanus.

This process of identification, which was commonplace in Classical Rome, extended to religion. Thus, Emperor Trajan, a warrior emperor, arranged the dedication of his column in Rome in 113 CE for the anniversary of the dedication of the Temple of Mars Ultor in 2 BCE in order to invoke the help of that god in the new war against the Parthian Empire, Rome's formidable rival to the east, and one that when it succumbed did not do so to Roman attack. If Rome is presented in terms of the antecedents of a Western military tradition, this point prefigures the more general relative significance of conflict between non-Western powers.

Acquiring the 'magic' of past leaders was an important aspect of military history and of its public resonance. This 'magic' ranged from specific keys to success, including those of technique, however defined, and more prominently new weapons, to broader ideals of cultural characteristics that would convey triumph if they were heeded. The latter was an argument adopted in Japan in the 1920s and 1930s, and notably by those who placed an anti-technical emphasis on the strength of will. This enabled them to discount the challenge of possible conflict with America. Indeed, histories of war in this sense posed both a caveat to, or affirmation of, the teleology of the future and, conversely, a means to pursue different, and often contradictory, accounts of military prowess, capability, and the triumph of fortune.

Although much mediated by the use of past sources, which are inevitably selective, and also by that of selected historical works, nevertheless, both the past, and our accounts, in the present, of the past, are in a perpetual tension. As a branch of history, military history is particularly susceptible to the latter, presentist approach, and frequently in a somewhat naïve fashion. In large part, this is because of the importance and interest of the subject, which includes immediate practicalities, as well as voluntary consumer interest. As an instance of such practicalities, military history, not least about the then-current conflict, was deployed at once as a recruiting tool, not only in international conflicts, but also in civil wars such as the American (1861–5) and Spanish ones (1936–9). This was necessary in order to elicit and maintain support, not least if conscription rather than voluntary service made the situation more problematic.[11]

Linked to this, military history is a branch of the subject in which compared to their dominance of other sub-disciplines, professional academic historians are notably weak, at least in modern Western states. Instead, there are powerful and numerous cross-currents, especially from writers for an interested public, as well as from those trying to make the subject relevant to the modern military. There are also social scientists using military history to support their theories. Some are facile, as in war made the state and the state made war, a longstanding thesis, refreshed by Charles Tilly and frequently repeated since, that ignores the extent to which war and its burdens can weaken or destroy states.[12]

In each case, there is a tendency to ahisoricism. This is especially pronounced when there are efforts to find universal laws for war, and thus lessons, for example on strategy, leadership or success.[13] Such works are frequent. Indeed, some writers have made almost an industry in producing such long-range thematic works. So also from the academic community, are collections of essays that are on common topics without, usually, sufficient efforts to search for discontinuities in the subject and its analysis.

At the same time, it can be very valuable to consider elements of continuity. A good example is the playing out of male bellicosity and the aggressive competition that was inherent to war, not only its causes, but also its conduct. Male brain chemistry and male bonding both played a major role,[14] but the understanding, acceptability and representation of these characteristics have varied greatly across time, as well as culturally.

The limitation of assuming common elements without, at the same time, stressing the strong constraints and discontinuities arising from contexts and contingencies, requires continued restating but, nevertheless, is relatively easy to discern. Less so is the related, but different, tendency to adopt a general analytical position that in practice reflects, often very strongly, the issues and ideas of a particular period. To some extent, such present mindedness is an inevitable consequence of the way we think and write about history, but the practice also risks imposing a pattern and therefore teleology on the past. Military history is no exception.

This teleology takes two forms. First, there is an assumption that development toward a certain situation, usually the present, was inevitable, and, secondly, that this was the key theme. Moreover, there is a linked tendency to adopt analytical constructions that arise from this approach, and make apparent sense of it.[15] The teleology becomes the context with the latter given dynamic force.

The most dominant example in the Western tradition is the idea that, with time, there was a move, indeed development, if not progress, to the 'modern' military and 'modern' warfare. These are usually defined in terms of conventional warfare, regular militaries, bureaucratic organisation, technological advance and industrial capability. In such accounts, the terms modern, industrial, total and conventional, are commonly, indeed insistently, deployed, and often in a loose and even meaningless fashion, albeit with different priorities and varying causal links.

The net effect, however, is the same. It leads to a situation in which history is apparently cumulative and unidirectional, the past is anachronistic and bound to fail, and problems are confronted and overcome by arriving at new solutions. These outcomes, moreover, are understood as new and as solutions, with the automatic implication and/or explicit statement that those who 'clung to the past' were doomed to fail. This is seen for example in discussion about delays in adopting firepower, as with the Mamluks of Egypt and their defeat and total overthrow by the Ottomans in 1516–17. In practice, the key battle reflected rather the absence of cohesion on the Mamluk part. Indeed, that was an important element in many battles.

Whether change is held to have occurred by means of revolutionary processes, or in a more evolutionary fashion (and however, and with whatever qualifications, revolutionary and evolutionary are understood, presented and counterpointed), there is a sense in much of the discussion of the necessity of change. In general, there is a focus on the new, a modernist bias, and an unwarranted credulity with regard to models of progress, notably of the rise of the state, the rise of the West, gunpowder technology and Western military organisation. Such models certainly make for arresting book titles and lectures, and for all the clarity of conviction. In contrast, it generally is not a career-gainer, -enhancer or -protector to argue for the restricted extent and impact of change, or, indeed, the only limited significance of the topic being studied. Such maturity is not in demand.

The standard approach, instead, entails ascribing the priorities of one age, notably that of today, to another age, and in a highly misleading fashion, indeed doubly so for there is generally a simplification of the present. For example, the focus on supposedly decisive battles, a focus which particularly, but not only, characterised commanders and commentators in the nineteenth century, led, when considering earlier periods, to an emphasis on battle, and on commanders who sought it.[16] A classic instance was Gustavus Adolphus of Sweden (r. 1611–32), not least for when he intervened from 1630 in the Thirty Years' War, leading to major battles at Breitenfeld (1631) and Lützen (1632). In contrast, far less attention was devoted to his earlier campaigning against the Poles. That is an instance of the nationally-slanted nature of military history, as campaigning in Poland has classically engaged less interest outside that country than is the case with that further west.

The commentators' quest for battle generally resulted in a downplaying of other factors, such as sieges. To contemporaries, there was a parallel with the glory to be gained from battle. Separately, the element of decisiveness was generally exaggerated in the case of battle, in practice supposedly decisive battles were frequently more likely to be but another blow in a series of blows (military, political and administrative) to prestige, authority and tax/manpower bases, although in monarchical systems the killing of a ruler could indeed be very important.

Great battlefield commanders could also be unsuccessful in war, as with Hannibal in the Second Punic War. He was eventually defeated strategically by the Romans before he was beaten in battle at Zama. Indeed, the emphasis on battle tended to lead to a neglect of strategy, a subject that rarely engaged public interest, certainly in comparison with battle. It was as if the shock of combat combined with the scale of battle drove out other considerations. As a result of the focus on battle, the role of other means of conflict, intimidation and pressure was also underrated. This was true in particular of the small-scale conflict sometimes described as 'small war' conflict that was far more frequent than battles and sieges.[17] So also, in the case of naval battles, of small-ship clashes, blockade, convoying and privateering.

More generally, and linked to the stress on scale and battle, the standard focus in discussion, both subsequently and at the time, was on symmetrical conflict, rather than on the need for armies to confront other forces, whether conventional or not, that sought to avoid battle, a practice that was not an easy way to win glory. By focusing on such conflict, and on battle, there was an emphasis on particular commanders, strategies, tactics and other factors, rather than an engagement with the range of operations and contexts. This emphasis was mistaken and misleading. There is the related issue of the definition of battle.

The idea of battle as essentially a one-day affair certainly prevailed into the nineteenth century even if several battles lasted for longer, for example Leipzig in 1813. However, the situation was radically different a century later. Breakthroughs could prove highly significant and might be obtained in initial fighting, but the subsequent stages in battles generally took longer. In part, this was because a breakthrough with trench warfare was a matter of a break-in followed by an engagement and then a breakout. While particularly the case with World War One, that process was also seen with World War Two. There were successful attacks, as with El Alamein (1942), and failures, as with Kursk (1943) and Operation Goodwood (1944). The common characteristic was that they took several days as, even more, did much that was termed battle, for example Verdun (1916), the Somme

(1916), and Normandy (1944). Instead, the term employed should have been campaign. As a related point, the delays that came from fighting through field fortifications, as at El Alamein and Kursk, helped ensure that it could be difficult to distinguish elements of battle from those of siege warfare.

So also for war at sea. Battles that lasted one or a few days, such as Coral Sea (1942), Midway (1942) and Leyte Gulf (1944), were very different in scale to 'the Battle of the Atlantic,' the long-term struggle against the German assault, particularly by submarines, on Allied commerce. In this case, again, campaign was a more appropriate term than battle. And so also for air assaults.

Linked to the customary focus on conventional operations, there was also an emphasis on state-to-state conflict, rather than on civil wars; or only on the latter when, as with the English (1642–6, 1648) and American (1861–5) Civil Wars, they approximated to conventional operations, or with that dimension stressed. This emphasis greatly affected the understanding and presentation of war.[18]

The standard approach in the literature is readily apparent, but it is far less clear how best to formulate a new approach. This is a significant point because historiography ought to involve pointing the way forward to new challenges, issues and subjects for research and publication work; rather than solely looking back. The former is certainly more realistic as a reflection of present concerns than the manner in which historiography is often considered by academics for, in looking back, there can be a tendency to underrate the extent to which works and events then were intended to influence the future.

In focusing on the way forward, it can of course be difficult to detect clear schools and developments, not least the military problems that will come to the fore. Nevertheless, aside from the variety of the histories of war, the existing divided tendencies of military history can each be sketched forward, as well as back. These include, and the tendencies overlap, the technological approach, the 'War and Society' focus, the 'Cultural Turn', the global perspective, and the dominant attention to campaigns and battles.

The proponents of each generally seek to argue for its consequence and frequently typecast other methods. Indeed, it is difficult to find much evidence as a result of a coherent subject as a whole, one that can be termed military history. For example, in a criticism of the 'War and Society' focus, Norman Stone commented on the tendency to focus on topics such as 'rape by soldiers, and other patriarchal activities'.[19] In practice, rape is very significant not only to the victims but also as a means of warfare and control, the last a topic indeed stressed in recent work.

However, Stone captured a lack of sympathy with 'War and Society' approaches that is widespread among many who are interested in the history of war, and notably that of campaigning. How these approaches will develop in the future is unclear. It cannot be said that there is a debate, for to do would be to imply a discussion and mutually-rewarding interaction that is not always obvious.

There is also, very interestingly, the academic literature that seeks to link war to questions of state development and differentiation. This approach goes back to the stadial theories advanced in the eighteenth century as Western commentators then attempted to devise a theory of history in which religion played little or no real role. This was a theory that did not rely on a providential account of Christian history and purpose, and that could readily incorporate non-Western societies and thus non-Christian accounts.

The stadial theories entailed a developmental model that today appears flawed, as well as prejudiced and Eurocentric; although it is not too different from many of the perspectives subsequently advanced by Social Scientists. In the essential argument, economic specialisation led, and leads, to levels of society and related organisation that have governmental and political consequences, as well as affirming and/or encouraging particular social and economic circumstances and trajectories. These all have military consequences, indeed leading to an ability to create, use and deploy resources that offsets the bellicosity of what were defined as simpler societies in which there is not any equivalent specialisation of labour and, instead, all men can act as warriors or be expected to act thus if they were to be treated as men. Ironically, with conscription, this practice was to prevail for much of the twentieth century, and in the case of societies that saw themselves as modern.

In the eighteenth century, the developmental approach was notably prominent in the West in the writings of Edward Gibbon, William Robertson and Adam Smith, writing that enjoyed a fame that was not restricted to Britain. A similar approach, also rejecting the past, was present in the writings of French *philosophes*, and there were other Western counterparts, including in America where the developmental model was to be employed to justify displacing native peoples as an aspect of modernity.

In effect, this developmental approach offered embracing historical change itself as strategy, with success equated as achieving modernisation; although the extent to which such a policy was planned, as opposed to being described, in part as a 'hidden hand' of change, was unclear in much of the writing. One of the most significant instances of specific government policies being seen as important came with Gibbon's discussion of Peter I, the Great, of Russia (r. 1689–1725), a warrior-ruler notably successful over Charles XII of Sweden, particularly at the battle of Poltava in 1709 and in the subsequent conquest of Sweden's possessions on the eastern shores of the Baltic. Peter's adoption of Western governmental and military methods was presented by Gibbon as making Russia a successful bulwark against any future irruption of 'barbarians' from the Asian heartland. This approach contrasts with the idea that Russia was a 'barbarian' power, a view widely voiced in the eighteenth century in Poland and Sweden, and from there, echoed further west, notably in France.

With Gibbon's assessment of Russia, military history is an aspect of total history. Rather, however, than this approach risking the loss of the value and distinctiveness of military history, it is more appropriate than treating the subject as a totally different dimension, not least because the wider nature of conflict is thereby captured with this totalising approach. Indeed, as tasking is a fundamental aspect of military history, so it is necessary to understand its parameters, context, role and dynamics.

Yet, an easy stress on tasking can also risk underplaying the extent to which it is often 'constructed' by commentators and thus agglomerated, in practice in the light of hindsight. Moreover, there is the tension between tasking as explicit or implicit, and, linked to this, between tasking as a 'natural' product of context and circumstances or the result of specific choices. Thus, while useful as a theory, the idea of tasking also has deficiencies, and has to be employed with an explicit conceptual awareness that is generally lacking.

Linked to tasking, the very nature of the present, whether military, geopolitical and/or ideological, always remains up for contention; and this is even more so for speculation about the future. Each, in practice, moreover, contributes to debate about the past. Teleological accounts of change should be seen as an aspect of this contention, and not as offering an apparently immutable proof, one that is subject to analysis but that allegedly remains a building block of the subject. This is a point that is often lost in the assertions about military change and modernisation. These are part of the rhetoric of war, a rhetoric seen in contemporary debates and also in subsequent historical ones.

Histories of war inherently tend to focus on outcomes, the majority making them desirable or at least likely, and, in general, seek to make these outcomes appear valorous and, indeed, do this whether they entail victory or defeat. Depending on the cultural and ideological perspective, these outcomes can be presented as inevitable or not, but generally are seen as providential, however much that is expressed in religious terms. That then poses pressures for a given narrative depending on whether the conflicts are international or domestic, and whether the combatants are presented as states, dynasties, nations, countries, religions, ethnicities or social groups.

In turn, however, these analyses, categories and desired outcomes could be contested at the time and now, and generally were. Thus, in imperial terms, Chinese writers sought the *tat'ung* or great harmony/unity, whereas, in the West, there was both this, and an interest in the balance of power, however fluctuating the latter might be. Any history or policy predicated on the desirability of the balance of power generally offered a different rationale to that of imperial expansion, for the balance represented an emphasis on restraint. Yet, in practice, harmony, unity and balance of power were subjective both as categories and in their implementation. So also with the balance of power, which is a rhetoric of politics as much as an objective assessment. That the balance has been seen very differently is particularly clear, as also its historical placing in terms of a West influenced in the eighteenth century by the mechanistic ideas drawing on the model and reputation of Newtonian physics. In contrast, in the nineteenth century, biological metaphors were to the fore, with an emphasis accordingly on vitalist points such as morale.

Today, teleology is tempting and commonplace in military history, understood as a general process, rather than as simply the narration of specific battles. In part this is because of the cult of technology, and notably the apparent objectivity of technological progress, as well as the ease of explanation it seemingly offers, including for these particular battles. But in reality there is no such objectivity for technological progress, as it involves costs, priorities and trade-offs that entail perception and politics. Indeed, there is no clearcut objectivity. Furthermore, if the emphasis for military capability, instead, is placed on administrative sophistication and, more generally, on the nature of the state or a society, civilisation, culture, people or ideology, then the course of military history in essence also becomes from this perspective an aspect of general history, and of the assertions bound up in it.

As a related point, competing powers are rival systems; consequently, the potential for conflict and the impact of war are each strongly mediated by pre-existing structures, both administrative and social. This then leads to a wider-ranging enquiry about the character of societies and their cultures. However effective a given state might be in raising resources, that does not explain the degree to which its people are willing to accept deprivation and risk death for its ends. Indeed, underlining the ambiguous relationship of states and war, the raising of resources may weaken this given state politically and damage it in both economic and social terms.

Yet, as a variant on divine favour and superior skill and/or will, a belief in technological potency and, separately, military professionalism is convenient for societies that cannot introduce, retain or match the mass mobilisation and ideological and social militarism of rivals; a trope seen from antiquity to the present. However, argument for the progressive evolution of superior military systems and, additionally or alternatively, economic development, an evolution that is discerned by some in a quasi-automatic, mechanistic fashion, need to be qualified by an understanding of the roles of fashion, ideology, prejudice and social patterns.

Another aspect of categorisation, and, with it, explicit or implied analysis, is provided by time. Indeed, a key device in histories of war is that of periodisation. Yet, this device is also a source of contention as well, separately, of confusion. Aside from the values to be placed on particular divides and periods, is the past (or any particular period of the past) different, such that attempts to find some fundamental criteria or state that does not change across time are misleading? Such an attempt of course has frequently been made. It can be found in terms of arguments in favour of lasting rules of war and thereby apparently relevant lessons. There are also alleged continuities in terms of the experience of battle, otherwise known as the face of battle. Furthermore, the religious analogy of the struggle between good and evil provided a metaphysical guide to the apparently lasting character of war in what was, for most cultures, its elemental form. The rhetoric and often practice of war today reveals that this metaphysics of conflict is still on offer, and in both religious and secular societies.

As against these approaches for, and from, continuity comes, in contrast, the emphasis on change. Change is description, analysis, explanation and rhetoric, each supporting the other but also confusing the response. Change also covers many facets in military history, not only changing circumstances but also key contextual elements, notably altering practices of thought and, also, different categorisations. The latter provide an instructive basis for variations in the periodisation adopted, for example by an 'Age of Cavalry.'[20] There are two prominent forms of periodisation. The first entails a period of time, such as the nineteenth century. The second focuses, instead, on different stages along a continuum based essentially on one criterion, for example firepower. Complicating such periodisation, as well as existing narratives and analyses of change, there are also newly-prominent concerns as applied to war, for example environmentalism in terms of the content of conflict, including immediate contexts and its consequences.[21] As this example indicates, these concerns do not necessarily match, closely or otherwise, other chronologies and analyses of military history.

Advocates of technologically-defined military transformation, or just change, tend, as already noted, to ignore the diversity of circumstances across the world, in favour, instead, of a presentation of the world as, in effect, an isotropic surface, uniform in all parts, both geographically and chronologically. Such an assessment, in practice, is naïve, both militarily and politically. Although not dependent on this point, this naïvety in many circumstances draws on histories of war predicated on technological superiority. These misrepresent the recurrent, indeed inherent, deficiencies and limitations of such superiority, as well as the contingencies of past success and the dependence on multiple factors.[22] A focus on technological superiority also captures the failure to engage with ensuring that victory is confirmed in terms of compliance. The last is crucial to the extent and nature of success.

Yet, to treat these or any histories as technical or value-free discussions of capability and effectiveness, as if they were part of an abstract discussion, is to ignore the multiple psychological factors that are crucially important to the production and reception of histories of war. This is far more so than for example of discussion of the geographies of war. The need for a belief in superiority is an important element in discussing and explaining conflict. It provides justification and explanation, and, in a crucial addition, also structures narrative and analysis, both explicitly and implicitly.

A belief in superiority in technological terms meets the ideological and imaginative demands of modern industrial society, and does so to the benefit of particular civilisational modes and moods, and individual states and peoples. America has been the most prominent site and beneficiary of this approach, not least as the state that invented, in 1903, and then, from the 1940s, dominated manned and powered air power, before moving on, also in the 1940s, to do the same with the nuclear age. A role as inventor and imitator obviously encourages interest in change, as does the very nature of American society with its focus on social and economic mobility, and its cult of the new. The cultural implications, instead, had a European state been the foremost power would probably have been great. The same element is very much affecting Chinese attitudes as well, not least because Communism presents itself as scientific and future-facing, while the leadership of China overwhelmingly has an engineering training.

From a very different perspective, there is a determination to use technology to overcome the multiple constraints of military operations, and that determination encourages an emphasis on its value. This approach to technology as the necessary, or at least desirable, answer however can lead to the mistake that overcoming constraints equates with abolishing risk, which is not the case as it is not possible to achieve the latter. The contrasting ways in which technology can be approached indicate the need to approach categories with care. So also with the use of the circumstances and requirements of hindsight to determine which technological developments in the past were of particular relevance and importance.

Military history, indeed, is an obvious field in which it is dangerous to adopt the perspective of hindsight. Linked to this, both staff rides, an established form of training in which the battlefield is viewed, and also war-gamers, devote time to an entirely reasonable pastime, asking whether battles, campaigns and conflicts could have had different results. This practice can be pursued at tactical, operational and strategic levels, and there are many outlets that do so.

The role of chance and contingent factors appears crucial when explaining not only particular engagements and campaigns, but also wars as a whole. At the same time, the counterfactualism of hindsight overlaps with that of contemporary reportage. The latter could be very insistent in its conclusions. Thus, as in 1782, Major-General John Burgoyne (who had been totally defeated by the Americans at Saratoga in 1777) commented on the French capture of the Sri Lankan port of Trincomalee, which Britain had earlier seized from the Dutch: 'I really believe the fate of the whole Carnatic (south-east India) to be involved in the loss of it. Had this remained in our possession, with such a fleet as the Admiral Hughes now has, we could have had nothing to fear.'[23] From the impressive protected anchorage at Trincomalee, ships could readily sail to the Carnatic.

Counterfactualism in many respects recovers the uncertainties of the past. It was much in evidence in 2022–24 during the Ukraine war, and is frequently advanced for other possible conflicts such as an Israeli air attack on Iran or a Chinese invasion of Taiwan. Indeed, far from there being clear divides, counterfactualism is a central aspect of planning, not least due to the time sequence of the latter.

Contemporary reportage was in part a matter of journalism but, more significantly for military development, of the relevant official processes of war, from immediate unit accounts to after-action reports, and also those of foreign observers. These processes could differ in their emphases or even conclusions, but combined to provide rapid histories. In turn, these contributed to the official histories that were to follow. That, however, was not their purpose. This is an instance of the more general situation of misalignment in history, notably the use of sources for purposes for which they were not intended.

More profoundly, there are readings by historians and other commentators between sources, attitudes, assumptions, circumstances and contexts that reflect links, causal and otherwise, resting on belief and assertion. This situation is present across history, and, indeed, perception and reasoning; but there should be no more of an acceptance of this slippage in some cases than in others. Histories of war tend to be particularly susceptible to this practice of assertion. Instead, they should show the necessity of the conditional nature of assessments, both sources and analyses.

In part, this failure of analysis is because wars always play a role in public memory. Moreover, these wars, and this memory, can be recycled by means of being relocated for new lessons. That is the case for oral societies and their folk memory, but also can be seen in the recent and contemporary use of wars in order to advance and interpret possibilities, threats and experiences.

A sceptical introduction to some of the issues involved in histories of war might conclude by arguing the inherent need for decentring any particular perspective. However much it is tempting to offer a panoptic survey, as if providing Olympian detachment, and an oracular judgment refracted through perfect knowledge, such an approach is philosophically bogus, conceptually naïve, and methodologically misplaced. Thus, as an instance of the need for caution, the historian as observer may note parallels, in for example East Asia and Europe, for example Han China and the Roman Empire, but there is a need for great caution in reifying these into an explanatory device. Moreover, the deployment of parallels is apt to be self-fulfilling in its selective use of evidence, indeed very deceptive.

Readers may not expect nor wish to be served caution, let alone doubt. Yet, the multitudes who have served in the military and will do so, deserve better treatment than to be employed to substantiate the platitudes so regularly deployed in discussion. By their very nature, conflicts are individual and specific, and the reasons for outcomes should be expressed with qualification, indeed scepticism. That this admonition does not capture standard usage helps in a way to make the situation more interesting and instructive. This is because histories of war express the need to advance particular agendas, whether national, social, cultural, intellectual, service or personal. Due recognition of this situation, and an exploration of its consequences, would contribute greatly to the subject.

Chapter 2

Mediums

The academic approach necessarily focuses on, or, to employ the generally misleading language of the present, privileges, scholarly discussion of the history of war. This approach will play a role in this study, but it is also necessary to devote due attention to the range of ways in which military history, the past of war, was presented, still is, and will be in the future. In doing so, there should be no assumption that one medium was and/or is necessarily more significant or progressive (however defined) than another, an assumption that seemed to be central to much scholarly discussion. Moreover, for each medium, it is appropriate to note differences of emphasis, and shifts in focus, across time, and by group concerned.

Fundamental contrasts rise from such factors as literary rates. These have varied greatly by period, country and social group, and thus affect not only the ability to produce works but also access to writings on war; this access being a matter for civilians and the military. It is also necessary to devote due attention to the contrasts between the history produced within and/or for the military, as in part of training and also of the collective military ethos, and, in contrast, other material and forms that lacked and lack this focus. Each of these elements deserves a book in itself. However, bringing them together serves to illustrate the need to move away from a silo approach to the subject, one of a particular method, format and language, whether understood in terms of the discipline of history or of other disciplines, for example those of the social sciences. Instead, it is important to note the extent and impact of links and broader relationships in ways to present and understand military history.

That is an aggregating approach. There is also the disaggregating one of the variety of content and medium that is available for assessment and citation, and, thus, the element of choice in histories of war. The last, the impact of choice and chance, should be addressed explicitly, rather than treated as a given or a hidden hand.[1] This is a crucial instance of the need for care in the presentation of history.

An obvious contrast is that of the differing views of combatants toward the same conflict. That, throughout military history, has been a feature, and both the legacies of the past and the pressures of current politics can be seen in wars in the world at the present time, notably, but not only, in Ukraine. As a result, the present is producing the sources, emotions and assumptions that will offer, in the future, contrasting views and, linked to this, the variations between more formal histories, as well as popular ones. In particular, as a key element of such views, there are the attempts by the victors to emphasise their merit in success and, alternatively, by the losers to excuse themselves in explaining failure.

There is a standard concept that the winner writes history, both about the last war and concerning previous conflicts. This argument, which was made by Hitler about the Armenian massacres, is true to a degree, but also less so than might be assumed, and notably so over the last century. In particular, the winning side not only profits from but lives success, and thus enjoys high morale; it does not need to explain it. In contrast, it is the loser that in military and political terms addresses failure by seeking to lessen and/or debate it through explanation, and also by providing a means to offer a rallying point for fresh efforts, whether military or cultural. Defeat as a form of testing by God is a frequent theme, one used by George III to explain failures in the American War of Independence (1775–83). As a result, he ordered national prayer days. Defeat in the Six Days' War by Israel in 1967, specifically the overwhelming destruction of the air force at the outset, led Gamel Abdul Nasser, the Egyptian dictator who had risen through the military, to blame American and British intervention, a false account that served as extenuation in the face of supposedly overwhelming attack and was also designed to engage Soviet support.

After the American Civil War, more explanatory effort was made by the defeated. The former Confederacy put up statues of American Civil War commanders, the famous defeated, such as Robert E. Lee, their most prominent general. This was done in particular, but not only, at times when the Confederacy's failures appeared confirmed by desegregation. The last point brings to the fore the extent to which memorialisation of the military past changes as a result of subsequent political conjunctures.[2] Key instances are offered by the statue removals, renaming and syllabus changes that followed the end of empires, notably, but not only, Western colonial ones and the Soviet one in Eastern Europe. Already, the Romanian nationalism of the Ceaușescu regime had led to the removal from Victory Square in Bucharest of the large statue of a Soviet Red Army figure erected in 1947. Moreover, the role of Romania in fighting Germany in 1944–5 was emphasised. Major political changes also have similar consequences.

The role of political conjuncture is an element that should never be extracted from the discussion of military history, because the concept of value-free analysis is flawed, as is that of value-free narrative. The aftermath of the American Civil War saw the defeated, led by Lee, seek to explain their failure by arguing that they were superior soldiers, but had been overborne by greater resources. This argument was also to be employed by, and on behalf of, the Germans after the two world wars. Indeed, the experience of the Civil War might have made some Americans sympathetic to this approach, one historical approach thus providing an automatic seedbed for another. This is a common process. It is also highly misleading.

On the other hand, there are other possible explanations, and they can be employed in a supplementary fashion, or as an alternative one. The most clearcut instance of the former is that in the Cold War the Americans needed to believe in the West Germans, once rearmed in the *Bundeswehr*, as crucial new allies in Europe against the Soviet Union, present need therefore helping explain instant history. In part, this valorisation of the 'weaker' side, which was how the World War Two *Wehrmacht* was presented against the size of the Soviet Union, accorded with a trope, used indeed by the Nazis, intended to be of value of heroic defence against 'hordes' from 'the East.' This was a politicised placing (and highly dubious reading) of Eurasian military history, one that was culturally driven and to a degree inherited by America when explaining its NATO commitment which began in 1949.

Certainly, assumptions are of great significance in both narrative and analysis, and more so in most writing than either the general tone of analysis or the presentation of the detailed story might suggest. Ironically, Russian intervention in Central and Western Europe had been seen by Britain in 1735–1815 on several occasions, notably 1735, 1748, 1799 and 1813–15, as crucial assistance against French expansionism.

The apparently seductive approach of an emphasis on resources overcoming honorable bravery is convenient for the defeated. The approach also counterpointed the apparently 'true' character of war as combat, which the Confederacy and Germans had allegedly won, with its false or lesser non-warrior characteristics: the male struggle on the battlefield, as opposed to the factories in which women and non-martial men were prominent. Thus, in explaining defeat, the losers offered a history of war that was culturally potent and heavily gendered, and one that, in turn, provided a commentary on justification and providence. This approach did not show favour to works suggesting that the fighting effectiveness, of the Confederates, the Germans, or others, either as a whole and/or of the supposedly more valorous, was more modest than generally claimed.[3]

The notion of winners and losers as recorded in statuary changed with time. Thus, the collapse of the Soviet bloc in 1989–91 not only ended the display of military hardware in May Day Parades, but also provided opportunities to rethink statuary, with statues to Soviet military liberation, satirised during the Cold War as statues to 'the Unknown Rapist', a theme ignored by the 'liberators', removed from Eastern Europe.

Such a process could be contentious, as with the 'Black Lives Matter' movement of the early 2020s in the West, one that led to a more general critique of imperialism. Thus, in Exeter, there was pressure from 2020 to remove the statue of General Redvers Buller, a leading figure of Victorian military imperialism (and nothing to do with slavery), but that pressure was blocked in 2021 by government action. Ironically, but in accordance with a frequent pattern, that particular statue itself, like the pressure for its dismissal, was a response to a very specific political conjuncture, namely Buller's dismissal when he was blamed for failure in the early stages of the Boer War of 1899–1902. This helped explain the emphasis on the public subscription for the statue, as well as the inscription 'He Saved Natal.'

Elsewhere, there has been less controversy. For example, the driving back of the Moors from Spain and Portugal left a legacy including placenames and statues. Thus, Vímara Peres, who conquered Oporto from the Moors in the ninth century, has a large, modern statue prominently displayed by the cathedral, while one of the major streets there is named after him. Évora has a statue of Gerald the Fearless, twelfth-century Portugal's El Cid, decapitating a Moor, and has him on its coats of arms, while its central plaza, the Praça do Geraldo, is named after him. In response to his vow to the Virgin in 1147 to do so, if he was able to capture Santarém, Afonso I of Portugal, in 1153, founded a major Cistercian monastery at Alcobaça, now a UNESCO World Heritage Site. Victory over the Moors at the battle of Río Salado in 1340 led Afonso IV to commission the *Padrão do Salado*, a monument with four arches and a cross in Guimarães.

Statues were not the sole form of iconographic military celebration. For example, like other visual forms of commemoration, the striking of medals presented a fixed account of war, one that tends to receive insufficient attention today. This could also be the case with the more ritual aspect of staged performances; although not of plays that aimed for fluidity and characterisation.[4] Many of the former overlapped with religious commemoration and thanksgiving for victories, which was another aspect of such staging. Furthermore, the extent to which rulers were sacral figures, as well as war leaders, accentuated the overlapping of forms of public celebration and commemoration.

In Western culture, paintings tend to leave a more permanent record, although it is a very varied one. Many paintings are instructive at a number of levels. For example, produced in the second quarter of the sixteenth century, Jan Mandijn's *Temptation of Saint Anthony* is his only signed work to survive. It incorporates elements of the fantasia style of Hieronymus Bosch. Set in about 270 CE, the temptation was a theme depicted in the arts from the tenth century. In Mandijn's painting, a primitive shooting armoured vehicle, one present neither at the time of the subject depicted, nor of the painter, was shown among the diabolical figures assaulting the saint. That was an instructive instance of the presentation of war, in this case that between good and evil, in terms of modernity, in this case gunpowder firepower. It clearly appears fanciful, but so also do modern examples of reading the issues of today back to the past.

Turning to the present, *F^{xxx} Abstraction* is a particularly blunt contemporary view of war in art, and the impressions thereby created for the history that will be told in the future. On 7 May 2023, Miriam Cahn's painting, displayed at the Palais de Tokyo, the Parisian contemporary art museum, proved too much for a protester who threw purple paint on it, being allegedly unhappy with what he saw as a representation of paedophilia in the form of the rape of a child. Cahn, in contrast, argued that her painting was a denunciation of the use of rape as a weapon of war, that the small figure in it shown being forced to perform oral sex on a much larger one, was an adult not a child, and that she had painted the work in response to reports of the Russian massacre and rape of Ukrainian civilians in Bucha in 2022. The gallery decided to leave the work on display with the paint on it. The discussion of this played through French politics, with complaints about the painting from the pro-Russian National Rally party.

In another context, the modern statue of Benkos Biohó in San Basilio de Palenque, Colombia, a village founded by him as the first free African town in the Americas, testifies to present-day concerns to offer a military history different from that provided earlier, one that incorporates previously excluded groups. Born in the Bissagos Islands off West Africa, Biohó was seized by a Portuguese slave trader and sold to a Spaniard at Cartagena, Colombia, escaping in 1599. With other escaped enslaved people, he thwarted the Spaniards, only to be treacherously seized in 1619 and executed two years later. Now he is judged worthy of public memorialisation, and as a part of a wider process in which there is considerable interest shown in slave rebellions.[5]

Paintings of conflict were (and indeed remain) frequently unrealistic, and notably so in the later stages of the age of firepower, as the combatants were usually shown closer together than was in fact the case. Thus, Robert Gibb's dramatic *The Thin Red Line* (1881) depicted an incident of 1854 from the Crimean War and was based on a battlefield dispatch by William Howard Russell, in which he wrote of 'a thin red streak tipped with a line of steel.' The painting shows the Russian cavalry far nearer the 93rd Highlanders at Balaclava than was actually the case, for the Minié rifles of the latter drove the enemy off and the Highlanders began firing at about 600 yards. Yet, realism was not to the fore when the impact of art was considered, and especially not in the case of casualties, as, for example, with the Franco-Prussian war of 1870–1.

Instead, it was the exemplary element that was considered central across the whole of history painting, a genre now taken forward by photography, which was conceptualised in this light as much as that of abstract realism. Thus, Benjamin West (1738–1820), an American Loyalist (opponent of independence), who was Historical Painter to George III from 1772, and became President of the Royal Academy in 1792, exhibited in 1780 paintings of *The Battle of Boyne* and the *Destruction of the Battle of La Hogue*. Produced in a period of national challenge and defeat during the War of American Independence (1775–83), this depiction of crucial English victories in 1690 and 1692, over the Jacobites in Ireland and over a French invasion fleet, greatly increased West's popularity. He also produced a series of paintings on fourteenth-century English victories. As an example of the construction of artistic nationalism, West (1738–1820) never returned to America after 1763, but, prior to the War of Independence, thus did not affect his status and his historical paintings were initially those of a British empire in which American interests played a major role, as in *General Johnson Saving a Wounded French Officer from the Tomahawk of a North American Indian* (1768) and *The Death of General Wolfe* (1770). In one sense, it was the American rebellion/revolution that produced the different context in which he painted *The Death of Nelson* (1806).

In the nineteenth century, parliamentarians were reminded that liberty had had to be defended: Daniel Maclise received £7,000 for painting both *Wellington and Blücher at Waterloo* (1861) and *The Death of Nelson* (1864) for Parliament when it was rebuilt after fire. His oeuvre, for example *Alfred the Great in the Tent of Guthruyn* (1852), a ninth-century episode, reflected the demand for an exemplary national history on canvas, especially a history of monarchs and war. Alfred shared with Arthur the happy role of providing distinguished ancestry for notions of valiant national liberty, and in 1873 the carving of a white horse in a hillside near Westbury that was held to commemorate Alfred's victory over the Danes at Ethandune (also known as Edington) in 878 was restored. The Westbury and Uffington White Horses were presented as testimonies to national survival and, therefore, identity.[6] In France, the Gallery of Great Battles which occupies the largest room in the Palace of Versailles was built in 1833–7 and in it King Louis Philippe displayed 33 paintings influencing the history of France from Tolbiac (c. 496, from 1930 also the name of a metro station) to Wagram (1809), thereby incorporating the Revolutionary and Napoleonic era. Most of the paintings were produced specifically for the gallery between 1834 and 1845, and it also memorialized in busts and bronze lists commanders who had died for France.

Novels made similar points. Charles Kingsley (1819–75), a clergyman who was Regius Professor of Modern History at Cambridge from 1860 to 1869, wrote a number of historical novels glorifying heroes from the past. These included *Westward Ho!* (1855), an account of the Elizabethan struggle with Philip II of Spain, and *Hereward the Wake* (1866) about English resistance to the Norman Conquest of 1066. These were long kept in print and made available in public libraries where I read the latter in the 1960s.

At the same time, there are, in the discussion of war, the changes in medium that occur due to, or linked with, technological, stylistic, social, demographic and political factors. The first can be obvious, as in the arrival of printing or film. Thus, the grip of the Mexican War of 1846–8 on the American imagination, a grip that owed something to the scale of American success, was enhanced by the extent to which it was covered in developing media, notably photography and lithography. The painterly representation of battle thereby changed greatly. The press also benefited from war reporters,[7] an occupation that became more common from mid-century, notably so for the British and the Crimean War (1854–6). This helped set a pattern, not least because the *Times*, the most prestigious newspaper, used a reporter. Telegraphy sped news of that war.

The nineteenth century onwards has been a period of particularly rapid technological change in the reporting of war, and in expectations accordingly. That does not mean that the earlier situation was somehow easier nor that changes, such as newspapers in the early seventeenth century West, did not occur, but rather that the pace of development has been particularly apparent. The technology creates organisational issues, entrepreneurial possibilities and audience responses. This can be seen in the move from film to digital photography, from bulky to handheld cameras and then to miniature cameras on mobile phones. It has become much easier to take photographs and transmit them. This makes it easier to report and harder to control war reporting, and thus greatly expands the visual space of military history.

Music is also significant. The practice of ordering celebratory music included Te Deums to be sung after a successful battle or campaign served to provide rituals to mark vindication.[8] In later periods, there were more secular versions of this, for example by Cherubini, Gossec and Mehul, and, later, Shostakovich's Suite on Finnish Themes and Symphonies numbers 7 (Leningrad) and 8 (Stalingrad). In terms of music styles, there are musical depictions of battles, from Janequin's *La Guerre* and Jilman Susato's *Battaglia* to Beethoven's *Wellington's Victory*, Tchaikovsky's *1812*, Liszt's *Hunnenschlacht* and Elgar's '*Spirit of England*.' Many operas have had a war-related theme, notably those by Lully glorifying Louis XIV, Handel's *Giulio Cesare, Orlando and Rinaldo*, and Prokofiev's *War and Peace*. More immediately, there was music in and of battle, such as bugles, signals, marches and patriotic tunes.

The various media could help provide choice in the history of war that was up for review, as in the paintings, books and later films concentrating on, and thereby accentuating, the prominent, such as the battle of Waterloo (1815). For the British, there was the possibility of focusing on different stages of the battle, and on infantry or cavalry, as well as the question of how much attention to devote to the Prussians. Separately, the representational and stylistic dimensions provided very different readings of such matters as heroism, of the officer class and the rank-and-file soldiers, or of the presentation of the enemy, as in the 1970 film *Waterloo* which extended to a criticism of some aspects of war.

Relevant demographic, social, economic and political factors ranged from literacy to purchasing power, numbers to censorship. Each can be seen as affecting the variety of media, which was inherently a product of these factors, both in terms of production and with regard to consumption. The last two were, and remain, central to histories of war, for media and histories are created but also received; and each plays a key role in affecting the others.

Helped in part by the dissemination of visual images, the cultural symbols and historical memories that shaped political imagination had a particularly military cast. So also with the placing of people and society. Streets, bridges, buildings and pubs took their names from episodes of war. In nineteenth-century Britain, military leaders, such as Napier, Wolseley, Roberts and Kitchener, joined sites of military glory, the Almas, Inkermans and Omdurmans which survive as street names to this day. London had Trafalgar Square and Waterloo Station, while Parisian avenues, bridges and stations recorded victories such as Alma, Austerlitz, Jena, Solferino and Wagram. Both the present and the past were honoured. Thus, in Japan, there was a memorialisation of battles and castles from the sixteenth century, the last period of significant conflict.

And so on for other countries, such as America and the Civil War, although also with changes that reflect political developments, a process that continues. In this respect, placenames are as one with statues in recording military success and failure, or at least the political dimensions, notably consequences, of both.

As another aspect of a grasp of the past, battlefields became more clearly the sites of monuments and destinations of travellers, although that process was far from new. In 1786, visiting Worcester in England, John Adams and Thomas Jefferson, later second and third Presidents of the United States, were shocked that the local population was not able to accept their view of the positive echo of Oliver Cromwell's total victory there over the Royalists under Charles II in 1651. Adams recorded:

'Edgehill [the first battle of the English Civil War, 1642] and Worcester were curious and interesting to us, as scenes where freemen had fought for their rights. The people in the neighbourhood appeared so ignorant and careless at Worcester, that I was provoked, and asked, "And do Englishmen so soon forget the ground where liberty was fought for? Tell your neighbours and your children that this is holy ground; much holier than that on which your churches stand. All England should come in pilgrimage to this hill once a year".'[9]

Yet, as a reminder of different histories, in part the popular response in Worcester was due not, as they imagined, to forgetfulness, but rather to a royalism which was to be seen in the popular response to the visit by George III) that owed something to the destructive character of Cromwell's victorious troops. Adams and Jefferson, however, captured the sense that the cause of liberty had now been taken over by the Americans, which was an unconscious echo of the interest of British tourists in scenes of valorous liberty on the Continent, as with visits to Roman battlefields in Italy and, later, to Marathon in Greece, of which George, Lord Byron wrote in 'The Isles of Greece' (1819):

> 'The mountains look on Marathon -
> And Marathon looks on the sea;
> And musing there an hour alone,

> I dream'd that Greece might still be free;
> For standing on the Persians' grave,
> I could not deem myself a slave.'

The poem continued by regretting that the modern Greeks lacked the determination of the Spartans who had sacrificed their lives at Thermopylae, and that the memories of the glorious Classical past were now lost.

Earlier, battlefields had a semi-sacral character, in large part due to the dead buried there. The past appearance in the battle of divine support was also important, as with the battles of the *Reconquista* in Spain and Portugal, notably the mythical battle of Clavijo (one much celebrated in art) in which saints, notably Saint James 'the Moor-Slayer,' had supposedly appeared,[10] as saints had also done in the First Crusade, particularly at Antioch (1097–8), where Saint George was allegedly present. As the result of a vision from Saint Andrew, the lance that had pierced the side of Jesus at the Crucifixion was found in 1098, and the Muslims defeated outside Antioch.

There were elements of the latter in more modern times. In 1914 spectral archers were alleged to have helped the British army in resisting German attack at the Battle of Mons. Yet, secularisation was more to the fore. Thus, founded in France in 1882, the *Ligue des patriotes* staged regular visits to battle sites from the siege of Paris in 1870–1. Its eventual President, the novelist Maurice Barrès, did the same for 1870 battlefields in Alsace from the 1890s. Defeats therefore could be celebrated. In recent decades, visits to the world war battlefields have become far more common. Propinquity and national commitment play a role, as with the British visits to the Somme. At the same time, there can be instructive variations as with British visits to the extermination camp at Auschwitz. Moreover, there can be an incorporation of other memories. Thus, the British show a great interest in Omaha Beach, which was an American landing beach on D-Day. In part, this may be a matter of different generations with the British beaches less central to attention once the generation of veterans has passed.

As a variant on battles, castles, maybe somewhat paradoxically as they were from the distant past, served in the age of nationalism as places of celebrating identity as well as encouraging popular interest in war. This was notably so in Europe and Japan.[11] Castles were also rebuilt in Japan in recent decades, not as bellicose sites but rather as places of local pride and identity.

The cult of the battlefield had a long genesis but became more popular in the nineteenth century, in part due to the development of train excursions, technology providing an enabler, as it was later also to do with car and coach visits. This was to become more direct with World War One and the visit of graves.[12] Interpretation was a key element of sites,[13] interpretation both by the site authorities and by those who visited them. In practice 'battlefields possess multiple truths.'[14]

Otherwise, the battlefield could be brought home, not least by historical paintings, panoramas, engravings and the instant history of photography. The last, however, could suggest a less than heroic reality, with casualties possibly to the vivid fore, as in some photographs of the American Civil War, for example of the battle of Antietam (1862). Photographs themselves could be misrepresented or staged, including famous ones such as Robert Capa's 'The Falling Soldier' published in *Life* in 1937, much reproduced, and depicting a misrepresented scene in the Spanish Civil War.[15]

The bringing home of war also happened onstage. Piper George Findlater VC, shot in both feet, sat up and played the regimental march to encourage his colleagues in the Tirah Expedition Force of 1897–8 in storming a hostile position. He had a second career re-enacting that episode from the North-West Frontier of British India (in modern Pakistan) on British music-hall stages. The demonstration of Findlater's bravery served to show how bravery crossed divides of military and social rank, a theme that was particularly common from the mid-nineteenth century. More generally, the focus on the hero clearly served a need for identification. Men invested in an image of masculinity they could admire and with which they could seek to identify. Thus, the somewhat foolish George Custer, who was killed by the Sioux at Little Bighorn in 1876, served as a personification of American bravery and expansion.[16] So also, with a more Christian gloss, with Charles Gordon's death at the hands of the Mahdists when they captured Khartoum in 1885. This was presented as a form of martyrdom.

Truth might appear as a secondary consideration to heroism in episodes such as Findlater's appearances. However, aside from the totemic character of heroism, the popular stage was scarcely unique in that. For example, misleading contemporary descriptions of the, in fact, muddled, but successful, Italian invasion of Albania in 1939 are a pointed testimony to the teleological as well as often inaccurate character of military commentary and history. Colonel Emilio Canevari, a leading commentator on, and later translator of, Clausewitz, reported the attack of non-existent motorised formations in close contact with the air force.[17] If deception, both of others and self-deception, was part of the depiction of war in reportage, this was seen across the past, and thus affected histories of war. The absence of any chronological divide between reportage and history was crucial in this respect, as in many others. This absence has been accentuated by the recent emphasis on the personal experience of individual combatants.

The depiction of war provides one of the fundamental markers of continuity and change. It was through this depiction that war was experienced for the many who did not serve, and was commemorated for all. The paintings of the nineteenth century, and notably of its second half, were to focus on advancing blocks of soldiers, albeit with their faces generally distinctive, rather than on their rulers and commanders. Separately, the photographs and film footage of the twentieth century, and (so far) of the twenty-first, for example of the Ukraine conflict in 2022–3, were to centre on the individual soldier and his experience, as does much of the literature, both fictional and academic, on modern war. Indeed, the emphasis on the individual that had very much come to the fore has been sustained.

Earlier, as in the Ancient, Medieval and Early Modern periods, it was the ruler as warrior leader that was the key theme and image. Moreover, this theme and image continued into the eighteenth century, as in Benjamin West's *Edward III Crossing the Somme* (1788), a reference to an English success of 1346 over the French. This theme of ruler as warrior leader did not lessen in intensity in the West until the second half of the eighteenth century. Georges III and IV and Louis XVI never served in the military; and after Peter the Great a series of Russian rulers, four of whom were women, did not serve in combat, although they were eager to reward success. However, the ruler as war leader was to be pushed forward anew by the challenge of the French Revolutionary and Napoleonic Wars, while, separately, George Washington helped set a pattern for American presidential leadership that was to be important across the nineteenth century with many having served in the military, a situation that was renewed in 1945–63 with Truman, Eisenhower and Kennedy.

In his play *Hamlet* (1611), William Shakespeare presented Fortinbras, the fictional nephew of the King of Norway, as a prince 'whose spirit with divine ambition puff'd', and who sought war with Poland in order to 'gain a little patch of ground that hath in it no profit but the name', in other words the prestige of being a ruler as opposed to being landless. Success, more generally, had a highly symbolic value. War was a struggle of will and for prestige, the ends sought being, first, a retention of domestic and international backing that rested on the gaining of *gloire* and, second, persuading other rulers to accept a new configuration of relative *gloire*. This focus led to a concentration of forces on campaigns and sieges made important largely by the presence of that ruler as commander.

This was a particularly notable feature of French campaigning in the seventeenth century, as in the campaigns of Louis XIII (r. 1610–43) and, far more, Louis XIV (r. 1643–1715). In the case of Louis XV (r. 1715–74), never a martial figure, this feature still continued with his campaigning in the 1740s, particularly at the siege of Freiburg in 1744 and the battle of Fontenoy in 1745, in each case a French success. In the latter, the opposing commander, William, Duke of Cumberland, who was to be victorious at Culloden (1746), was the favourite son of a king, George II of Britain, who had been victorious at Dettingen (1743). Louis XV did not campaign thereafter, nor Louis XVI (r. 1774–92) at all; but royal generalship was to be revived, in a very different form, by Napoleon (r. 1799–1815). He exercised the command Louis XV did not enjoy nor Louis XVI seek, and made the army a pattern for the society he sought to inculcate, notably with prestige focused on military service.

French monarchs were far from alone in campaigning in person. Most rulers did so in the seventeenth century, and many in the eighteenth. Tsar Alexis took a major role at the siege of Smolensk in 1654, and Peter the Great was a frequent campaigner. Monarchs who were not noted as war leaders could still lead their forces, as did Philip IV of Spain (r. 1621–65) in 1642 when he joined the army that unsuccessfully sought to suppress the Catalan rising of 1640.

The French monarchs were particularly important due to the prestige of France. They proved especially adept at associating themselves with the glory of victory. Moreover, in doing so, the kings sought a resonance with past glories, the past glories of the dynasty, of the French Crown, and of the Classical inheritance. This was shown in the arts. Peter Paul Rubens's painting *The Triumph of Henry IV* (1630) was intended for the gallery devoted to him in the Luxembourg Palace in Paris, although neither painting nor gallery were finished due to the disgracing of Henry's widow, Marie de Medici that year when she supported opposition to Cardinal Richelieu, the leading minister of Louis XIII. Neither Marie nor Richelieu were warriors as Henry very much was. The sketch depicted Henry (r. 1589–1610) entering Paris in a chariot crowned by a winged figure in the manner of a Classical Roman triumph. This was a frequent and resonant theme, one seen in the iconography surrounding both Napoleon and the Italian Fascist dictator Benito Mussolini (r. 1922–43); the latter, who had many parallels with Napoleon, including eventual total failure, had his conquest of Ethiopia in 1935–6 presented as if akin to a Roman victory. Henry, indeed, had first entered Paris as king in 1594, and only as a result of military victory and of political success. Rubens also produced paintings depicting the glory of Habsburg victories, including the successful siege of the Dutch fortified city of Breda in 1625 and the defeat of the Swedes at Nördlingen in 1634, and these works cast much light on the preferences of patrons. Military success was a dominant theme.

Henry IV's elder son, Louis XIII (r. 1610–43), was not an impressive leader, politically or militarily, but was nevertheless depicted as a great heroic figure, being compared, as was commonplace, to Alexander the Great and Hannibal. Engravings were matched by pamphlets emphasising his successes.[18] In turn, Henry IV's elder grandson, Louis XIV (r. 1643–1715), who was encouraged to model himself on his grandfather not his father, looked back to a childhood in which civil war, in the shape of the Frondes (1648–53), had challenged both the authority and the power of the French crown. Once the Frondes were overcome, Louis's forces were able to campaign, generally, from 1658, with great success, and he personally could serve as the focus of triumph, as in Charles Le Brun's *The Second Conquest of the Franche-Comté, 1674*, a painting of 1678–9. Louis's victories, such as the contested crossing of the Rhine in 1672, and the successful sieges of Maastricht (1673), Ghent (1678), Mons (1691) and Namur (1692), were all celebrated with religious services, commemorative displays and paintings. This reflected the significance of sieges, and also Louis's preference for their sometimes predictable and stage-managed character, which contrasted greatly with battle. In the impressive *Salon de la Guerre* at the royal palace of Versailles, finished and opened to the public in 1686, Antoine Coysevox presented Louis as a stuccoed Mars, the God of War. This was the setting for Louis' life, and somewhat of a contrast to the reliance of his campaigning on the management of financial systems, both domestic and international, a management that failed in the 1700s.[19]

Louis was scarcely alone. His contemporary, Frederick William, the 'Great Elector' of Brandenburg-Prussia (r. 1640–88), presented the victory over the Swedes at Fehrbellin in 1675 as a major success. Its date was celebrated as a holiday until the 1910s, while Frederick was thereafter known as the 'Great Elector' and commissioned Andreas Schlüter to design an equestrian statue depicting him in armour and holding a field marshal's baton. The battle was commemorated with a statue erected in 1875 on royal initiative.

An opponent of Louis XIV, Victor Amadeus II of Savoy-Piedmont (r. 1675–1730), was presented as triumphant in the royal palace at Turin. His victory in the battle of Turin in 1706 over French besiegers became a key element of the dynasty's sense of mission. During the Dutch siege of Maastricht in 1676, William III of Orange spent much time in the trenches and was shot in the arm. In 1678, he was described at the battle of St Denis as armoured with breastplate and helmet 'with thousands of bullets about his ears'.[20] William was to gain control of Britain through invasion and conquest which he commanded in person in 1688–90 and then returned to campaign in the Low Countries. However, although present on campaigns and at battles, some monarchs depicted on canvas in martial poses were far from successful, notably Charles I of England (r. 1625–49).

Paintings, like architectural devices, helped set norms for heroic behaviour. For example, Frederico Bassano's somewhat misleading 1589–90 painting of Charles VIII of France receiving the crown of Naples in 1494, a painting showing him as doing so as the result of a battle that did not in fact occur, was subsequently in the collection of George, Duke of Buckingham, an unsuccessful war leader for Charles I, and then in that of the Austrian Habsburgs.[21] Eugene of Savoy's (1663–1736) recently-restored Winter Palace in Vienna included a hall with paintings of battle scenes, as well as stucco reliefs with military themes.[22] These recorded and glamorised his impressive military commands, which included a string of victories, the most impressive of the age as far as European battles were concerned.

The last qualification is one repeatedly necessary when assessing command skills although there is a strong tendency on the part of Western writers to fail to advance this qualification. Thus, for Eugene's lifetime, the Kangxi Emperor of China or Nadir Shah of Persia might rank as a more impressive commander, not least because they led not only on campaign but also directed the military system. This raises the question of whether such comparisons are helpful, which is one way to ask about the problems posed by compilations such as those of great commanders. In practice, compilations can be instructive as well as useful, but only if the conceptual and methodological issues involved are understood and explicit. This is only rarely the case.

While the celebration of victory was one aspect of the history of war, histories of war at a basic level involved reporting on conflict, a pattern that remains true to the present. Thus, in 1685, the English Ordnance Office sent Jacob Richards to the war front between Austrian and Ottoman (Turkish) forces:

> 'You are to set forward on your journey toward Hungary with all convenient speed, and there to survey, learn and observe the fortifications and artillery, not only of Hungary but of places in your way thither ... and when you come into the next campaign in the Emperor's[23] army to observe all the marching and countermarching and in the besieging of any town to observe their making approaches, mines, batteries, lines of circumvallation and contravallation ... make ... draughts of places and fortifications.'[24]

He did so, taking part in the successful siege of Buda in 1686 and, after returning to Britain, played a role in the campaigns of William III (r. 1689–1702).

Such reporting is now made more vivid and immediate in television, film and other visual media. The latter, of course, were/are a medium, not a message, and range in purpose as well as content. Thus, in considering the reporting of the war in Ukraine, it is necessary to remember Russian reporting. Alongside the war reporting of current conflict, there is also the depiction of the past. Both are open to visual scrutiny, and each affected by questions of accuracy.

Moreover, these media of depicting war have particular requirements, from the commercial to the ideological. These could be conflated, although the possibilities are very varied, with profit less possible in some contexts[25] than others. Ironically, profit can also be sought through decrying profit, in this case the policies of the English East India Company, which deployed considerable forces. Thus, William Dalrymple's history book on eighteenth-century India, *The Anarchy*, was acquired in 2023 for filming by a Bollywood producer, Siddharth Roy Kapur, the author telling *The Times*, as it reported on 25 April:

> 'The idea is to do it on a massive scale. Either you don't do it or you do it guns blazing with a cast of a thousand elephants ... a contemporary resonance that sees the weaponization of profit on a level that boggles the mind ... it is something we have barely been taught and, when we have been, it's been taught in all sorts of ways that obscured the corporate nature of it: the fact that this was a corporate exercise undertaken by a company for profit.... These are not glorious stories or national heroism.'

More generally, military history in such formats matches the earlier tendencies with paintings, novels and other forms, in that there is an ahistoricism in which characters and drives are presented as if present-day and thus unchanging. This is also seen in much writing with notions such as the inherent and constant character of war, not least the often implicit argument that victory had an unchanging meaning. Those in the past are given motives and reflections that relate to the present, rather than the period in question. Indeed, this is a tendency that extends to the mythical creatures depicted in many films, their plots providing a particular commentary on conflict. That ahistoricism can lead to unintentional humour. It certainly can take making history approachable so far as to leave it really nonhistorical other than in terms of analogy; although that can indeed be significant. Approachable equates with usable, but not necessarily with accurate. Military history is scarcely unique in this.

This presentation of military history, however, does not work well for the clearly extended agenda of military history in recent decades. Thus, current war and society topics, for example the role of women,[26] do not transfer well to the standard stage of combat-linked military history. So also with the stance of governments toward war, and, notably, the means and styles in celebrating martial prowess. Women in wartime often had some agency and, if they could, had to get on with life in as accustomed a fashion as possible. Thus, if their treatment is largely as victims, heroines or military auxiliaries, it is inadequate.[27] The ethical challenge of drone warfare was explored in the film *Eye in the Sky* (2015) in which Helen Mirren plays a UK military intelligence colonel.

Presenting the histories of war as if there is an obvious content or process, matching, moreover, an intellectual optimum of rationality, risks downplaying the significant roles of both change and politics in analysing the subject. Indeed, as with other topics, for example strategy and geopolitics, there can be a misleading tendency to depoliticise the analysis and, in doing so, to present a 'rational' account as well as a fixed approach. The supposed rationality is of course in part a matter of perception and assertion. Indeed, there is no fixed rationality in any form of historical analysis. Even the general modern conventions of source-based analysis are in practice limited in their popular support and, moreover, politically and culturally specific. Furthermore, but paradoxically, far from there being a source-based analysis that emphasises the particular character of individual wars, there is a widespread stress on the universality of combat through the supposed commonalities of 'face of battle', as well as the memorialisation from a distance, now celebrated through the use of photography and film and by monuments that are far from the seat of conflict.[28]

How the situation might develop over the next few decades is unclear, but one factor worthy of consideration is the rise of 'the Global South,' also clear in the development and expression of a distinctive narrative about the history of the last two centuries, notably the age of Western imperialism and the Cold War. This narrative overlays particular national accounts in that area and makes the Western history of war appear to be just that. rather than one that is the obvious global narrative and analysis. Alongside accounts that emphasised the role of external intervention,[29] this process is likely to become more pronounced. It will be matched by generational changes that more generally encourage different priorities, not least as new wars come to the fore while some earlier ones will appear less relevant, as has already happened with World War One. And all this with the continual change in the media of representation and communication.

Chapter 3

Official Views

Official histories of war can be readily differentiated in a modern perspective between those that were produced for, and from, the military, and those that reflected broader patterns of state engagement, both with the past and with war. The latter include museums, commemorative iconography, annual memorialisation and a range of activities. In each case, the priorities between and within conflicts are pertinent.

It is, however, questionable to provide too rigid a categorisation of official views, and certainly that offered in the previous paragraph, and more to the point one across time, geography and culture. In large part, that questionable character reflects the extent, instead, to which there is often a clear overlap, both historically and in the present, between the military and the state. Not only are there military-run states today, such as Egypt, Sudan, the Central African Republic, Niger, and Myanmar, as well as others affected by civil war in which force is the clear component of power, for example Libya. Furthermore, more generally, it is also highly mistaken to imagine that the attempt in some countries to define separate military and civil spheres is matched elsewhere, whatever the formal constitutional provision to provide such a separation. Whereas, in some countries, there is an ultimate military guarantee for authority, in many states the military is the more immediate arm of the government, and vice versa. This is particularly the case given the large number of states in which the military do not, as an additional goal, wage war against external foes; but, instead, concentrate on domestic control or are prepared for that task.

This element helps capture the extent to which the Anglophone world provides a poor context for discussion of global military affairs, let alone history. America and, in the past, Britain are atypical in the power they wielded, in its focus on sea and later air capability, in their relatively limited engagement with conscription, and notably with peacetime conscription, and in their distinctions between military and political spheres. The last has then led to a misleading account of strategy (military) as opposed to policy (political) when, in reality, they are to a degree coterminous and, if not that, on a continuum. The Anglo-American idea that, as an aspect of divided power and civilian control, policy is handled by the politicians and strategy by the military, does not describe a feasible situation even in those countries, and notably so for most countries where no such distinction is attempted. Nor is there any clear basis for establishing a norm of effectiveness nor a hierarchy thereof.

Furthermore, that current situation was more than matched in the past. In particular, the prestige and often legitimacy of leadership reflected the role of ruler as war leader, with the fame that thereby accrued through success. Indeed, many members of the British public were surprised in 2022–3 that the funeral of Elizabeth II and the coronation of Charles III both saw a leading military role. They seemed unaware of the significance of the monarch being *ex officio* head of the armed forces. This was taken further, not least with the role of members of the royal family as colonels in chief, as at the 2023 Trooping the Colour in London, the naming of warships after royalty, and many other ceremonial aspects.

As a result of the close links across much of history between ruling groups and military command, indeed their cohesion, commenting on current and recent struggles involved a marked degree of celebration about leadership. That in practice, indeed, was a prime purpose of such accounts. This was military history that had a clear mission, and indeed validation, and is probably the most obvious aspect of the presentation of war, one that is seen for example in China with the celebration of Communist military successes. Within states, the validation relates to varied constituencies, generally national, service, type, unit or individual. Yet, there is a common focus on the use of the discussion to demonstrate the virtues and value of the subject in question. This process is also extended to cover particular methods of war making, and thus accounts of change.

To present such an approach as unscholarly, while tempting, is not necessarily helpful. This is not least as the judgment of unscholarly implies a clear hierarchy in proficiency which can in fact be absent, as well as a contrast between scholarship and strategies of validation, a contrast that is not always the case. In many countries, the universities, indeed, are part of the power structure of the state and an established means for its validation. More generally, there is a tension in the presentation and therefore evaluation of military history, because there is both the need for it, and yet no clear and agreed agreement on the sources or methods of such presentation and evaluation.

In large part, the subject of this chapter is a prime topic of this book, and the key themes require elucidation. The most important is the appreciation that, despite assumptions, appearances and the tendency for simplification in the pursuit of clarity and categorisation, there is no one official view about the presentation of military history but rather a range. This point can also be seen more generally with regard to histories of war, as for example with the practice of reference to national and/or popular views. Indeed, the contrast, a unifying *zeitgeist* (spirit of the age) is a misleading concept in this respect, not only because it underplays the plurality of views but also because, whatever the *zeitgeist* is conceived to mean, it is refracted through a variety of prisms. So also with the related tendency toward reification: turning ideas into activating principles.

The idea of a strategic culture, or indeed the concept as a whole, can be regarded in this respect as similar to that of a *zeitgeist*, for it is in practice necessary to accept the very different views that can be held about national interests. Indeed, these are frequently present both in periodic strategic reviews and in continuing debates about prioritisation in tasking, implementation, procurement and doctrine. The lack of one official view is true even of the most authoritarian of states and the most choreographed of societies, even if the evidence for this situation (and its causation) may be limited and require careful unearthing. In particular, the agencies of such states compete as much as do those in more liberal societies, even sometimes more so because there are not the release-valves that free expression, public accountability and democratic transfers of power permit in the latter. Thus, in Nazi Germany, there was acute competition between institutions including the *Wehrmacht* (army), *SS*, navy and *Luftwaffe* (air force); and providing a tale of bravery for one was far from without point in terms of fixing attention and striving for benefit. The last included the attention of Hitler and the availability of resources, which were in short supply throughout, notably steel for weapons manufacture, but which weapons?

That the German army had an institutional continuity and history that the navy, air force and, even more, SS lacked was a factor in the tension between them. So also was the ability of the army to avoid responsibility for the defeat of 1918. Blaming Germany's failure in World War One on internal dissidence, notably Socialism and strikes, was not only a political tool but also a military one. The latter avoided attention both to the failure of the army on the crucial Western Front in 1918 and to its broader lack of apt strategic conception in that conflict. This lack prefigured the failure of the army's strategic insight during the Nazi era, a failure seen both in relations with the Nazi leadership and in the conduct of the war.

In so far as the internal dissidence in World War One was linked to the strains caused by the Allied naval blockade, there was also an aspect of advancing a history that shifted blame away from the army. This is more generally the case in offering accounts of the past, for example navalistic ones as opposed to 'continental' or land accounts. Such accounts assert interests, define responsibility and, less positively, serve as repositories for credit and firing-grounds for blame. Yet, they are also necessary in drawing attention to important clashes over priorities.

In the case of the alleged responsibility for defeat in World War One, the argument was invested in not only by the military, but also by politicians on the Far Right, particularly those who gathered under Adolf Hitler and the Nazis. As a result, the history of the war took on a powerful political element, and that has lasted to the present. At the same time, the Far Left came to see what happened in 1918 as a demonstration of their power then and their continued possible influence thereafter, which was not in fact the most accurate way in which to view their role in 1918.

To summarise in terms of one facet, as in *the* Nazi account of military history, or the German one of that period, is therefore mistaken. Instead, it was the case of several accounts. This would also have been an aspect of states for which evidence is lacking, in other words those across history. The presentation of their motivation is often overly simplistic. Conversely, the presence of a dominant account is itself significant, but frequently again the evidence is patchy and the dominance therefore problematic.

Yet, at another level, any use of propaganda, or focus on it subsequently, entails an emphasis on a dominant account or at least on a clear-cut rivalry, whether (or both) domestically and internationally, that can be discussed in terms of success and failure.

Moreover, although propagandist accounts of such types were not new, as religious conflict such as crusading amply illustrated, such an emphasis became more, or at least differently, pronounced with the combination of mass politicisation, the affirmation of home fronts and the technological opportunities and challenges of new media seen from the twentieth century. The last was very much the case with the extensions to sound and sight offered by radio and cinema.

Propaganda became an aspect of the branding of war, one that was pursued hard by the Germans, notably by Hitler as he branded the military as Nazi, not least employing the swastika logo, and by Goebbels with the visual presentation of success by his Propaganda Ministry. The British, in contrast, struggled, being associated with repeated failure in 1940–1, which led to the BEF (British Expeditionary Force) being nicknamed 'Back Every Friday', a reference to the retreat of forces from the Continent. In turn, America took time during World War Two to brand its war effort effectively, not least in order to justify a citizen's war against Germany.[1]

Similar issues can be seen in more recent decades. Thus, a moralistic branding in terms, for example, of state building did not necessarily convince the military, home opinion or other states, and risked setting unconvincing military goals and methods.

Returning to divisions within militaries, tension between commanders was repeatedly at play in debates over strategy, procurement and doctrine, as well as in the competing accounts of success (and failure) that underlay 'the' official account. This tension could be very prominent, as in American military history. For example, during the Mexican-American War of 1846–8, the rivalry between Zachary Taylor and Winfield Scott, potential presidential candidates from within the American military, was significant for the attention devoted, both in resources and publicity, to contrasting operational options. The support for Scott's expedition to Mexico City in 1847 was one result. This was very much war as politics, with opportunities created accordingly. In 1848, Taylor defeated Scott for the Whig nomination. In the Civil War, the frequent removal of Union commanders was a product not only of failures but also of the inherent tensions in the command system.

World War Two saw military politics and geopolitics bound up in contrasting American strategies, both between the European and Pacific theatres, and within each, for example the tension between Nimitz with the Central Pacific axis and MacArthur with the South-West Pacific axis. Since strategy is about priorities and these are inherently political and subjective, the apolitical and objective tone of some of the official presentation of war is at least implicitly misleading, if not worse. Moreover, this is not only the case for the Soviet Union but also for democracies.

As a separate issue for World War Two, the official histories of both America and Britain were written during the Cold War. This had implications, the present in this case influencing the past, with, in particular, a determination to keep intelligence information secret, for example the British 'Ultra' system of signals' decipherment. This secrecy had major consequences for the coverage of both the strategic and the operational dimension. As a reminder of the authorial voice, I was initially going to write controlling rather than influencing in the penultimate sentence. On reflection, I decided that controlling was inaccurate, a word too far, but such caution is not always on offer from commentators and is actively discouraged by those trying to push their book. Moreover, as a reminder of the role of media, there may be more caution in writing than in speech.

Military commanders may doubt the relevance and value of official histories, and have other things on which to spend the money.[2] From a different perspective, these histories are frequently criticised for their content, notably lacking an adequate contextualisation and spending too much time on a detailed and dull campaign narrative. There can also be criticism of the histories as overly dependent on government approval. Doubtless all of these can be the case. There have been frequent controversies. For example the official histories of the Second Afghan War (1878–80) were suppressed, while those of the Boer War (1899–1902) were censored to a degree, and different to the *Times History of the South African War*.[3]

Yet, it is not necessarily so. Thus, the British naval history of World War One proved a subject for contention, with pressure brought to bear by the Admiralty in influencing the official account, only for this pressure to be but partially successful. The most instructive historical argument was that of Sir Henry Newbolt, one of the official historians as well as a poet of patriotic verse, particularly *Admirals All* (1987), notably 'Vitai Lampada'

'the voice of a schoolboy rallies the ranks:
"Play up! play up! and play the game!"'

Newbolt had been Controller of Wireless and Cables at the Foreign Office. He felt that the contrast in 1917 between the British decision for convoys and that of Germany for unrestricted submarine warfare reflected the superiority of civilian over military decision-making.[4] This was an analysis that cut across the military criticism of civilian decisions, the latter most frequently captured in Western societies, especially America and Britain, in the argument that strategy ought to be a separate sphere under military direction. Indeed, tension over this can be found in much discussion of war.

As with launching the war on the Western Front in 1914, the German leadership confused operational and strategic planning, and also based both essentially on hope, an element far more frequent in strategy than is usually appreciated. In 1917, the capabilities and impact of the submarines were exaggerated, and the ability of the Allies to respond, underrated. Turning to a submarine warfare that in practice brought America into the war as anticipated but did not, as promised, knock Britain out, can be discussed in the 'rational' terms of poor situational awareness and analysis. However, to do so risks underrating the psychological and ideological drives affecting German perception and helping determine policy choices and their implementation in strategic and operational terms. The ascendancy of individuals and groups who despised their opponents on ideological terms was a major factor, as also was the willingness to accept, even embrace, risk. The German leadership also failed to respond adequately to the issues on the Home Front, including the public response to the propaganda it produced.[5]

As separate but related issues over World War One, there are the contested topics of the degree of pre-war preparedness, notably in terms of understanding the developing nature of war, an issue that remained pertinent during the conflict, and of the quality of leadership; strategic, operational and tactical. These questions fed through into the veracity of the official histories and the response to them.[6] This response was active due to the degree of shaping that contemporaries sought to provide and the high level of contention over the conflict. Institutional, service, factional, personal and civilian politics all played a role, as in the response in Britain to the failure of the 1915 Dardanelles campaign. Winston Churchill, the First Lord of the Admiralty, fell as a consequence of his advocacy of the campaign. Then he used the subsequent scrutiny, by a Royal Commission in 1916–17, the official history, and more widely, to present his own view of success narrowly missed.[7] Churchill's fame is such that this episode has received extensive attention. However, the same process of justification and debate was also pertinent for many other individuals. Furthermore, the consequences of past intervention to establish and protect reputations affect the situation today; past politics thus influencing present history. The tensions over army and naval leadership were similarly contested. Indeed, military memoirs became semi-official accounts of war due to their author's standing.

The addition of new capabilities did not change the situation. Not only were individual reputations at stake. As far as the world wars and other struggles were concerned, the lessons that wars offered of the limitations of strategic bombing and the value of joint rather than stand-alone operations were unwelcome to airpower exponents and therefore not effectively incorporated into air force doctrine, notably in America.[8] In particular, insufficient weight was given to tactical bombing, and, in the British case, to the use of aircraft in support of maritime trade, as convoy escorts and by attacking submarines.[9]

So also with the problems posed for official histories by counter insurgency warfare. By their very nature, these histories provide the counter insurgency perspective, and not that of the insurgents. This represents a real problem in understanding, not least that reference to asymmetrical warfare can lead to a failure to follow through on the logic that brings together differences between insurgencies and counter insurgencies over goals and means that are possibly best addressed separately as well as together. Moreover, linked to this, there can be a process of clumping or running together, of aggregating insurgencies and, in contrast, counter insurgencies for analytical reasons, or indeed for the rhetorical ones that are so important to the usage of the past.

This process creates not only difficulties but fundamental misunderstandings, notably reading from one conflict to another in a fashion that underplays their distinctive character. This tendency is seen in discussion of periods of widespread 'crisis,' for example that of the mid-seventeenth century. A more recent instance was when the 'War on Terror' of the 2000s led to far greater interest in counter insurgency struggles on the part of American and British military commentators, academic and popular historians, public and publishers. An awareness of the issues involved in running together for discussion of the conflicts of today should induce caution about doing so in the past. It may appear possible to classify the wars of the early twenty-first century as a 'New Cold War', or 'Wars of Environmental Degradation and Resource Competition', or whatever is the new classification, criterion and cliché to attract one-dimensional writers; but, however suggestive such titles might be and helpful in terms of books sales, that lumping is not an appropriate approach.

Another issue challenging 'the official mindset' was that differing practices and tones in official histories affected the description of coalition operations, as with clashing American and Turkish approaches in the Korean War of 1952–3.[10] This is most obviously a matter of the differing approaches of allies, as with World War Two and Anglo-American tensions; but can also be seen in the contrasting views of operations held by differing services for these are also as it were in alliance. Thus for America, in the Pacific War of 1941–5, there were major tensions between army, navy and marines. The independent report on the debacle of the Ajax armoured vehicle programme commissioned in May 2022 by the British Ministry of Defence published in June 2023, concluded that 'relationships between different entities within or associated with MoD (Ministry of Defence) were at times fractious and involved guarding of territory.'

The perspective of official histories can offer much in terms of slowing down the account and anatomising the supposedly clear-cut building blocks of military history. Instead of these building blocks, what emerges is not 'the official view' or 'mind,' but rather a complex refraction of differences in command and, linked to that, more significant issues of purpose, implementation and the methodology of handling contention in military history. Official perspectives do not suffice but they are highly instructive.

The official view of the past resonates through commemoration, celebration and education. Moreover, legacy can be long term, as the contextual political circumstances of one period affect what comes later. Thus, the Crusade of 1444 ended at Varna in Bulgaria with total defeat by the Ottoman (Turkish) army. There was no reason to commemorate this in Bulgaria during the long centuries of subsequent Ottoman rule, while, after that ended, the emphasis was on the Russian military role in bringing that rule to a close in 1877–8. However, under Boris III (1918–43), there was an interest in Varna, with the memorial bearing the name of King Wladyslaw III of Poland and Hungary, who was killed during the battle, opened by the king. In part, this represented the engagement of Bulgaria with other conservative, anti-Soviet Eastern European states. The latter were the source of the crusaders of 1444. In turn, under the Communists from 1946, there was an emphasis on the extent to which the Varna force came from other Communist Eastern European states, while from 1952 Turkey was a NATO power and therefore hostile. At present, there is not that echo in Bulgaria. Nevertheless, the resonance of past accounts influences present memories, a process encouraged by the many decades during which schoolchildren were taken to the monument and told about the battle. And so also for elsewhere.

The most basic sense of an official view is a history of war in which current geographical demands and political categories are to the fore. The former has been particularly pressing as states have gained independence, a process that is far from new. Indeed, the modern topics of imperialism and decolonisation have a long historical background. This poses many implications for military history, not least the risk that participation in imperial armies is written out or down or misrepresented. Thus, for the Austro-Hungarian empire (Austria for short), which ended in 1918, there was a tendency subsequently, notably in Czechoslovakia which in 1918 became independent, to emphasise discontent, a process given literary form in Jaroslav Hašek's satirical novel *The Good Soldier Švejk* (1921–3). In practice, the extent to which soldiers then were motivated by a different sense of identity and loyalty, not least a masculinity linked to military service, was important, and the disillusioned Czechness that was to be emphasised was less significant than a willingness to fight for the empire.[11]

Chapter 4

The Popular Buzz

The present makes the popular buzz of military history very apparent. In particular, war is important in film, television, internet games, fiction and popular history and is celebrated by re-enactors and in displays, as in the British 'We Have Ways Warfest'. War as background and foreground suffuses many genres, such as romantic fiction and detective novels, for example the British television series *Foyle's War* (2002–15), a detective series set during World War Two and in part based on true stories. The genre of wartime detective stories, one set in earlier conflicts, developed with relevant works by Alan Furst, Robert Harris and Philip Kerr. There has also been a reprinting of detective novels written during World War Two and set in military life. These provided histories of war that slid from thrillers to 'secret histories' in which real characters appear.

As a result of the scale of the general activity today, there is no previous period for which there is so much military history, however defined and whatever the allowances made for quality and, separately, for a fictional dimension. This situation is far from surprising given the size of the world's population, which became eight billion in 2023 compared to three in 1960, its relative wealth, and the unprecedented rate of literacy. These varied factors of relevant scale are all important. Much attention is not devoted to military history, but there is much that is. Moreover, the popular buzz of military history that was focused for its audience (and subject) on the wealthiest part of the world – Western Europe and North America – has now expanded to include much more of the world, not least because of the rise in the relative prosperity of China and India. Each is highly active in presenting military history, particularly in the shape of film. In addition, popular history can be found in some of the conferences organised by larger museums such as, in Britain, the National Army Museum or publishers like Helion or societies such as the Gallipoli Association. They attract quite a bit of interest from the general public, and it is instructive that they often have a tendency to feature non-academic authors or speakers (often soldiers turned historians) who can present familiar facts and questionable interpretations as if new revelations.

The popular buzz scarcely began with the present parameters, and it does not help solely to discuss that situation. Nor, as a key related point, is it only the case that a present categorisation, means, scale or definition of a popular buzz should be read back into the past. In particular, what was seen as in the popular sphere has changed greatly, in terms of content, context and role, with acceptability also being an important aspect. War reporting and war artists represents a clear instance of this change in method. Moreover, it is one that is clearly going to go on being highly significant for combatants, not least as the electronic nature of dissemination makes it easier to affect reporting in opposing countries. As a result, the character of morale, both civilian and military, can be influenced through aspects of cyberwarfare. This will be an important aspect of the 'hybrid warfare' that has always been more significant than was suggested when it was presented as such, in the aftermath of the Russian seizure of Crimea in 2014, indeed as somehow novel.

That point opens up another sphere for histories of war. Not only will it be necessary to understand, record and evaluate such conflict, none of which is easy. Taking a related, but also distinct, technological point, it will also be pertinent to determine how much space to devote to the discussion of cyberwarfare in more general histories of war. In part, a focus on cyberwarfare raises the question of how far to focus on conflict as a whole that does not involve fighting, certainly fighting as conventionally understood. That is an issue in which standard assumptions are very much to the fore, but possibly have always also required qualification. Cyberwarfare extends to activities such as systems penetration and information seizure that can be continuous, hostile and harmful, but not necessarily regarded as war.

To underline the variety of the modern world, the complexity of the popular sphere and buzz can be understood differently if the varied role today of religious readings of past (and present) conflict are assessed. Thus, the situation in Iran, where there is a popular buzz, is both varied (as is the case in all societies), and includes a significant engagement with religious tropes as a means to contextualise, encourage, consider and present war, including fuelling a paranoia about alleged threats, one that leads to military preparations and aggressive rhetoric and actions. So also, more generally, with the use of religious division as an explanation for reasons for conflict in the past and still to this day, as in the European Wars of Religion of the sixteenth and early seventeenth centuries.

The word present in the sentence before last is instructive for it nicely captures a major issue with language and the corresponding need to address it when applied to war in contextual terms and with care. Present refers both to a period of time, the present, and to a process of representation, to present; and they are totally separate.

Mention of religion underlines the extent to which the definition of the popular buzz varies geographically, culturally, socially, politically and chronologically. There is a teleology in both the liberal and the radical Western traditions that is based on the assumption that the popular world becomes progressively more potent (that itself a form of progress), and, unless there is a form of 'false consciousness,' allegedly misleading the population, for example religious commitment, does so to the benefit of that particular tradition. That approach, which rested on a developmental account of change, analysis as well as politics as progressivism, looks less secure with the strengthening authoritarianism of the twenty-first century, including in democracies, the crisis of the liberal world order that is currently in evidence, and the growing strength of confessional politics and policies in a number of major states, including India, Russia and Turkey.

In this background, there will be not only a multiplicity of popular impulses but also a series of national contexts that give them weight, and infuse and monitor accordingly the discussion of war. The latter is as part of a general concern with the presentation of history. Thus, in India, the Hindu assertiveness strongly seen with the governing BJP (Bharatiya Janata Party) of Narendra Modi, Prime Minister since 2014, is focused on a rejection of the Mughal Emperors that gained power from 1526 as Muslims and, instead, a validation of their Maratha Hindu opponents of the seventeenth and eighteenth centuries. In Turkey, President Erdogan focuses on Ottoman greatness and successes in the fifteenth and sixteenth centuries.

Heroic defeat or challenges finally overcome are classic themes in national military histories, as with the British and the retreat from Dunkirk in 1940. These themes can offer triumph. At the same time, for most societies, decline and catastrophe, past, present and future, are expressed in terms of defeat, both the tendencies leading to it and the final crisis itself. Indeed, science fiction from that perspective is generally a form of military history, even if the history in question is an analogy located in the future. So also for the past with the use of apocalyptic images, both religious and historical, as offering an account of what might happen. This was seen in particular with the fall of Rome to Attila the Hun in 410 CE, but other ancient cities, from Troy to Palmyra (destroyed by the Romans in 273 after the defeat of Zenobia's rebellion), could be depicted to the same end, as with Herbert Schmalz's painting *Queen Zenobia's Last Look Upon Palmyra* (1888). The more unplaced sense of past defeat could also offer resonant history. Eugène Delacroix's dramatic painting *The Death of Sardanapalus*, hung at the Paris Salon of 1827, depicts a mythical Oriental tyrant, both cruel and weak, who chose to die surrounded by his slaughtered possessions (including slaves) as his state succumbed to rebellion.[1] This anticipated the outcome, though not the style, of the overthrow of the reactionary Charles X of France in 1830: history as future.

That a painting had a considerable following, in the sense of critical acclaim and extensive reproduction, does not itself substantiate the use of the term popular buzz, but that is itself a phrase that is open to various definitions, as well as contestation in its application and content. In part, we are anew with the idea of the *zeitgeist* or spirit of the age, one that is more complex in application than in assertion.

Allowing for that important point, there has been an important democratisation over the last two centuries as the numbers to be reached or who can be reached have grown while the ethos of representation has changed in a popular direction. There may be authoritarianism, but it is authoritarianism claiming a popular ambit and responsibility. That indeed helps explain the significance of school syllabi in public policy, and indeed 'history wars', as in America and Britain over the last four decades. They are not only a matter of control, but also a response to the real and apparent need to define, respond to and guide the wider public sphere. There is a clear utilitarian aspect, with a focus on the next generation of troops and voters and, indeed, troops, but also a wider sense of cultural need, which is felt by governments and commentators due to the significance attached to history as well as the extent to which it is under state control or regulation, with the latter therefore attracting controversy.

A very different instance of popular buzz, in terms of both medium and applicability, was found in the short video game *Counterstrike*. Created for the Finnish newspaper *Helsingin Sanomat*, it highlighted Russian atrocities in the Ukraine conflict of 2022–4, and used the medium of an online game to provide reports in Russian written by the paper's war correspondents in Ukraine, including information on Russian atrocities and casualties. Allegedly four million people play the game in Russia, a game set in a Slavic City called *Voina*, which means war in Russian. According to the newspaper 'The purpose is to make Russians see that the terrors of war are happening in places that look very familiar to them.'[2]

As a reminder that there are a number of ways to present war to the public, the same issue carried an article 'Putin's children: how the Kremlin indoctrinated a generation' that looked at how pro-war accounts are shared on Russian social media including the presentation of Ukraine and NATO as neo-Nazi. Putin's backers present the invasions of Ukraine in 2014 and 2022 as defensive acts similar to the resistance to German attack in 1941, which is a misreading of military history intended to validate action in the present.

Video games shared in the wider practice of infographics, visual representations of information, that have become increasingly significant for military history.[3] Yet, allowing for the undoubted appeal of such works, there is a dependence for accuracy on data, which is frequently lacking or partial or available without adequate comparative opportunities. It is more than likely that graphics will be a future for histories of war, with CGI dominant in the visual for popular histories, and graphs, in contrast, for their academic counterparts. How far this will lead to a ready transferability of images between cultures lacking in the world of print is unclear. Hitherto, the world of film has had few consequences in terms of any standardisation, at least at a global level; although, arguably, the situation within the West has been different as a consequence of the dominance of Hollywood. The current strength of America, China and India as image producers suggest that there will be no future standardisation or uniformity in histories of war at the level of popular imagery. Yet, there may be similar expectations and methods.

Chapter 5

Refighting The Last War?

'Waterloos' were the name given to sets of false teeth in early-nineteenth century Britain: sets were made from the real teeth of the many soldiers who had died in the decisive battle with Napoleon on the long day of 18 June 1815. These teeth proved a welcome replacement to the rotten counterparts of all too many of their seniors. They were also the last opportunity for such a harvest, as Britain did not see another major battle until conventions had changed. The young teeth of the soldiers, which were still recorded in catalogues in the 1860s, were carefully harvested as part of the gruesome process of pillaging the dead, one that continues to the present in some conflicts, as with Russian soldiers taking clothes from dead Ukrainians and a more general pattern of seizing weapons from the defeated.

Planning for the last war is the proverbial occupation of generals, but it is far fairer to say that most people tend to live under the shadow, or in this case using the teeth, of the previous major period of conflict; and this is particularly so after a sustained time of such warfare, such as 1914–45. These world wars, which were unprecedented in scale, frame the experience and understanding of war of both combatants and non combatants: it directly affects those who fought, or who were related to those who fought, and remains a powerful and living memory for the many who followed the war from a distance and those who framed, in some fashion or other, what was, in the twentieth century, to be called the Home Front.

Moreover, those who were too young to take such roles as combatants or non combatants during wars, nevertheless, still grew up in a mental world framed by the indirect experience of conflict, and, more particularly of specific wars. Literary and other works gave shape and lent force to this mental force, whether the grandeur of Leo Tolstoy's novel *War and Peace* (1865–9), with its epic account of Napoleon's invasion of Russia in 1812, the largest prior to the twentieth century, or the mundane fate, in Elizabeth Gaskell's novel *Cranford* (1851–3), of a much-revered paternal boot that had served at Waterloo. Tolstoy, who had commanded an artillery battery during the Anglo-French siege of Russian-held Sevastopol of 1854–5 in the Crimean War, also wrote about that costly but eventually successful siege. Children's fiction was peopled with characters who had fought in the wars, such as those in the novels of William Earl Johns, notably Biggles (1932–68), Steeley (1936–9), Worrals (1941–50) and Gimlet (1943–54).[1]

The mental world of the shadow of war was, if not uniform in its immediacy, close to being so; although its configuration varied greatly. For example, in America, the experience of conflict was felt most strongly after the bitter Civil War of 1861–5. This left a trauma of unresolved defeat for the Confederacy. There were also major consequences for the victorious Union, not least in the shape of the five veterans who, between 1869 and 1901, subsequently became Presidents: Grant, Hayes, Garfield, Harrison and McKinley.

This experience of conflict was then to recur after World War Two, which, for America, was 1941–5; whereas, after the short-lived Spanish-American War of 1898, World War One did not have a comparable impact, and is now somewhat of a forgotten war for Americans, although many were killed in 1918. Moreover, as an instance of counterfactualism, many more would have been killed had the war continued, as was expected into 1919. By that campaign, the Americans would have provided the largest Allied contingent on the Western Front. As a result, the history of that war would have been very different, an obvious point but one that tends to be overlaid by a sense of the need to explain what happened rather than what had seemed likely. Indeed, in the spring and early summer of 1918, with Russia having left the war and the Germans putting considerable pressure on the Allies through repeated attacks on the Western Front, it would have appeared implausible to most that Germany would have to accept armistice terms that November. In 1941–2, in contrast, despite greater territorial and numerical losses, the Soviet Union did not leave the war. This was a reflection in large part of the contrast between the Bolshevik takeover and Stalin's grip. Yet, this contrast was also a reflection of the failure of German strategy in 1941–3 compared to that in 1917–18, indeed an inability to learn from the past. In 1917–18, the Germans in effect mounted a political offensive to create and sustain political divisions and offer terms in a way that they did not even try to do under Hitler.

The events of any period could be shaped by contemporary and later commentators into developments and trends. This shaping was especially significant for those seeking to understand how best to win wars or, at least, to avoid the traumatic defeats that had been seen in recent conflicts. Such an understanding was a particular issue in Europe after the extensive warfare of 1792–1815. Then, alongside a desire not to repeat the experience of the wars, not least because of the continuing burden of having to pay for the debts to which they had given rise, aspects of the military agenda seemed to change little in the decades after 1815. While Clausewitz, Jomini and others were writing, the same places were fought over, notably Belgium, Poland and northern Italy, while figures from these wars, such as Radetsky (Austria), Soult (France) and Wellington (Britain), remained prominent in their country's military establishments. Generally known for his victories in Italy in 1848–9, Radetzky (1766–1858) became an officer in 1786, a Major General in 1805 and was Chief of the General Staff in 1809–12 before playing an important role in the campaigns against Napoleon in 1813–14. Soult (1769–1851), a Napoleonic Marshal, was Minister for War in 1814–15, 1830–4 and 1840–5. In the Spanish Civil War of 1833–40, the key Carlist commander until his death in 1835, Tomás Zumalacárregui, was a veteran of the struggle against Napoleon, a struggle that served as an important model for the rebel Carlists. So earlier with the French invasion of Spain in 1823 in which commanders on both sides had served during the earlier Napoleonic invasion.

A similar process could be seen in America, with the legacy of the War of 1812, the term given for the conflict waged with Britain from 1812 to 1815. Commanders from the wars of 1792–1815 who continued to be prominent, such as the American, Winfield Scott, the key figure in the Mexican-American War of 1846–8, and one whose influence continued into the early stages of the Civil War. Scott's planning of operations in Mexico in 1847 was influenced by his reading of the Peninsular War, particularly Napier's history of it.[2] In addition, much of the establishment of post-war militaries consisted of those who had fought in more junior capacities in recent wars. In China, there was no dramatic break until the successful attack by Britain in the Opium War (1839–42) and in Japan until the arrival of American naval pressure in the shape of Commodore Perry's warships in 1853.

The habit of looking back was well engrained. In Britain, the legacies of Nelson at sea and Wellington on land proved potent, and, in 1854, Lord Raglan, the British commander in Crimea, was praised by comparison with his former patron, Wellington:

> 'If the poor old Duke had lived to see your triumph, how justly proud he would have been of victories won by his pupil and by his dearest and most trusted friend. Indeed he still lives in the army which he trained and in the general whom he taught to conquer... This is indeed treading in the steps of your great master.'[3]

Modelled on the command style and success of Horatio Nelson, the decisive naval battle was held up as a model for subsequent naval operations, leading to British disappointment in World War One: Jutland (1916) was no Trafalgar (1815), a point that was well understood. At the same time, there was marked continuity in the importance of convoys and blockading.[4] The failure to give due weight to them in the most popular discussions of naval history helped affect the priorities adopted in World War One, notably that of the public.

It is true that learning from or recollecting major battles, such as Napoleon's defeat at Leipzig (1813) or Waterloo, meant little in the case, for example, of the Polish uprising of 1830 against Russian rule. However, the legacy of the Napoleonic Wars also comprised both insurrectionary (and counter insurrectionary) warfare, notably in Calabria and Spain, as well as conflict outside the West. Both of the latter, indeed, were at stake for Western powers in the decades after Waterloo.

Alongside practical points, any reference to refighting the last war, however, is apt to be pejorative. In part, this reflects the particular views of a modern age that was and remains disparaging about reference to the past, and reverence of it, a set of values that came to the fore with nineteenth-century utilitarianism. More specifically, the disparagement of the past was part of the criticism of World War One commanders, particularly British generals. In practice, this was not a correct judgment, for the commanders of the period proved very able to adapt to the difficulties of the conflict.

There was no constancy in the tactical, operational or strategic dimensions of the war. If in 1914 there was a looking back to pre-war planning, doctrine and practices, that was scarcely surprising, but by the end of the war there was a response to the deadliness of firepower by turning to trench warfare. That was scarcely a case of fighting the last war, no more than the use of submarines and response to them was the case at sea. Moreover, the nature of trench warfare changed greatly and repeatedly on the Western Front by 1918. Thus, the 'history' of World War One as a case of fighting the last war, although often affirmed, is simply inaccurate. Looked at differently, this very affirmation is an important aspect of the history of war understood in popular terms and also with reference to later debates among military commentators.

Instead of learning from the past, the standard argument now is that one should embrace the future, for example missiles rather than aircraft-delivered nuclear bombs in the 1960s.[5] This approach reflects a particularly strong dynamic in modern Western thought on war, that of teleology. In practice, it is crucial to learn from recent experience. Thus, rather than being fixed on victory in the civil war of 1946–9, a victory in which there had been a major shift from the guerrilla techniques in the 1930s, the Chinese Communists sought to learn from the much more difficult conflict in Korea in 1950–3, a conflict in which they had fought the Americans. They sought to learn not only to improve their own military but also to develop that of North Vietnam.[6] In turn, that effort was a way to increase Chinese political influence but that proved unwelcome and was ultimately rejected, such that the two powers fought in 1979, beginning a conflict that continued until 1991. The failures of the Chinese invasion in 1979 provide an interesting context in which to consider earlier French and American failures. Indeed, military influence could be less successful and sustained than might be anticipated, a lesson the Soviet Union was to learn from Egypt in the early 1970s.

Separately, an understanding of the diversity of conflicts, past, present and future, offers important correctives to narratives of modernisation. Moreover, success and failure were generally the result of local conditions and demands, rather than reflections of the supposedly inherent benefits of certain technologies or systems. The contextual nature of success is not one that lends itself to simple analyses of proficiency. Thus, for example, the emphasis on Western proficiency in the sixteenth century needs to take note of failures, notably, but not only, in Morocco and Mozambique, and in the nineteenth century likewise, including for, respectively, Britain and Italy in Afghanistan and Ethiopia.

In reality, long-term developments are not only present in retrospect, but can also be apparent to contemporaries. Yet, at the same time, the significance of change, though, of course, easy to suggest and a key part of the content and rhetoric of politics, including military politics, can in practice, be difficult to grasp. It is both hard to understand the particular significance of individual conflicts, let alone campaigns, battles or sieges and to separate out and assess capability, potential and developments.

The learning process is problematised because hindsight, both then and now, is very much a matter of the play of the present, with the pressing concerns of the latter framing the questions asked of the past, and thereby the understanding and discussion of it. Answering (as well as questioning in order to produce answers) is seen as demonstrating the value of military history, not least in the settings in which for long it operated.[7] Nevertheless, a commitment to certain answers can guide the questions asked, indeed generally does. This is true of military learning, academic teaching and popular speculation.

Such a commitment is inherently present in contentious issues, for history that is contentious is an opportunity to debate issues of identity and to explore what are presented as the discontents of modern civilisation; with both fired up by the ability to draw on different positions. Thus, the appeasement of the dictators in the 1930s and the Vietnam War served to encourage and discourage subsequent Western, notably American, intervention in international crises, for example the possible American roles in Angola and Somalia. As a result, scholarship on these apparent lodestars became controversial. Thus, arguments that the Vietnam War was winnable by America and South Vietnam, for example Mark Moyar's *Triumph Forsaken: The Vietnam War 1954–1965* (2006), were challenged, as by John Prados's *Vietnam: The History of an Unwinnable War, 1945–1975* (2009). In this longstanding argument, there was a degree of politics, of culture wars and of the pressures of current military issues. Each is significant and it is possibly naïve to suggest that they can be avoided. Comparison and contrast with the Chinese-Vietnamese war of 1979 is instructive.

This debate about the Vietnam War remains active at the present moment, although it can suffer from the difficulties of linking the discussion adequately to the often obscure nature of decision-making within the North Vietnamese government. The motivation of the latter has been clarified to a degree by scholarship, as have divisions within it and their linkage to the relationships with China and the Soviet Union as the two powers moved apart. At the same time, the extent to which these could be influenced by the actions of America and South Vietnam remains unclear, and that raises fundamental issues about the context for evaluating the latter. This issue is more generally the case with the assessment of strategy and also with the consequent analysis of histories of war. Unfortunately, much of the more accessible popular American treatment of the Vietnam War displays this tendency of only really looking at one side of the hill and treating opponents as if a 'horde' with an uncomplicated strategy and ethos expressed simply in terms of a willingness to take heavier casualties. In part, this approach primitivises the North Vietnamese and Viet Cong, and thereby places all the burden and choice of strategy simply on the side of the Americans. There is a tendency to do the same when assessing Chinese failure in 1979. More generally, there were tendencies of what have been termed 'forever war' in American policy,[8] but also the limitation of not using the world's most potent military, in part due to a wish to avoid nuclear conflagration.

And so also for other powers, and unsurprisingly so given the extent to which America, Britain, France and many other states had not only to confront insurrectionary forces but also to face a variety of military tasks during the twentieth and early twenty-first centuries.[9] This meant that tradition and doctrine alike were under pressure from the needs for a workable military history able both to support a variable present and to contest other interpretations. The last is an important aspect, for the value of arguments for rhetorical purposes is a significant aspect of their use. Indeed, positions can in part be taken partly or largely to contest the rhetorical debate.

Due to changing tasks, the past is therefore presented anew. The concern with counter insurgency in the 2000s, as a result of the serious difficulties facing American-led coalition interventions in Afghanistan and Iraq, led to a sustained reconsideration of the earlier military situation in both countries, with an interest also in earlier instances of such episodes. How far value was gained by considering say the Napoleonic conflict with insurgents in Spain in 1808–13, or the later difficulties the British had repeatedly encountered in successive interventions in Afghanistan in the nineteenth century is a matter of opinion. Yet, such reflection did not mean being trapped in the past. Instead, in marked contrast, there was a flattening of the past in order to try to provide pertinence for the present. However, in terms of counter insurgency, the British assumed that they were experts following their long experience yet clearly stumbled badly in Iraq and Afghanistan. There was too much complacency, not least the idea that Basra was 'more Palermo than Beirut.' Some of the British commentary on American methods appears questionable.

A similar process can be seen in discussion of the conflict in Ukraine that began in 2022. The popular account of the initial Russian failure that year owed much to discussion of a new, more nimble technology, notably destruction delivered by and thanks to drones. Yet, that approach was subsequently qualified, as attritional conflict focused on artillery came to the fore, by references to World War Two on the Eastern Front, and notably the battle of Stalingrad (1942–3). The latter was resonant because it was a total Soviet triumph, and one waged close to Ukraine. More particularly, attritional conflict in early 2023 was very different to the fighting at Stalingrad, for the letter was the prelude to a successful use of manoeuvrist warfare. The relevance of Stalingrad to the present is unclear militarily. Moreover, in political terms, the battle was a totally inappropriate comparison, as at Stalingrad the Soviets had been the defenders against German aggression, whereas in Ukraine the Russians are the attackers. Indeed, the Russian use of World War Two as an indicative parallel is simply wrong.

Of course, the very mention, indeed focus, on Ukraine in a book written in 2023 is itself a form of presentism, and is so in terms both of the content of history and of its analysis. The specifics of alleged parallels and particular case studies should be assessed within a more cautious process in which decisions are not elevated simply by outcomes, or indeed only by the alternatives offered. The frictions of place, time, performance and the role of the other side need to be assessed, not least in terms of the experience of the key decision-makers.[10]

Furthermore, it would be misleading to suggest or imply that it is only in the modern period, however defined, that powers have had to adjust to a variable present of different military tasks. This was the case for example of Ancient Rome,[11] but also of a wide range of weaker powers that had to face international opponents but also domestic insurrections. The need to discuss confronting challenges however was affected by the degree to which there was a validation of certain rivals as honorable while others were not seen in that light, notably 'barbarians' as well as rebels. Thus, histories of war in part record sociocultural and political assumptions rather than being based on any abstract notion of rivalship or means of challenge. The latter, however, scarcely exists separately to these assumptions. Repeatedly, the role of assumptions emerges as a central issue in this book.

Chapter 6

Prior to the Last Half-Millennium, –1500

Creation accounts, whether of the world, of humans, or of the social order, generally involved conflict, fundamental and thus metaphysical, bitter conflict, as with that of the world in the *Purusha Sūkta*, the *Hymn of Primeval Man*, from tenth-century BCE India. If creation and religion were about conflict and rivalry, with god(s) in competition with those with rival claims to divinity, it was not surprising that bellicosity or warfulness was a key to the resulting social norms. This situation reflected not just the need for a will and readiness to fight in order to survive, but also the connotations of individual masculinity and collective bonds.[1] Oral and other histories proclaimed war in terms of need and pleasure, survival and excitement. History was part of the ritualisation of conflict and of its historicity. Indeed, this was a prime purpose of history. Symbolic rituals centred on military leadership, and success was important to the maintenance of prestige. Sin was long the explanation of defeat; sin frequently being seen as a lack of resolute godly purpose.

Sin was also the characteristic of the defiance of gods, both by humans and by superhuman figures, such as those that played a prominent role in Japanese, Indian, Greek, Māori and many other mythologies and storytelling. In one respect, winning the support of gods and superhuman figures represented a way to gain the equivalent of an advantage in technological capability but that was also conceptualised in moral terms, as with Homer's account of the Trojan War.

Shrouded in myth, and therefore eminently usable, the war over Troy was central to a Greek tradition that was to be important to Western culture and a lasting source of reference, one that took precedence over what might otherwise have been influential, not only Egyptian and Mesopotamian history, but also the rival legitimacy offered to the West by Old Testament accounts. The Trojan War, fought in about 1194–1184 BCE, or rather the later presentation of that war, captured the extent to which the histories, the presentation of experience, by which humans made sense of themselves, related to conflict, both between gods and between humans. Thus, Homer's *Iliad*, the epic account of the Trojan War, is the earliest war story to survive, albeit in a much later account. Moreover, as was normal, command decisions were explained in accordance with the norms and moral commonwealth deemed appropriate.

Although rivalry between the gods did not resonate in monotheistic Christianity, the theme of individual heroism echoed from the Greek treatment of the Trojan War. Thus, neoclassical works drew on the conflict, as in Donato Creti's painting *Achilles Dragging the Body of Hector round the Walls of Troy* and François-Pascal Gérard's *Achilles Mourning Patroclus*.

In the *Iliad*, honour was the key spur, honour in the shape of control over a woman, Helen, taken to Troy, but also, and more consistently, in this and other war stories, of relations between men and between deities. Men who fail to honour deities make not only themselves, but their causes vulnerable, a process to which oracles provide warning. Indeed, oracles provided a form of instant history that ranged into the future while also offering an explanation.

Honour and deities played a part in India, with the role of dynastic feuds and major battles in the great Sanskrit epics, the *Mahabharata* and the *Ramayana*, notably the battles of Kuruksetia and that of the Ten Kings. Similarly, war took a central role in more explicitly religious narratives, such as the Old Testament of the Bible, with the children of Israel capturing Jericho and other targets. That account was part of the markedly historical character of the Bible. Divine intervention was seen when the pursuing Egyptian army was drowned crossing the Red Sea. Mandated authority, whether for monarchs, dynasties or people, all were reflected in cosmic forms of history. In turn, some religious rites required conflict in order to feed their needs. Thus, the human sacrifices used by the Aztecs of modern Mexico were provided by captives, which was a particularly brutal type of slavery. The latter more generally represented a human aspect of the history of war, with slaves a consequence of conflicts. Indeed, this is one of the major long-term results of war, one sometimes the reality underlying territorial conquests.

War is important in rituals, for example those that have survived to the present in the South-West Pacific, and are re-enacted, notably for tourists, as in the Solomon Islands. These rituals, as in New Guinea, frequently depict struggles against other clans and against creatures that are semi-animal and/or semi-gods. In narratives and rituals, gods were usually presented as warlike. While particularly the case with male gods, this was also seen with some female ones. The rulers are representatives of the gods, a situation that pertained in Japan until the end of World War Two when, as a result of defeat and occupation by the more secular Americans, this divine mandate was removed. The extent to which rulers, both hereditary and elective, military and civilian, still wear military uniforms and attend military ceremonies is an aspect of the same process. The annual Bastille Day ceremony in Paris in the presence of the French President very much captures republican militarism, and the same is seen with the commemorative military role of American presidents, although this has been compromised to a degree by public attacks on commanders, notably by Donald Trump.

The rituals of the past were part of a process in which tribal success over other tribes involved conflict between gods in an inherently competitive system, a process, moreover, that led to the spiritual union of conquerors with the land they had conquered, as both gods and peoples were defeated and displaced or brought into servitude. Thus, conquests of Jerusalem, notably by the Assyrians and the Romans, saw the destruction of Jewish religious sites, particularly the temple. The polytheistic nature of most religious systems encouraged narratives of struggles between gods. In turn, for monotheistic religions, such as Judaism, there was struggle between the 'true God' and pagan cults, such as those of Baal. Thus, the Jews' war with the Philistines was a religious conflict at all levels, politics being religion in part because religion included everything.

This was a position also seen with Christianity, for which indeed conflict was necessary in order to resist the Devil and all his agents, such as witches and works, including the temptation to sin. As a result, to avoid conflict was to accept a lack of vigilance and a weakness that constituted a false peace.[2] In *St Michael Striking Down the Rebellious Angels* (c.1650–2), the Spanish-born painter Sebastián López de Arteaga (1610–52) depicted St Michael, sword in hand, leading a host. This was religion as war.

This approach presented war as normative, and could see the enemy not only as non Christians but also as bad Christians. The latter was an approach that spanned international and domestic opponents, as indeed was to be shown with crusading. Its targets included not only non Christians such as Muslims and pagan Lithuanians, but also Christians who were treated as enemies, for example the Albigensians/Cathars of southern France and the Hussites of Bohemia. The latter looked toward the assault on Protestantism in the sixteenth century. It was seen as a heresy that required destruction, and the emphasis was on 'holy war.' As a result of this, it is not helpful to treat 1500, or any year nearby, as a firm boundary between periods, one, for example, defined by the large-scale use of gunpowder in the West. Instead, the gunpowder-definition of modernity requires considerable qualification, not least with religious warfare, between and within religions, such as the Protestant-Catholic rivalry in Christianity and the Sunni-Shia divide in Islam, offering continuity. At the same time, there has been continuity at many levels across history, and that does not lessen the need to distinguish and classify.

The interaction of conflict and religion was scarcely an approach restricted to Christendom. In the *Aśvamedha* in Vedic India (*c.*1500–1100 BCE), the wandering of a sacrificial horse followed by warriors provided a claim to suzerainty and a cause of conflict. If anything, Islam offered a more bellicose sacral culture[3] as the emphasis was less on conversion by missionaries than in the case of Christianity, and more on conquest. That did not necessarily mean the extirpation of other religions, but such was certainly a major theme as was the enforced conversion of the slaves gained by the raiding that was an important aspect of Islamic warfare. More generally, the memorialisation of places, and the recording of the battles that took place, helped convey a sense of territorial control and collective identity, the histories of war offering explicit associations with deities and kings, in a process of ancestor exposition as well as worship. This practice of memorialising places and recording battles, such as the Athenian victory at Marathon in 490 BCE, in order to convey control and strengthen identity, can be seen in the present as well. If the latter is not usually with a religious dimension then it is with the apparent equivalent of one in terms of mission.

There was both a mythic quality in military history and one that was anchored in the creation of new accounts, accounts that demonstrated providential support and affirmed militaristic culture. This was seen with empires and their varied forms as far back as records go. Thus, describing his capture of Susa, the capital of Elam, in the south-west of modern Iran, in 653 BCE, King Ashurbanipal, an especially successful war leader of particularly militaristic Assyria, recorded:

> 'Susa, the great holy city, abode of their Gods, seat of their mysteries, I conquered. I entered its palaces, I opened their treasuries where silver and gold, goods and wealth were amassed ... I destroyed the ziggurat of Susa. I smashed its shining copper horns. I reduced the temples of Elam to naught; their gods and goddesses I scattered to the winds. The tombs of their ancient and recent kings I devastated, I exposed to the Sun, and I carried away their bones towards the land of Ashur. I devastated the provinces of Elam and on their lands sowed salt.'[4]

This was very much a conquest of past, in the shape of temples and tombs, a struggle between religions, and history as a descriptor, affirmation and record of the triumph. This approach was given later poetic resonance, but also the criticism of time by Percy Bysshe Shelley in his atmospheric sonnet *Ozymandias* (1818), a comment on the inherent fragility of histories of war, and not least by a widespread possibility for reference from the Pharoah Rameses II (Ozymandias was a Greek name for him) and Ashurbanipal of Assyria to Napoleon and, more ironically, the unmartial George IV:

> I met a traveller from an antique land,
> Who said—"Two vast and trunkless legs of stone
> Stand in the desert.... Near them, on the sand,
> Half sunk a shattered visage lies, whose frown,
> And wrinkled lip, and sneer of cold command,
> Tell that its sculptor well those passions read
> Which yet survive, stamped on these lifeless things,
> The hand that mocked them, and the heart that fed;
> And on the pedestal, these words appear:
> My name is Ozymandias, King of Kings;
> Look on my Works, ye Mighty, and despair!
> Nothing beside remains. Round the decay
> Of that colossal Wreck, boundless and bare
> The lone and level sands stretch far away."

In practice, while frequently asserting his magnificence, notably in temple building and enormous statues, Ramesses was not a great general. His major battle, with the Hittites at Kadesh in 1274 BCE, was a close-run draw, but Ramesses needed to assert success in order to preserve his domestic and international position. His monuments frequently mentioned Kadesh.[5]

In small part, the fall of the statue imagined by Shelley is a lay reprise of the Prophet Daniel's interpretation of the dream of the Babylonian ruler Nebuchadnezzar in which the collapse of a golden-headed statue acts as a prediction of that of a series of empires, with eventually, very differently, the arrival of the rule of God. The role of prophets provided an equivalent to the Greek use of oracles. Predictions rested not on a developmental knowledge of the future as different, but rather on a sense of time as a continuum and with both past and future part of it.

There were, indeed, plentiful instances of the overthrowing of triumph. At Himera, the first Greek settlement on the north coast of Sicily, an imposing Temple of Victory can be seen. It commemorates victory in 480 BCE over the Carthaginians; although, ironically, the latter were to capture the city in 409 BCE. Somewhat differently, occupied by the Spaniards from 1614, La Mamora in Morocco was successfully besieged by Sultan Ismail Ibn Sharif in 1681, and renamed al-Mahdiyah. The statue of Jesus in the church was taken as loot, as were Spanish captives for slaves, including women and girls. A mosque, madrasa and traditional inn were constructed as part of the restoration of the twelfth-century kasbah.

Conflict was seen as natural, necessary and inevitable, part of the divine order, the scourge of divine wrath, and the counterpart of violence in the elements, as well as the correct, honourable and right way to settle matters. Early cultures saw war as just. It was sacral, legitimate and rational. As a consequence, early ethical thought about war, for example those of Egyptian, Hittite and Jewish cultures, had a commitment to war as right and justified on both general and pragmatic grounds,[6] and there was no interest in restraining or condemning it.

This point serves as a corrective to the view that war, conquest and imperialism were products of the age of Western capitalism or some other apparent pathology of development of the West. These views expect to see validation of early societies as pacific, a view widely held in the West in the 1960s and 1970s that, however, is not supported by archaeological evidence. Instead, as with so much in terms of the histories of war, the view speaks to a particular moment in later Western culture, and carries with it an accompanying ahistoricism. This presentation of early societies is not shared to the same extent in other major cultures, notably China. Moreover, competition with animals was a major cause of conflict.

As a result of the apparent naturalness of war, history was part of the show element of providence, one that it was necessary to record. History was duty and, as such, exemplary and admonitory. Thus, the remains of the Colima culture, which thrived in west Mexico from 100 BCE to 300 CE, show that its shamans (religious figures) communicated with the gods on behalf of the people, and were also great warriors depicted, accordingly, with the heads of the defeated. The treatment of the defeated in this fashion was a way to gain their potency and magic, and to demonstrate victory over the living and the dead. Terror, the terror of show, was important to this process and a vindication of it. Other cultures saw aspects of such desecration of the defeated, as with the cutting off of scalps or penises.

The history in question was not necessarily only or even partly a matter of writing. Thus, in the Tahitian archipelago, 'Oro, the god of fertility and war, was a formidable figure who received offerings of dead men. The defeated could expect slaughter and the destruction of their traditional temples. The clan war of 1768 over who would be paramount chief of Tahiti led to genocide for the defeated and a wall of skulls built by the victor. Similarly, in New Zealand, war dances and priestly incantations celebrated the power of gods and ancestors.

Religion, in both theory and practice, doctrine and belief, linked past, present and future. Thus, Hannibal made a vow in the Temple of Baal in Carthage to take revenge against the Romans for their defeat of Carthage in the First Punic War. Such vows were a significant aspect of the mission aspect of war, and provided a personal history of commitment. The role of religion in conflict of course has lasted to the present, even if much writing on military matters is apt to forget this level of motivation and experience, not least a feeling of providential piety. This is true for Western traditions[7] as well as non-Western ones.

Although just war and holy war are not synonymous, the notion of just war long focused on religious considerations. Thus, aside from more specific goals, millenarian beliefs focused on the First Crusade (1096–9), with the sense of mission linked to the demise of Islam and the creation of a new Christendom centred on Jerusalem,[8] which indeed fell in 1099 with a large-scale massacre of the defenders as well as many Muslims and Jews. Muslim holy sites were converted into Christian counterparts. The scale of the First Crusade was unusual for Christendom, but a similar theme of devastation was seen on many other occasions, while that crusade also helped to make it normative.

Religious identity and violence linked conflict, conquest, conversion and control, as with the Muslim impact not only on Christendom but also more widely, for example in India.[9] As monotheistic religions became the pattern, so this process was accentuated.

The long range of history was largely complete by 1500, for only just over half a millennium remained then. That only one chapter is devoted to this period therefore may appear mistaken, distorting both the overall account and that period itself. However, there are clear issues in terms of source availability for history prior to 1500. In addition, as a multiple of time versus population, there is a reason to look far more favourably on the last half-millennium than would otherwise have been the case. The major issue therefore is not one of relative space distribution within a book, but, rather, the problem that the whole period prior to 1500 can be covered too rapidly, indeed generally is done in histories of war, thus underrating differences and the extent of change.

Moreover, as a separate issue underlining the value of this organisation, 1500 itself is a date of no special significance within Western history, and also has no comparable meaning for the numbering system of other cultures. As a result, the year can be used without creating a classification that misleadingly suggests a particular analysis; but such a classification can be all-too seductive.

There is also the problem of primitivisation in terms of downplaying the sophistication and importance of discussion with reference to monarchs and religions, as if they were simple factors and spheres, neither of which was the case. That misleading approach is particularly apposite for developmental accounts of history, and, indeed, warfare. In addition, other elements were active in the historicism of war prior to 1500. Thus, proto-nationalism was part of the equation, with all of its implications of wider public engagement. The conflicts of that period, like those since, involved the mobilisation of resources.[10]

The surviving sources for this long period tend to emphasise an epic account of war, whether in terms of the Terracotta Army in Xian, the carvings on Assyrian palaces and Egyptian columns, or the tale told by Homer. It is probable, however, not only that other societies that currently leave no comparable traces would have had such sources, but also that the surviving sources were only part of a richer and more varied account of war, one in which there were a range of activities and foci, from the state to the family. The lessons learned would have been the standard ones of fortitude, dynastic and tribe legitimacy and divine favour. Thus, war, and in particular battle, served to inscribe broader lessons. Learning solely about conflict, and its means, was far from the central point. Instead, moralised notions of good and ill were crucial, with warrior status, exemplary purpose and chivalric values all valued. Prowess and courage had to have purpose. There had to be a readiness for violence.[11]

Honour and glory were key injunctions from the past conflict as they affirmed personal, family and dynastic position. An exemplary history was therefore important, and part of a living past. Thus, Henry VI of England (r. 1422–61; 1470–1) backed the canonisation of the ninth-century King Alfred of Wessex, in order to link to a great warrior of the past. Warrior predecessors were regarded as important forbears. For the Crown of England this list ranged from Arthur and Alfred to Richard the Lionheart, Edward, the Black Prince and Henry V. Campaigns were represented in illustrations and writings, as in John Page's poem on Henry V's successful siege of Rouen in 1418–19.[12]

And so also elsewhere, with commemorative histories accordingly commissioned. Manuel I of Portugal (r. 1495–1521) commissioned, from the historian and chronicler Duart Galvào, the *Chronicle of El-Rei D. Afonso Henriques*, the life and deeds of Portugal's first king which dealt with the victory at Ourique over the Moors in 1139 as well as the capture of Lisbon from the Moors in 1147.

Dynastic references in China were similar. Thus, the emperor, Kao-tsung (r. 1127–62) of the Sung dynasty initially admired Han Kuang-wu-ti (r. 25–57) of the later Han dynasty, who had restored the Han after it had been overthrown, providing a model for a hoped-for-response by the emperor to the Jin who had taken control of northern China from the Liao in 1126. From 1141, in contrast, Kao-tsung started to admire Wen-ti (r. 180–157 BCE) of the Western Han dynasty on the basis that he had sought to attain success through peace, an approach that in part reflected Kao-tsung's attempt to maintain the peace with the Jin.

The deeds of rulers could be those of lawmakers, but warrior roles were more frequent and significant as sources for prestige and renown, as with the anonymous *Holy Wars of Sultan Murad, son of Mehmed Khan*, an account of the Ottoman Sultan Murad II (r. 1421–51). Subsequently, by Mehmed II conquering Constantinople, the centre of Orthodox Christianity, in 1453, and by Selim I taking over from the defeated Mamluk rulers of Egypt, the guardianship of the Holy Cities of Mecca and Medina in 1517, the Ottomans drew through victory on powerful historical resonances of authority, as well as contributing to the significance of these victories through these resonances. Doing so was important to the domestic prestige of the Ottoman dynasty, to the competition for primacy with other Islamic dynasties, notably the Safavids of Persia, and also in providing a context for the continuing struggle with Christendom. Conquest set a pattern for Ottoman rulers, who in effect competed with their predecessors.

It is possible to rationalise the Ottoman pattern of expansion, and to apply specific assessment, for example one in which a key element is the drive to gain control of maritime trade routes, thus making a number of territories, including Mameluke Egypt, particularly significant. Yet, that element might have been less important than the bellicosity of rulers and social elite.

Yet, just as the religious ethos, energy and experience of crusading did not preclude a process of careful planning and organisation that can be described as characteristically rational,[13] so the same was the case for the Ottomans. Alongside more limited purposes for specific rulers, both Ottomans and others, manifest destiny, messianic imperialism and universalism were all refracted through the prism of glory. However, it might be mistaken to suggest that the two aspects, religious and rational, should be seen as separate or necessarily divergent; and a similar point could be made about bellicosity and rationality.

Reputation was a dynamic that enforced action and therefore was bathed in bellicosity, which helped ensure that it was necessary to handle the reputational blow of defeat. Whether old or new, forms of warfare served to display valour and leadership, the two being regarded as linked, so that individual prowess related also to the leadership of the group. Histories of war demonstrated merit, as with the accounts of those who led storming parties into the breaches of walls or, at sea, in boarding parties. Valour was seen as a constant, which cuts across progressivist accounts of war. Indeed, the latter drew and draw on modern terms such as professional, the application of which can be anachronistic and seriously misleading,[14] unless loose categorisations and linkages are employed.

Thucydides (*c.* 460–400 BCE), the Athenian author of *The History of the Peloponnesian War* and Herodotus (*c.* 485–425 BCE), the other renowned Greek historian of the fifth century BCE, are widely seen as key figures in the development of Western historical writing, providing a less mythical account than Homer. For each, conflict was a key theme: Herodotus, who defined history as what could be reliably discovered, rather than just stories about the past, set out at the very beginning of his narrative to trace the origin of the hostility between Greece and Asia. He advanced a set of stories that rationalised myths, and then rejected them in order to concentrate, instead, on King Croesus of Lydia. About 425 BCE, Herodotus (I, pref.1) wrote:

'This is the display of the research of Herodotus of Halicarnassus, made so that human achievements should not fade with time, and so that great and wondrous deeds displayed by Greeks and barbarians should not be without lasting fame: my particular concern is the reason why they went to war with one another.'

Thucydides, meanwhile, began:

'Thucydides from Athens wrote his account of the war which the Peloponnesians and the Athenians fought against each other, beginning from when the war broke out, because he expected that it would be major and the most worthy of discussion of previous events.' (1.1.1)

Thucydides also wrote consciously as he put it:

'not for immediate applause but for posterity, and I shall be content if the future student of these events, or of other similar events which are likely in human nature to occur in after ages, finds my narrative on them useful.'

Surviving writings provide evidence of the existence and significance of military factors that otherwise cannot be so readily assessed. Thus, Thucydides has Nicias seek aid from Athens for its force at Syracuse in these terms:

'Our fleet, as the enemy also have learned, though at first it was in prime condition as regards both the soundness of the ships and the unimpaired condition of the crews, is not so now; the ships are waterlogged, from having been at sea for so long a time already, and the crews have wasted away. For it is not possible to draw the ships up on shore and dry them out, because the fleet of the enemy ... keeps us in continued expectation that it will sail against us.'

Also for Sicily, the Greek historian Polybius (*c.*208–125 BCE) in his *Histories* commented on the Carthaginian establishment of a position: 'Hercte commands a harbour very well situated for ships making the voyage from Drepana and Lilybaeum to Italy to put in at, and with an abundant supply of water.' In his *Hellenica*, Xenophon, with reference to the last stage of the Peloponnesian war, noted the significance given to controlling the grain trade:

'Agis, who could see great numbers of grain-ships sailing into Piraeus [the port for Athens], said, that it was useless for his troops to be trying all this long time to shut off the Athenians from access to their land, unless one should occupy also the country from which the grain was coming in by sea.'

In practice, aside from the lasting tension between the generation of eyewitnesses and subsequent generations,[15] it was not of course open to these authors to have a comparative reading of the sources from both sides, let alone to pursue, understand and apply archaeological evidence, or to contextualise well-known conflicts in terms of others that are far less well-known.[16] All of these possibilities are far more pursued today, obviously so when literary sources are absent, but also as a way to consider the latter.

In terms of fitness-for-purpose, which is the key issue in military affairs and military history alike, Thucydides served up an impressive account that linked strategy to fighting. It is inappropriate to offer diachronic (across time) comparisons in judgmental as opposed to descriptive terms. Nevertheless, Thucydides was clearly offering an account in a very different context to that earlier supplied by Homer.

There is also the cross-cultural perspective offered by other 'early' works, a diverse category that ranges from China to the Norse saga. The ethos of the latter affected not only what are classically seen as sagas but also early histories such as Saxo Grammaticus's *Gesta Danorum* which was completed at the end of the twelfth century. In this, ancestors fought pagans in a world in which gods, demons, wizards and witches all played a role.[17] Given the modern suppositions of popular culture, this approach might appear less fanciful than was once the case.

The problems of assessing success frequently arose from differing contexts in a fashion that is still seen in the present. This was apparent for example in Roman expansion. The case of the conquest of Iberia (Spain and Portugal) is particularly instructive. Having conquered the Carthaginian bases and territories in Spain during the Second Punic War (218–201 BCE), bases essentially on the Mediterranean coast, Carthage's nemesis, Rome, eventually sought to extend its power across the entire peninsula. From the Guadalquivir valley in nearby Andalusia from 208 BCE, the Romans began to press on nearby southern Portugal. Yet, the Romans found that there was a major difference between overthrowing another foreign imperial presence, in the shape of Carthage, and subjugating the rest of Iberia. The former was more vulnerable to attack, and more focused on cities, notably ports, that could be besieged. The targets in the remainder of Iberia were far more diffuse.

This helps explain the length of time it took for the Romans to conquer Portugal, but, as a reminder of the difficulties of producing histories of war, there were more significant issues, notably the culture of conquest and, separately, alternative commitments. The Republican system with its annual consulates and praetorships functioned to give the officeholders brief opportunities for military glory, ideally winning triumphs as well as the profits to be made from war including slaves. So it was in the interests of the ruling élite in Rome to win victories and take loot, but, at the same time, keep the war going almost indefinitely.

The same situation occurred later in the early Islamic period. The Umayyads could in practice have eliminated the small Christian states in the north of Iberia in the eighth, ninth and tenth centuries, but needed them as targets for annual campaigning, to advertise their credentials as Islamic rulers.

Returning to the long time the Roman conquest took, Rome, having defeated Carthage, was, instead, drawn into a series of wars with Macedon that left it in control of Greece, but that had absorbed much of Rome's energy through to 148 BCE. There were also other major struggles, including war further east with the Seleucid king, Antiochus, in 192–189 BCE, as well as the Third Punic War with Carthage (149–146 BCE).

Nevertheless, Rome made gains in this period in Iberia, and these gains were followed in 139–133 BCE by the successful conquest of much of the peninsula. The Lusitani, a tribal confederation, probably Celtic, between the Tagus and Douro rivers, had provided firm resistance from 194 BCE, notably in 147–139 BCE under Viriathus, but his poisoning was followed by Roman conquest. The Roman account was that Viriathus was killed in his sleep by his companions who had been bribed by the Romans, only for them to receive execution as their reward on the grounds that Rome did not pay traitors.

The Roman conquest involved local support, a practice also seen elsewhere. The city of Olisipo (Lisbon) provided help against the Lusitania from 138 BCE, and the Romans fortified the settlement. In 137 BCE, Roman forces, moving north, crossed the Douro and, the following year, reached the Minho River. The Roman troops proved reluctant to cross the rivers, fearing that they were the Lethe, the river of forgetfulness. The sense of a known world beyond which campaigning was risky was more generally captured as with the Macedonian reluctance to advance eastward across the Indus as Alexander the Great wanted.

Julius Caesar, Governor of Hispania Ulterior, and after whom the town of Beja was named Pax Julia, campaigned in modern Portugal, north of the Tagus, conquering local tribes, in 61–60 BCE. Aside from conquering, the Romans also faced rebellions, both from the indigenous population and, as elsewhere in the empire, from Roman rebels. With reference to Caesar's campaigns against Pompey's sons in Iberia in 45 BCE, a Roman writer noted: 'in view of the constant sallies of the natives, all places which are remote from towns are firmly held by towers and fortifications… they have watchtowers in them.'

Resistance to Roman conquest continued in north-west Spain and northern Portugal until 17 BCE, and this impressed Roman commentators, as well as providing a way to praise their own successes. As with many items in the history of war, there is no particular proof for the latter, which is in fact a suggestion. That is a frequent problem in a subject that benefits greatly when source evidence is available, but the absence of this evidence does not itself lessen the possibility that the argument may be correct.

In the nineteenth century, this resistance attracted interest from nationalist commentators and artists engaged with the idea of an exemplary pre-Roman national origin and, in the case of Portugal, concerned with tracing differences from Spain to the nature of pre-Roman tribal identities. However, there was also a marked preference, instead, for claiming a Roman legacy and for focusing, not on the resistance to the Romans, but, instead, on the eventually successful later medieval resistance to the Muslims. The latter resistance could be presented as having an exemplary Christian character, which was not the case of the resistance to Roman conquest.

Alongside the strength of the resistance came the many challenges to the Roman troops posed by the environment, notably those of operating in the mountains, of the climate and of logistical support.

In turn, the rapid fall of Iberia to Moorish invaders in, and after, 711 was one of the many dramatic successes of the forces of Islam. Explanations in Christian Iberia of its fall were for long religious, providential and moral: 'God testing his People' as well as the 'Coming of Antichrist' were key themes that were frequently to provide a context for military history. There was also a narrative and explanation of judgement in a story of rape, revenge and betrayal, in which a rape by Roderic, the last king, played a central role. In practice, however, Visigothic failure was due to Muslim strengths as well as Visigothic disadvantages, notably divisions and other military commitments including that against the recalcitrant Basques. Moreover, rapid changes in territorial control had been the pattern across Europe and the Mediterranean since the start of the fifth century. It is continuity that requires explanation rather than its absence.

Crossing the Straits of Gibraltar in 711, as part of a much wider process of Islamic expansion that also soon after took Islamic forces up against the Chinese (over whom they could not prevail), the Moors defeated and killed Roderic that year or the next. They followed up by rapidly taking over most of Iberia. The Moors pressed on to invade France, where, in contrast to north-western Iberia, the south provided readily accessible targets as well as desirable ones because of the cities and rich agricultural land available for looting. Initially successful, they were, however, heavily defeated by the Franks at Tours in 732 or 733, with the crucial loss of leaders, and were then driven out of modern France, losing the major city of Narbonne in 759.

Meanwhile, the Cantabrian Mountains had helped make the north, more particularly the north-west, of Iberia difficult for Muslim attackers to access, and had thereby provided refuge for the Christians. This refuge served as the foundation for a medieval Christian Portugal and Spain that were defined by war with the Moors and based for long in the north. At the same time, as a reminder of the need for care and context in histories of war, the inhospitable lands of the north were of only limited interest to the Moors, other than for raiding, notably for slaves. In contrast, having been exploited for taxation and labour, much of the Christian population in the Muslim areas eventually adopted Muslim culture and language.

Conflict enforces the need to understand opponents, and this is the case irrespective of how the war develops. Yet, this understanding operates within a dynamic context. For example, the rapid expansion of Islam meant that a Europe initially defined for Arabs as solely Byzantium, the Eastern Roman Empire, which indeed ruled the abutting areas, instead became more extensive and complex. For a while, the need by the Islamic world to respond to this complexity was limited, as raiding and/or conquest were to the fore. In this context, modern geographical distinctions and political boundaries were not of significance in fixing limits: geography was not destiny. Nevertheless, both taking control of Christian settlers where conversion to Islam was often limited, and reaching buffers of expansion, however transient, forced upon Islam a more varied reaction to Christendom. As a result, conflict came to include the necessity of information as well as pragmatic opportunities for links. In turn, undermining any idea of war being between civilisations, there was no unity among Christian or Muslim rulers. Thus, the First Crusade succeeded in part due to bitter rivalry between the Fatimid ruler of Egypt and the Abbasid ruler of Baghdad. The Near East was therefore a buffer zone in which it was relatively easy to expand, as opposed to Egypt where Crusaders encountered major problems in expanding and could not achieve any medium-term success.

Narratives and analyses can fail to grasp this is not the key context, as with the Mamluk Sultanate of Egypt defeating the Mongols, who had taken over Syria, at Ain Jalut near Nazareth (1260) and Homs (1281), which left the Crusader positions fatally vulnerable to the Mamluks with the Near East no longer a buffer zone. The Crusades therefore fitted into a longstanding pattern in which far from the role of local 'peoples' being crucial, they were fought over by incomers, or the descendants of incomers. This had been seen, for example, in the struggle between Macedon and the Persian Achaemenids, between Rome and the Parthians, between Byzantium and the Sassanians, Arabs and Seljuk Turks in sequence and, after the Crusades, was to resume eventually in the struggle between the Ottoman Turks on one hand, and the Habsburgs and Venice on the other.

Moreover, far from the expansion and energy of Christendom being the crucial element, the history of the eastern Mediterranean was in large part a product of the Asian nomadic world, its longstanding pressures for action, and the opportunities for sedentarisation (settling down) offered by wealthier lands, notably Mediterranean coastal regions. This nomadic world had greater military resources than the Crusaders, and especially so once benefiting from the takeover of the wealthier lands.

In turn, struggles interacted, which underlined unpredictability and risk. Thus, Timur's total victory over the Ottoman Turks in 1402 at Ankara won some time for vulnerable Constantinople. Yet, Timur then turned east, dying in 1405 as he prepared to invade China. As so often, choice the key element in strategy, however much it might be constrained, provided the context for what came later. There was no determinism, geopolitical or otherwise. Whereas the Mongols had created polities, some of which survived for over a century, Timur's empire rapidly fell totally apart, which underlines the uncertainty of the period.

Constantinople fell to the Ottoman Sultan, Mehmed II in 1453, and he enforced the history of success, taking the sobriquet 'the Conqueror' and the Byzantine title of 'Caesar.' Further successes help explain why, in a case of backward projection, one of the four horsemen of the Apocalypse was frequently presented as a Turk, as in Albrecht Dürer's woodcut of *c.*1497–8. This was a potent placing for a history of war. There is also a resonance to the present. Thus, in 2023, many of his supporters expected Erdogan to win re-election in Turkey with 53 per cent, which would have been, they believed, a sure sign from Mehmed II who was the first to convert Hagia Sophia into a mosque, as Erdogan had himself done.

There was also the more immediate history of reportage, one that was dependent on correspondence, but widened in terms of diffusion and impact by printing. Thus, the first printed and illustrated accounts of the unsuccessful Turkish invasion of Malta in 1565 appeared in Italy and Germany within a month of the Turkish withdrawal. The interplay between reportage and historical resonance was frequent. Thus, the use of gunpowder weaponry differentiated the Christian naval victory over the Turks at Lepanto in 1571 from that of the Greeks over the Persians at Salamis in 480 BCE, but the latter provided Christian Europe with a resonant and apparently relevant historical image in terms of defending civilisation. Continuity operated in images as well as action.

Aside from continuity in terms of resources and technology, there were also elements of the same suggested by scholars. Thus, the case of continuity in warfare from Roman methods and organising practices to that of the Carolingians of the eighth and ninth centuries has been argued with great energy,[18] but also contested by those dubious of the scale and sophistication of Carolingian organisation.[19] That creates a cautionary context for other such arguments for continuity.

This is particularly significant for this period as it is such a long one and there is therefore a tendency to search for agglomerating or clumping in terms of finding continuity and reifying it as an explanatory device as well as a description.[20] This tendency is accentuated by the idea that modernity comes subsequently and, with it, the end of continuity and its replacement by the very different form of continual change.

Chapter 7

Toward the Modern? 1500–1770

This period was given historical cohesion at its close in what became a prominent work of Western history, a book that has had an influence that has lasted in the West to the present. That indeed is despite most readers having heard neither of the title nor of the author. In his *History of the Reign of the Emperor Charles V with a View of the Progress of Society in Europe from the Subversion of the Roman Empire to the Beginning of the Sixteenth Century* (1769), the Scottish historian William Robertson was to date the onset of the modern European system to the outbreak of the Italian Wars in 1494, and the establishment, he claimed, as a result, of a European balance of power linked to the development of modern firepower and the limitations this posed to attacking forces.

Musketeers and cannons have continued to define modern discussion of conflict in this period. With the standard interest in the new, that approach is understandable and indeed separately, to a degree, reflects concerns then with new weaponry. Yet, a focus on gunpowder weaponry, whether or not this approach directs, or is fitted into, paradigms of change, revolutionary, evolutionary or episodic, is unsatisfactory. For many other elements played a role in conflict in the period, not least the continued primacy of cavalry and infantry not armed with gunpowder weaponry in many areas, and, separately, the degree to which the impact of gunpowder weaponry could be lessened by a variety of means, from copying the weapons to 'anti-tactics' that were designed to limit their impact. Such tactics included for example the African opponents of the Portuguese in Angola fighting in dispersed order and using cover, thus avoiding providing a concentrated target.

'Anti-tactics', indeed, is the most underrated element in discussions of military change. It captures human ingenuity and how that is not restricted to copying. Indeed, adaptation can involve rejection. Moreover, the Africans had missile weapons of their own, both javelins and arrows, and, although these might lack the specifications of gunpowder weapons, they were still effective and also easier to supply.

For the period of the chapter, the concept of an early-modern 'military revolution' has attracted much attention from the 1950s. Indeed for military historians and others it became an academic building block in Anglo-American writing, with history seemingly explained in a theory and adage that appear to work across time while, at the same time, apparently conveying all that needed to be known about military affairs and their processes of change.

Linked to this, is the progressivist account and shaping of military circumstances and developments. This progressivism draws on and applies assumptions about modernity and modernisation to military history, and of such history to the discussion of modernity and modernisation. Indeed, the assertion of an early-modern 'military revolution' can be located as a facile application of modernity and modernisation to military history.[1]

As ever, the use of language is a key element in suggesting meaning, as with the application of the term revolution, which, in practice, serves to provide a metaphor rather than to offer an analysis. Metaphors are readily accessible and potent, but that is what they are, and the metaphor of revolution is both highly resonant and totally overused. Similar comments can be made about other aspects of the language of military history, for example decisive.

A similar sceptical approach could be more widely taken across a sub-discipline that is, by its very nature, Whiggish in character and, as a separate issue, under-theorised. The latter is in the sense of frequently adopting simplistic analyses. These analyses are the context, instead, for a more general frequently descriptive focus on the tactical and operational levels of war. This process of focusing was accentuated by the 'face of battle' approach that became so influential from the 1970s and, correspondingly, encouraged interest in battle.

As a result of the simplistic nature of much of the conceptualisation, it is necessary, instead, to rethink the subject. This is a situation encouraged by the growing strength of world history in recent decades. This is not the simplistic world history of the extension of Western power and models, but, instead, a more sophisticated global history that notes the strength and autonomy of individual traditions whether affected by Western power or influence or separate to them. The latter approach is one that undercuts the standard approach of the global and analytical primacy of the supposed early-modern European 'military revolution', and that, indeed, underlines the conceptual, methodological, historiographical and empirical poverty of the concept.

This point can be taken further not only by arguing that a focus on a supposed military revolution is inherently flawed, but also by considering the degree to which the very vocabulary and nomenclature of circumstances and developments varied and vary; and to a degree that far surpasses any issues of translation or becoming 'lost in translation.' As such, it is necessary to be cautious about the application of say British concepts, or ideas from the Anglosphere, unless noting that this was essentially what they were/are and considering what the latter means. Within Europe, yet also more widely, there were, and are, very different conceptualisations and vocabularies. In particular, the British concept of an early-modern European 'military revolution' has only limited meaning in French terms or those of many other countries.

In academic terms, therefore, caution should be to the fore. This is true both for concepts and for their chronological fixing. In response, adopting a long timescale in order to bring in developments and later academic concepts in a range of countries, does not address the issue.

And so also for the concepts influencing contemporaries. For example, the long-standing idea, particularly strong in Christendom, of conflict with diabolical agents in a war that would end only with the Final Judgment was extrapolated from the Old World to the New, as in the attitudes of Spanish clerics in frontier missions. This was seen in the convent murals in New Spain (Mexico) depicting conflict with the allegedly demonic Chichimec with whom there was war from the mid-sixteenth century.[2]

Linked to this, the question of emphasis can readily lead to a misleading impression about priorities. Thus, a standard approach in constructing an early-modern period separate to that of the Middle Ages, is to focus on transoceanic European expansion and to see this as leading to radically new goals. Aside from the problematic nature of this account of transoceanic expansion, there is the need to put that in the context of a continuing commitment to nearby goals that can be regarded in terms of continuity, as with the Portuguese in Morocco. So also with the Spaniards in the

Mediterranean, with ideas of just war and Christian universalism applied not only to affirm support for conflict with Muslim opponents but also for justifying an expansionism in Christendom presented as designed to help these goals. Ferdinand of Aragon used this argument to explain his conflict with France in Italy, took the title of King of Jerusalem, and became the Guardian of the Order of Saint John.[3]

An understanding of the limitations of the early-modern European military model, or what has been presented as this model, notably gunpowder weapons fired in volleys, has been part of a reconsideration of conflict in sub-Saharan Africa. In this, the weakness of European powers prior to the late-nineteenth century emerges, most notably with the Portuguese in Angola[4] and Mozambique. Related to that comes an appreciation of the linked European and African interests involved in the misery of the slave trade. More generally, any discussion of the relationships, and specifically military balance, between Western and non-Western powers should not centre simply on initiatives by the former, a point that is abundantly clear when considering the earlier example of Ancient Rome.

In addition, the Spanish-Moroccan alignment in the sixteenth century, as well as longstanding enmity between the Saadian dynasty of Morocco and the Ottoman Turks (who had backed their Wattasid predecessor, overthrown in 1554), are reminders of the mistake in thinking in terms of wars of civilisation, in this case between Christendom and Islam. The frequency of war with the neighbouring Ottomans, who controlled Algiers from the late 1520s, helped distract Moroccan attention from what otherwise might have been more of an effort for expansion along the Atlantic littoral against the bases of Christian powers and to the south against other Africans.

The selectivity of military history is readily seen in coverage. Countries where there was considerable military power and a history of consequence tend to be underplayed or even ignored in standard military history texts, for example Madagascar, Morocco, Myanmar and Thailand. Some countries, notably Macedon and Mongolia, attract attention for a short period, and are then ignored.

Yet, it is far from clear why states that collapsed into military failure, such as France, deserve the far greater coverage they are commonly given.

To take a contemporary of Louis XIV, Ismail Ibn Sharif (r. 1672–1727) was able to defeat several family members in order to gain control of Morocco. He then enforced his control southwards to the Senegal River, also reimposed that over the far-flung Pashalik of Timbuktu on the other side of the Sahara, drove the English from Tangier and the Spaniards from La Mamora, Larache and Azile, subjugated the unconquered Berber tribes, and, far less successfully, fought the Ottomans and besieged Spanish-held Ceuta and Melilla. Where best to place the balance is unclear. Ismail was very much a power on land and had no opportunity to reshape the larger Atlantic world by sea power. Furthermore, he was not capable of extending his control south of the Senegal River, nor of invading Spain, nor of allying with rulers in sub-Saharan Africa. Yet, he was an impressive military leader.

One criterion that is worthy of consideration is that of multi-sphere capability and success. Thus, a leader and military able to confront a range of tasks and environments deserves more praise than one, however successful, who only confronts one. For example, Frederick II, the Great of Prussia (r. 1740–86) fought his European neighbours, but did not have to confront rebellions, naval warfare, or trans-oceanic conflict with both European and non-European powers and could provide no example for these. In terms of this criterion, the British proved more successful in 1688–1815 than France, and America during World War Two than the Soviet Union.

A point that deserves attention here, and throughout the book, is the difficulty of addressing the naval dimension alongside that of land warfare, in general terms, with reference to specific regions or countries, and in determining how much weight to place on land and sea. Separately to the latter, the wisdom of any separation of land and sea is questionable, not least due to the use of joint operations, particularly in amphibious attacks, a process frequently seen in a number of regions, notably the Mediterranean. For example, the Turkish ability to add a major naval capability to that on land after the capture of Constantinople in 1453 became an important aspect of Mediterranean power politics in the sixteenth century.

However, the projection of this strength into the Indian Ocean proved less significant, in part due to the lack of the necessary infrastructure, but also to more episodic attention. Moreover, in organisational terms, the Turks lacked the equivalent of the East Indian Companies of many Western states and also did not develop Indian bases, nor sustained alliances. This was despite the Turkish empire being nearer than Western Europe via the Red Sea and, far less prominently, the Persian Gulf.

Aside from capability and operations at sea, river warfare was significant. This was especially so in the Low Countries and China, but also for example on the Brahmaputra and the Danube. However, river capability and warfare tend to attract insufficient attention.

For both land and sea warfare, the notion that conservative societies lack the capacity for reform, and that they are therefore necessarily weaker than revolutionary counterparts, is deeply flawed. This conclusion is also of significance today. As a result, the conceptual can be joined to the empirical in rejecting the notion of the *ancien régime* (the term generally employed for European societies and states in the early-modern period, but also applied more widely) as, allegedly, inherently redundant and waiting for the revolutionary trends and moment to overturn it from the late-eighteenth century.

In a fashion that stretches to the present, as for example with Xi, Putin and Erdogan, the ambitions of rulers were a crucial element in the military history of the period, and not least with Philip II of Spain, the major Western ruler in the late-sixteenth century. Although he commanded in the Low Countries against the French in the 1550s and, in 1580, reviewed the Spanish army before it invaded Portugal, Philip was not a warrior like Suleiman the Magnificent of Turkey (r. 1520–66) or Gustavus Adolphus of Sweden (r. 1611–32), and thus did not implement policy and engineer military developments as the latter did. In large part, Spain's forces fought at a distance, notably in the Low Countries and northern France. In addition, for most of his reign, Philip did not represent the peripatetic military rulership seen with his father, Emperor Charles V (r. 1519–56) and, to a lesser extent, Suleiman. As a result, and on a more general pattern, there was a potential difference in the tone of celebration of war. Whereas Charles could be depicted centrally in battle, as with Titian's splendid equestrian portrayal of him in victory at the battle of Mühlberg (1547) over John Frederick, Elector of Saxony, the leading German Protestant prince, Philip was not present at the repeated victories of his Army of Flanders over Dutch and French opponents, nor that of Lepanto (1571) over the Turkish fleet.

Nevertheless, Philip was still crucial to Spain's military history. His ambitions, and those of other Western rulers, such as, in the first half of the century, Henry VIII of England, Francis I of France and James IV of Scotland, were significant to any assessment of capability, as they established the goals that were formulated. Each of these monarchs was proud to serve in person and James was killed, alongside much of Scotland's nobility, in the English victory at Flodden (1513). In peacetime, the emphasis on hunting as well as on tournaments and other forms of mock combat dramatised valour and prowess, and marked a major continuity in élite behaviour.

In India, the Mughal rulers, who dominated the north from the mid-1520s and were active warriors, supported the compilation of historical works in order to assert their position and, in some cases, wrote their own memoirs. In contrast, their Chinese counterparts in the sixteenth century were less martial and, crucially, failed to gain prestige that way. However, that pattern changed with the early Manchu rulers who seized power in the mid-seventeenth century, notably the Kangxi emperor (r. 1661–1722). He led the army that heavily defeated the Dzungars at Jao Modo (1696). This battle is one of the many deserving the epithet decisive that is generally left out of compendia of such battles. In geopolitical terms, it was part of a pattern of conflict between Inner Asian powers, one of which had taken over China and was therefore a hybrid force.

After it abandoned conflict in Korea at the end of the 1590s, Japan saw domestic consolidation that was a background for a lengthy peace and not for the renewed assault on Korea. Ming weakness might have encouraged the latter by lessening the chance of the repetition of intervention in Korea against Japanese action seen in 1592–3 and 1597–8: there was to be a repetition of such Chinese action at the expense of the Americans in 1950.

In contrast to Japan in the seventeenth and eighteenth centuries, war, and in all cultures, proved the most established way to gain the renown that was then repeatedly displayed. The ceremonial entries of French monarchs celebrated royal valour and success. Less prominent rulers also sought to gain fame and enhance their position through war. Francesco II Gonzaga, Marquess of Mantua, presented his performance at the battle of Fornovo in 1495, where he had fought bravely and captured many prisoners, albeit failing to block the French march north, as a victory, and Andrea Mantegna's painting the *Madonna della Vittoria* was produced accordingly. Francesco also displayed what he saw as an apt comparison; Mantegna's earlier series *The Triumphs of Caesar*, offered an exemplary reference for rulers a millennium and a half later. Separately, rulers, both Western and non-Western, frequently played an active role in the development of weaponry and tactics,[5] although far more so on land than at sea.

The major role, indeed ambience, of glory and honour was such that military activities that provided both were necessarily effective in a fashion that, however, can be difficult to compare, both across space and time. In part, this is because so much depends on the specific political and cultural context, which, indeed, could change during reigns.

So also for the value and values brought to the social élite by military service, a value and values that was readily apparent in Castile, the political core of Habsburg Spain[6], as well as in other states. The hierarchy and collective discipline of officership could work, and could be made most effective, if it rested on a definition of noble honour and aristocratic function in terms of military service. Nobles were treated as especially suited to this service thanks to their nobility.

This process was encouraged by the presentation of war in glorious and chivalric terms. Chivalry certainly remained strong as both concept and idiom. The definition of aristocratic honour with reference to military service was encouraged by the emphasis on honour, service and glory by, as well as for, rulers, this proving a key element of continuity. Aristocrats looked back to heroic members of their families who had won and defended nobility, and thus social status, indeed social existence, through glorious, honourable and honoured acts of valour. The role of inheritance, in wealth, prospects and status, further helped lead to looking back in defining appropriate behaviour. Renown was important. These traditions were sustained, both by service in war and by a personal culture of violence in the form of duels, feuds and displays of courage. The public bearing of arms contributed to this culture as, separately, did the social significance of hunting, which was a marker of status. As far as conflict was concerned, the same sociocultural imperatives underlay both the international and the domestic spheres. Despite ideas of legality, loyalty and order, there was frequently scant separation in this respect and that is a key variable in military history, one that is neglected when the emphasis is on the how of fighting, rather than the why and to what ends.

At the international level, there was a contrast in ideological imperative between conflict within a zone of similarity, such as the Catholic world, and across zones, for example between the latter and Islam. This imperative pertained both in international conflict, as with war between Spain and the Ottoman (Turkish) empire, and internal conflict, as with the unsuccessful rebellion in Granada against Spain in 1568–70. The rebellion did not enjoy international support; the partial legitimacy that made negotiations possible. That and the scale seen with the Dutch Revolt against Philip II.

A key similarity, one, moreover, that should take analytical priority over differences between and often within cultures, was that of the willingness of leaders and combatants across much of the world not only to kill large numbers, but also to accept heavy casualties. In addition, glory was presented as involving both. This willingness, which was amply seen in the case of Spain, and owed much there to the potent practical and psychological legacy of the *Reconquista*, was part of an important continuity with preceding and subsequent centuries.

In contrast, this attitude has been far less common in the case of regular forces over the last half-century. A functional explanation of this contrast draws attention to the cost of training modern troops and the expertise required, and therefore the folly of losing them, unnecessarily. This is certainly a factor as far as military commanders were concerned. However, social, cultural and ideological factors are more significant in explaining the concern about casualties. This was/is notably so in the West and in this case as far as expeditionary warfare is concerned, a point highlighted when the latter are described as 'wars of choice,' as with the American-led invasion of Iraq in 2003.

In contrast, the willingness in Ukraine to take heavy losses in defence suggests that very different criteria pertain depending on the tasks involved. This willingness has in part been conceptualised with reference to the idea of resilience. Indeed, determination and persistence as ideological and psychological characteristics require a social and institutional network of resilience.

Concepts of duty and fatalism, in the contexts of a much harsher working and demographic environment, and in markedly inegalitarian systems, were significant across the world in the early-modern period. This situation acted as a key enabler of bellicosity and of the normative character of war. As a result of the continuation of this crucial cultural dynamic for, and of, war from the Middle Ages, however defined, into the twentieth century, and across the world, it is less helpful to think in terms of paradigm shifts in warfare, at least, in this respect, prior to the last half-century. Furthermore, there are clearly many elements of this dynamic in the present day, albeit in some contexts far more than others. This is a factor, for example, in the serious domestic instability referred to as 'failed states.'

The long-term effect of culture on the conduct of war challenges the emphasis on change, notably of the disruptive understanding of technology and of the impact of logistics on war by those who write in terms of an early-modern military revolution. As is so often the case when analyses are debated, these emphases in practice are not incompatible, and war indeed is a multivalent process that requires nuance in analysis. Nevertheless, there is a crucial contrast in focus between these analyses. That point is pertinent more generally when considering the need to assess war; both the circumstances of a given period, and with regard to change in terms of independent, albeit interactive, variables, rather than a single underlying pulse.

As part of the tension over analytical focus comes the degree of understanding devoted to whatever was the previous situation supposedly displaced by the possibilities and exigencies of change, indeed a previous situation that was allegedly rejected. This can rest on a failure in analysis. Thus, the misrepresentation of medieval warfare as limited in sophistication and development rests on misunderstandings that reflect later assumptions.[7] This process serves both to affect the perception of the medieval situation (itself very varied) and to lead to a flawed presentation of the later position in both the early-modern period and more generally. Change, however, cannot be understood unless the previous position is grasped.

In societies that were reverential of the past and referential to it, and profoundly so compared to the present situation, there was a widespread pattern of turning back for validation, and, very differently, inspiration. This process was encouraged by the frame of reference provided by available experience and analysis, each of which were far more limited than what was to follow. However, that did not mean an inability to engage with factors other than the past. Thus, the Europe of the fifteenth and early-sixteenth-century Renaissance was capable of thinking through new solutions even as it looked back to antiquity in its search for validation, as with the attention devoted to Flavius Vegetius' *De Re Militari*, a Roman text of the fourth century. This was a major source for fifteenth-century military manuals.[8]

Printing made earlier manuscript works more accessible and was an important aspect of the potential for change that was so apparent from the fifteenth century. The use of movable metal type by European printers from mid-century ensured that the already frequent circulation of military manuals was stepped up. This was important not only for a self-conscious revival in the Renaissance of Greek and Roman knowledge, but also for making more recent manuscript works more accessible. Thus Leon Battista Alberti's *De Re Aedificatoria*, with its call for sloped and lower fortress walls, was written in the 1440s but first printed in 1485. The prestige of the Classical world was such that a 'return to the past' served to validate new emphases, and in military matters there was a fascination with the past. In particular, from 1487, the Roman writers Vegetius, Aelianus Tacticus, Frontinus and Modestus, were published by Eucherius Silber in Rome. In turn, Julius Caesar's *Comentarii* were published in an Aldine edition in 1513, and this served as the basis for another Latin edition published in Paris in 1543. Drawing parallels for contemporary rulers with Caesar encouraged the apparent relevance of the latter's example and writings. Published in Lyon in 1554, Guillaume Du Choul's study of Roman fortification and military discipline appeared in new editions in 1555, 1556 and 1567.

A range of conflict could be addressed in this fashion. Thus, literature, like other media such as sermons, engaged with terrorist violence, which was notable in the Wars of Religion of the sixteenth and early-seventeenth centuries, in order to provide explanation. This was common in religious and Classical terms, for there was plenty of rebellion on offer in Roman history.[9] Moreover, ideas of tyrannicide were common in ancient history and could be readily transferred.

More generally, ideas and vocabulary associated with Classical Rome were frequently applied in order to validate developments. For example, Battista della Valle's *Vallo Libro Continente Appertinentie à Capitani, Ritenere e Fortificare una Città con Bastioni*, a very popular work on fortifications that went through eleven editions from 1524 to 1558, drew heavily on Classical sources. If the Classical world, however, could provide only limited guidance to many of the challenges and opportunities of the period, not least transoceanic warfare, the Romans had still devoted much space to what they saw as warfare with barbarians, not least in Caesar's *Gallic Wars*.

A classic instance of the application of Classical models was the Dutch development of continuous volley fire in the 1590s which was advanced by William Lodewijk of Nassau, Governor of the Dutch province of Friesland and a scholar of Classical literature. The *Tactica* of Aelian written in about 100 CE provided the key text, and in 1594 William wrote about it to his cousin, Count Maurice of Nassau, the talented commanding general of the United Provinces (modern Netherlands) in its war with Philip II of Spain. Aelian provided much detail in matters of drill, and this detail proved of great value to the army organisers of the period as did his critical account of earlier works on the art of war. Editions of Aelian included a Leiden one in 1613 and *The Tactics of Aelian or Art of Embattailing an Army after the Grecian Manner* (London, 1616).[10] Maurice was impressed by Aelian's account of the drill of Classical pikemen and slingers, and he took steps to improve and standardise drill and the army.

Reference to Aelian reflected the authority of antiquity and the habit of comparison with Classical methods, which were well-established in the literature on war, as with Imperiale Cinuzzi's *La Vera Militar Disciplina Antica e Moderna* (Siena, 1604), Hermannus Hugo's *De Militia Equestri Antiqua et Nova* (Antwerp, 1630) and Jacques Ozanam's *Traité de Fortification, contenant les methodes anciennes et modernes pour la construction et la deffense des places* (Paris, 1694). Authors who wrote on modern military history, such as Johann Jacobi, also published on Classical warfare, in his case *La Milice Romaine* (Frankfurt, 1616).

The continued reprinting of Classical texts testified to their authority, as with Justus Lipsius's *De militia Romana libri quinque commentarius ad Polybium* (Antwerp, 1630). This reprinting was not simply the case in the early decades of the seventeenth century. For example, the *Ars Tactica* of Flavius Arrianus (*c.* 96–175) was published in Amsterdam in 1683, and the *Strategematum* of Polyaenus (fl. *c.* 163) at Leiden in 1691. Works also appeared in translation, as with Julius Caesar's *Commentaries*, for example in London in 1682 and 1694, and Frontinus' *The Stratagems of War* (London, 1686). Andreas Cellarius's *Architectura Militaris* (Amsterdam, 1645), the second edition of which appeared in 1656, included engraved plates showing the use of Classical techniques: the Roman testudo and the battering ram. The authority of antiquity extended to Byzantium, the Eastern Roman Empire, as with an edition of Emperor Leo VI's *Tactica* (Leiden, 1612), and a translation of Procopius' *The History of the Warres of the Emperor Justinian* (London, 1653). In contrast, there was less attention to the warmaking of other European states of the period.

References to the Classical period continued during the eighteenth century, most notably with the active and important French debate from the 1720s over tactical formations, methods and ethos for the infantry. Continuing into the 1790s, this debate captured elements of the lasting tension over the value, both functionally and in terms of morale, of taking the offensive. The formations and weaponry that could, indeed should, be thereby used attracted attention and advocates. In part, there was interest in the Classical use of the pike by attacking phalanxes. The debate over tactics was also in part a matter of the response to the possibilities and problems of combining success with firepower, and not least when the capability potentially offered by the latter was limited by the degree to which both sides were thus armed. In addition, possibilities appeared changed by the major shift from combined infantry forces of pike and musket units to troops armed with a musket that was equipped with a bayonet. This was different to the Classical model of infantry armament.

Nevertheless, continuity in reference remained a theme. For example, Caesar's *Gallic Wars* continued to be much read across the West, while Major Robert Donkin based his *Military Collections and Remarks* (1777), a call for the reorganisation of the British army, on his studies of the armies of the Roman Republic.

There were, moreover, references to Classical strategy. Thus, the *Monitor* of 4 December 1757 referred to the Punic Wars between Rome and Carthage, when calling in the Seven Years' War (1756–63) for a more vigorous strategy of amphibious attacks against France:

> 'A fleet is our best security: but then it is not to lie by our walls; nor be confined to the navigation of our own coasts. The way to deliver Rome from the rival ships and hostilities of the Carthaginians was to carry fire and sword upon the African coast [i.e. to attack Carthage itself]. Employ the enemy at home, and they will never project hazardous invasions.'

Tobias Smollett's bold claims for the British navy extended to Antiquity:

> 'I do believe, in my conscience, that half a dozen English frigates would have been able to defeat both the contending fleets at the famous battle of Actium [31 BCE], which has been so much celebrated in the annals of antiquity, as an event that decided the fate of empire.'[11]

In practice, motivated in large part by the exigencies of domestic politics, notably the need to assuage criticism of the commitment of forces to a land war on the Continent, the amphibious attacks launched by the British against the French coast during the Seven Years' War had only mixed success and, separately, did not prevent the major French invasion attempt of 1759 which, instead, was beaten as a result of British naval victories off Lagos in Portugal and in Quiberon Bay.

It was necessary to address the impact of gunpowder not only on the understanding and practice of war, but also on its representation, with the latter stretching from fact to fiction, war-winning to ethics. The last included both positive and condemnatory engagement with the deadliness of gunpowder and with its displacement of heroic warriorship, or, rather, its reconfiguration.[12] The last was a widespread cultural issue not only in the West but also, for example, in the Islamic world, China and Japan. However, some earlier military techniques proved readily compatible with gunpowder, not least horse-archery.

The continued practice of comparison was shown by the publication in London in 1678 of Louis de Gaya's *Treatise of the Arms and Engines of War ... both Ancient and Modern* and in Wilhelm Dilich's *Krieges-Schule* (Frankfurt, 1689). Such comparisons had a degree of basis in practicalities, including constraints, technologies and social norms and drew on the extent to which conflict looked to established themes.

That did not mean that this conflict was necessarily 'backward looking' as it might have appeared in terms of a model of modernity. For example, the European Wars of Religion of 1559–1648 rested in part, for both Protestant and Catholic sides, on well-established but still apparently highly pertinent themes not least those of religious warfare, crusading and the rivalry between popes and princes. Thus, the Jesuits were a new, although not fighting, version of the medieval Christian Military Orders such as the Templars and Hospitallers. So also with the European witch hunts of the sixteenth and seventeenth centuries: the struggle between Devil and God appeared as strong as ever. The Islamic-Christian wars of religion of the early-modern period also sat in terms of a continuity of goal and culture.

The search in this period for best practice in the further past, as with the European interest in the Classical, has a similarity with more recent and current models of military development that assume some mechanistic search for efficiency, and a related maximisation of force. Each was limited, if not seriously flawed, as they do violence to the highly complex process by which interests in new methods, which certainly existed, interacted with powerful elements of continuity; and will continue to do so. In part, the notion of effectiveness was framed and applied in terms of dominant cultural and social patterns, a pattern that continues to the present and one that can be regarded as necessarily the case. However innovative, military technologies repeatedly ended up accommodating entrenched conceptions of power and social relations,[13] and this, again, will continue. Military structures and command policies both reflect these conceptions.

In the early-modern period, a stress on the value of morale and on the importance of honour came naturally to the aristocratic order that dominated warmaking. Traditional assumptions about appropriate conduct were very important in force structure and tactics, and this was particularly so for individuals conscious, as was generally the case, of lineage and reputation, and not psychologically committed to change. Yet, referring to dominant cultural and social patterns, and using terms such as accommodating, should not imply that there were no other significant reasons for continuity in military arrangements. In particular, it is all-too-easy to find fault with past practice, a situation that remains the case to this day, but such fault-finding may be mistaken. So also with the related quest for the new.

As a related point, the consequences of the misleading and teleological treatment of the state, both as a whole, and more specifically for the West in the early-modern period, are a particular problem in that they seriously affect the consideration of military developments. There is a misleading tendency to treat 'the state' as an essentially bureaucratic entity, and one automatically seeking greater power and therefore efficiencies to that end. This account underplays multiple divisions within government and affecting governance, and their close relationship with social dynamics[14], as well as the varied understandings of the idea of power. Moreover, the accompanying role of court, aristocratic and, as an overlap, military factionalism and of military entrepreneurship[15] is such that accounts of statecraft in terms of supposedly modern concepts, both of 'rational' decision-making and concerning the development and rationale of power and goals, are misleading. This is a corollary to the similarly misleading emphasis on rationalism and efficiency in the literature on the 'military revolution,' indeed its inherent 'Fordism', with its focus on allegedly optimal production of military resources and methods. In all cases, instead, fitness for purpose owed much to specific tasks and particular circumstances, and, as a result, optimal criteria have to be contextualised. So also accordingly with the use of history.

The circumstances of conflict included, to a degree now understood, more of a focus both on 'small war' between regulars, and of guerrilla and other conflict involving irregulars, than used to be discussed when the focus was almost exclusively on battle. Thus, in place of the English Civil Wars discussed in terms of major battles such as Marston Moor (1644) and Preston (1648), has come, instead, a greater emphasis on a range of conflict including skirmishing, not least to secure or disrupt resource raising and movement, as well as rioting of an insurgency character with bloody street fighting as a result. This emphasis has consequences in terms of considering topics such as motivation, recruitment and command.[16]

So also in handling the discussion of points that are more general to these particular civil wars (and warfare itself) as a whole, such as the respective weight of campaigning and resources in explaining success.[17] This approach risks underplaying the moving, and yet more movable, understanding of success during a particular conflict, as well as the interactive character of the factors summarised as campaigning and resources.

In addition, resources are not a static factor subject to ready measurement and evaluation. Instead, resources are a complex mixture of quantity, quality, availability, maintenance, understanding, doctrine, training and usage. Resources are also open to the possibility of political (and other) redefinition, and required, and still do, very careful management, and notably so in wartime.[18] Peacetime, in that light was often a preparation for wartime. Failure produces a sense that something must be done, as with the French after defeat by Britain and Prussia in the Seven Years' War (1756–63),[19] and therefore has many owners in the sense of commentators. For failure can readily be grafted onto pre-existing or new solutions, and gives them rhetorical and practical force when there are demands for action.

The nature of the context varied greatly. A specific impact of geopolitics and thus strategic environmentalism for Britain emerged from the *Craftsman*, the leading London opposition newspaper, and an opponent of a standing (permanent) army of any size, the latter the goal of the government. Seeking to draw the lessons of history alongside the practicalities of a physical and thereby political environment that defined strategic culture, it declared on 13 July 1728:

'History does not afford us one instance of a people who have long continued free under the dominion of the sword … the very situation of our country, which is surrounded with rocks and seas, seem to point out to us our natural strength, and cut off all pretence for a numerous, standing, land force.'

The emphasis on 'a people' was understandable for Britain, given its recent history, constitution and active press.

This was an argument that was to be repeated in America once it gained independence. In that case, the Democratic Republicans under Thomas Jefferson, president from 1801 to 1809, emphasised militia forces and opposed the Federalists' stress on a standing army and navy. Ironically, this led to major problems when war was declared on Britain in 1812. Militia forces were more appropriate on the defence than in invading British-held Canada.

The emphasis in such rhetorical arguments also captured the need in war, as in international relations as a whole, to decide how best to conceptualise and appeal to public support, however understood, and how much weight to place on this element, both then and now. It was scarcely new or 'modern', not least because rivalries within Christianity, Islam and the Buddhist world spanned power politics, religious division and the measure of public support.

The extent to which these rivalries were of declining resonance, at least in Western Europe, after the mid-seventeenth century, and notably the Peace of Westphalia (1648), is a matter of controversy. Opposition to Louis XIV of France (r. 1643–1715), notably from William III of Orange, who ruled in Britain from 1689 to 1702, could be presented in Protestant Europe in religious terms, and this was to recur when Frederick 'the Great' (II) of Prussia (r. 1740–86) attacked Austria in 1740, and during the Seven Years' War (1756–63) when Prussia fought Austria and France, while Prussia's ally Britain fought France; although Britain did not fight Austria.

However, as with earlier divisions, for example between popes and antipopes, popes and lay rulers and over the Albigensian and Hussite heresies, there were also contrary power politics, in William's case alliance against France with Austria and Spain, which were the other major Catholic powers. A failure to give due weight to these earlier elements challenges some of the discussion on 'post-Westphalian' novelty in international relations and the resulting context of Western war after the Peace of Westphalia. There is a parallel with misleading claims to novelty in French Revolutionary warfare.

Moreover, public debate and commitment in international relations and warfare were not new, as any reading of the history of republican Athens and Rome would indicate.[20] Nor would Louis XI in the late-fifteenth century have had much to learn from Louis XIV's expansionism.[21]

In part, these discussions of continuity are points that are parallel to the debate over the 'military revolution.' This parallel is significant because assumptions feed on each other as causal and consequential links are sought. However, it is important to be cautious in establishing, still more validating, explanations on the basis of analogies and parallels, as with the contemporary discussion of a revived Cold War. The comparisons that are made, not least as chronologies are established, are frequently problematic.

Separately, the extent to which the past was a model, indeed learnable, potentially clashed with the presentation of it as closed. Thus, in his *Decline and Fall of the Roman Empire* (1776–88), Edward Gibbon addressed the question whether 'barbarian' invasions of Europe could recur, deciding that European advances in technology and their dissemination, notably to Russia, made this highly unlikely.

As a reminder, however, that it was possible to adopt very different contextual accounts, Peter the Great of Russia (r. 1689–1725) had been seen very differently earlier in the eighteenth century. Thus, in terms of content and method, the *Plain Dealer* of 7 December 1724 announced:

'While, like the provinces of the declining Empire of Old Rome, we are fretting, and disturbing ourselves ... the Goths are at our gate ... There seems to be rising near us, that NORTHERN LYON, which has, so often, been prophesied of.'

Russia in short was a new iteration of a long-lasting 'barbarian' challenge, and not the block to it. The paper pressed on to argue that past success was no guarantee to the future, with history raided widely to make the point. Such raiding is par for the course and can be actively unhelpful. Alternatively, such raiding offers a change to the use of familiar episodes presented in an unproblematic fashion.

Although, again, analogies have to be used with care, the closure suggested by Gibbon prefigured to a degree the early 1990s' idea of the 'End of History.' Yet Gibbon's suggestion did not mean that the relevance of the past had ended, only that it had changed in this particular case. Indeed, in one respect, Gibbon's history was an illustration of how knowledge of the past could help throw an understanding from, and on, the then present. Moreover, that knowledge was denied those in the then past who might have sought to predict the future.

The identity, character and dating of the modern is a matter of discussion, rather than the triumphant and obvious assertion so often presented. So also with so much involved in the writing of histories of war, not least analytical terms, fundamental assumptions and parameters such as total war. For example, there is a tendency to link total with modern in warfare, but the two are very separate. The destructiveness of total war is far from restricted to the modern, while many modern conflicts have been limited, as with the Falkland War of 1982 or the Gulf War of 1991. The latter saw many casualties and much destruction on the side of the rapidly-defeated Iraqis, but was short and did not extend to an attempt to conquer Iraq. In addition, the modern is a movable feast, one that necessarily should change as time passes and a different modern is on offer. As a consequence, the 'path to modernity' will look different, as will modernisation.

In addressing this and other points, there is also the serious lack of contextual knowledge and understanding, as, again, with the oft asserted but erroneous view that the French Revolutionary and Napoleonic Wars were total, and also new in being such.[22] In practice, their anti-societal violence was less than in successive Russo-Turkish conflicts, for example those of 1768–74 and 1787–92, and both the French Revolutionaries and Napoleon sought, albeit differently, to incorporate territories and people, rather than to destroy them. In terms of historical writing on war, however, there is a teleology that sees the modern as more 'total,' a view that looks increasingly questionable as we understand the very clear absolutes involved in religious hatreds and in large-scale enslavement. Compared to Chinggis Khan or Timur, let alone Classical usage,[23] the Revolutionaries and Napoleon scarcely seem 'total,' whatever the rhetoric of the Revolutionaries.

To end the chapter with theory would be inappropriate, for it would not capture the range of histories of war that were on offer to contemporaries; from established forms that predated the culture of print, to entrepreneurial works focused on the latter. Thus, active writers for the market produced military histories. This was particularly the case where printing was strongly developed and not under government control. Thomas Lediard provided *The Naval History of England* (1735), which presented the revival of naval success after the Glorious Revolution of 1688 as looking back to a national tradition. He also wrote a life of John, 1st Duke of Marlborough, the leading general of the 1700s. John Campbell offered *Military History of the late Prince Eugene of Savoy and the late John, Duke of Marlborough* (1736), the same year as Lediard's *Marlborough* (John, 1st Duke of), as well as *The Lives of the Admirals and other Eminent British Seamen* (1742–4). So also with the life of Frederick the Great published by Joseph Towers in 1788. John Banks wrote not only a life of Christ but also books on Cromwell, William III, Peter the Great, Marlborough and Eugene, as well as the history of the current-day; for 'The History of Our Own Times', to take a title employed by Henry Fielding in 1741, was what today would be more commonly described as journalism or commentary. Thus, on 8 February 1746, the *Westminster Journal* advertised Banks's *Compendious History of the House of Austria, and the German Empire* which, it claimed, gave 'a more exact and clear idea of the motives and nature of the present war (the War of the Austrian Succession, 1740–48), and what may probably ensue, than is to be met in any other work.' As ever, the advertising of a work gives valuable guidance to its intentions and/or the way in which it could be sold.

The history of the present was given a more fixed form in prominent statuary. Erected in 1730, the Column of Victory at Blenheim Palace bore an inscription to John, 1st Duke of Marlborough written by Henry, Viscount Bolingbroke, a former political rival:

> 'The Hero not only of his Nation, but his Age: Whose Glory was equal in the Council and in the Field: Who by Wisdom, Justice, Candour, and Address, Reconciled various and even opposite interests; Acquired an Influence, which no Rank, no Authority can give, Nor any Force, but that of Superior Virtue; Became the fixed, important Center, Which united in one common Cause, The Principal States of EUROPE. Who by military Knowledge, and irresistible Valour, In a long Series of uninterrupted Triumphs, Broke the Power of FRANCE, When raised the highest, when exerted the most; Rescued the EMPIRE from Desolation; Asserted and confirmed the Liberties of EUROPE.'

The survival of similar works was to be affected by the inroads of politics, as with the destruction of French royal commemorative monuments during the Revolution. Yet, they, the Blenheim Column and similar legacies in non-Western cultures, all underline the need and expectation to establish histories of war.

The Blenheim column also showed the highly political nature of such accounts. In 1730, Sarah, Duchess of Marlborough, the Duke's widow, and Bolingbroke were both strong critics of the foreign policy of the government of Sir Robert Walpole which, at this stage, included alliance with France and opposition to Emperor Charles VI, ruler of Austria. During the War of the Spanish Succession (1702–13 for Britain), Marlborough had fought in cooperation with Austria, not least at his most famous victory, Blenheim (1704), but, in 1725–30, Britain prepared for war with it. Bolingbroke argued in his inscription on the column and his journalism in the newspaper, the *Craftsman*, that this policy threatened both national and European interests. Thus, the history of war he offered was a clear critique of the then present, a situation more generally seen.

Ironically, in 1731, the Walpole government changed tack, negotiated an alliance with Austria and nearly fought France, although, despite other crises, hostilities were not in fact to occur until 1743.

Bolingbroke's politicisation of military history thus swiftly lacked focus, and has come to lack apparent point, which serves to underline the need to explain and contextualise the histories of war we have from the past, as well as those we produce today. Without such explanation, there is, as it were, an archaeology of objects and texts that lack explanation and point. That, indeed, is the general situation.

Chapter 8

Revolution and Technology, 1770–1914

'I saw the smoke banks on that October evening swirl slowly up over the Atlantic swell, and rise, and rise, until they had shredded into thinnest air, and lost themselves in the infinite blue of heaven. And with them rose the cloud which had hung over the country; and it also thinned and thinned, until God's own sun of peace and security was shining once more upon us never more, we hope, to be bedimmed.'

Referring to the overwhelming British naval victory at Trafalgar in 1805 over a combined Franco-Spanish fleet, the last sentences of Arthur Conan Doyle's historical novel *Rodney Stone* (1896), was typical of the most common writing on war in the nineteenth century, although this novel is now essentially forgotten, as is most of that literature, including Doyle's Brigadier Gerard Napoleonic stories, which in a sense are stories from the 'other side of the hill,' in this case the French.

Military commentators might focus on technological change, and the supposed lessons of latest conflicts and predictions for the next. Those were also discussed in the press, but they were far less prominent than popular accounts of war that focused on heroism and notably the clash of battle. That of course did not preclude discussion of technology, but heroism, as a constant, took precedence over technology as a changing factor. It involved charging forward and risking life.

The emphasis on heroism was understandable for a number of reasons, not least that it reflected established patterns and, as thus, provided a way to honour continuity by matching the patterns of the past. Heroism brought together the human interest that always played a major role in the discussion of conflict, with its affirmations of masculinity, the individual, the family and the group, each on its own, and all together, offering exemplary pride. In addition, the focus on the heroic was related to, but scarcely dependent on, the conflation of nationalism with what in effect was the competitiveness of Social Darwinism. This conflation characterised the portrayal of war and therefore also of military history. There was no separation between past and present. Instead, the valour and success of those presented as ancestors was the predictor of what could be strength at present and in the future, and therefore an inspiration that should be followed and inculcated, not least with the attraction of a narrative which emphasised setbacks and victory.

As a result, we shall begin this chapter not with the conventional discussion, of Clausewitz, the military thinker, the Prussian/German commander Moltke and breech-loaders, the firepower multiplier. Instead, we shall look at storytellers, however defined and as increased by an expansion in print and lithography, and notably so in the Western world,[1] with the storytellers, for example war reporters, playing a major role in shaping public memories and attitudes.[2]

Some storytellers were very explicitly focused on grand themes, as with Jacques-Louis David's portraiture of Napoleon, including *Bonaparte Crossing the Great St Bernard Pass* (1800) and *The Distribution of the Eagle Standards* (1810), or his equivalents.[3]

However, even those not associated with martial process had their military heroes, and Doyle, most famous as the author of the Sherlock Holmes stories, provides an instructive figure. That he did so reflected the extent to which the idea of character was one that brought together a range of values. Across the world, exemplary masculinity was focused on military heroes. In Britain as in America, they were presented as national icons in a fusion of martial prowess, Protestant zeal and moral manhood. In Britain, this looked back to Francis Drake and Horatio Nelson. Charles Wolfe's poem on the burial in 1809 of the heroic Sir John Moore after holding off the larger and pursuing French army at Corunna, was a classic of the nineteenth-century anthology and schoolroom. It was a tale of heroic withdrawal anticipating that from Dunkirk in 1940: the survival of the troops took precedence over strategic and operational debates.

In another instance of failure, the zealous Charles Gordon, who died unsuccessfully defending besieged Khartoum against the Mahdists in 1885, was presented as a quasi-saint resisting a vast force of Muslims, and sacrificing himself to that end. He is celebrated near where I live by a lamppost, not the most martial of memorials, but a local testimony to commitment. Separately, in the Doyle short story 'The Resident Patient,' Watson looks at his newly-framed picture of Gordon.

In Doyle's 'The Blanched Soldier', which is set in 1903, there is an instance of hereditary bravery, not only Godfrey Emsworth, who had played a brave role in the Boer War (1899–1902), but also his father Colonel Emsworth – 'Emsworth, the Crimean V.C.', a reference to the Crimean War of 1854–6. There was, indeed, no shortage of VCs in the pages of detective novelists. In 'Murder by Proxy' (1897) by Mathias McDonnell Bodkin, Colonel Peyton, a positive character, 'had distinguished himself in a dozen engagements, and has the Victoria Cross locked up in a drawer of his desk.' The moral authority of the police repeatedly emerged in fiction from the extent to which in novels (as in reality) so many had been senior army officers.

The culture of print actively engaged with the Napoleonic Wars and notably so in Britain. Thus, the Peninsular War of 1808–14, in which successive victories were obtained over the French, was treated in works such as William Napier's *History of the War in the Peninsula* (1828–40) and James Wyld's *Maps and Plans, Showing the Principal Movements, Battles and Sieges, in which the British Army was Engaged during the War from 1808 to 1814 in the Spanish Peninsula* (1840). Napier was also involved in controversy about Moore's campaign in Spain in 1808–9, publishing *Observations Illustrating Sir John Moore's Campaign* (1832) in response to criticism expressed by another veteran, Moyle Sherer, in his *Popular Recollections of the Peninsula* (1823). Sherer also published a commercially-successful *Life of Wellington* (1830–32), while Napier defended his brother's campaigning in India in *The Conquest of Scinde* (1844–6) and the *History of Sir Charles Napier's Administration of Scinde and Campaign in the Cutchee Hills* (1851). George Gleig, who became Chaplain of Chelsea Hospital in 1834 and was Chaplain General from 1844 to 1875, published *Waterloo* (1847), *Sale's Brigade in Afghanistan* (1847) and biographies of Robert Clive (1848) and Arthur, Duke of Wellington (1862). He also published his account of Peninsular service in *The Subaltern* (1825), just as Captain James MacCarthy's *Recollections of the Storming of the Castle of Badajos* appeared in 1836 and the *Recollections of Rifleman Harris* in 1848. Such works testified to widespread and sympathetic public interest in the military.

Extensive and sympathetic popular accounts of conflict continued to be written by well-informed participants, for example John Frederick Maurice's *A Popular History of the Ashanti Campaign* (1874). Maurice, who had been Major General Sir Garnet Wolseley's private secretary during the Asante campaign, went on to be a professor at the Staff College.

Furthermore, the stage went on being a form in which military heroism was depicted, although this theme was not adopted uncritically. Thus, Richard Brinsley Sheridan's brilliant play *The Critic* (1779) ridiculed the patriotic depiction of the danger of the Franco-Spanish invasion of 1778 in the shape of Puff's absurd play-within-a-play, *The Spanish Armada*, an implausible historical reference in this case to the defeated Spanish invasion attempt of 1588.

Heroic drama was far more common and prefigured the dramatic, indeed, histrionic gestures of revolutionaries and other warriors. The theatre saw many heroic plays on historical subjects, such as Richard Cumberland's *The Battle of Hastings* (1778), George Colman the Younger's *The Battle of Hexham* (1789) and *The Surrender of Calais* (1791) and Edward Jerningham's *The Siege of Berwick* (1793). The *Surrender of Calais*, depicting Edward III's capture of the French fortress in 1347, closed with:

> 'Rear, rear our English banner high
> In token proud of victory!
> ...
> Where'er the English warrior rides,
> May laurelled conquest grace his name.'

This was military history as nationalist drama. Providential support was an aspect of the same, because not least it was presented in a nationalist fashion by what in effect were state churches. Thus, Edward Nares, an ambitious clergyman, preached in 1797 on a day of public thanksgiving for a series of British naval victories:

'From the first invention of letters, by means of which the history of post ages has been transmitted to us, and the actions of our forefathers preserved, it has ever been the wisdom of man, under all circumstances of public and general concern, to refer to these valuable records, as the faithful depositaries of past experience, and to deduce from thence by comparison of situation whatever might conduce to his instruction, consolidation, or hope ... in the course of human events, a direction marvellously conducive to the final purposes of Heaven, the constant and eternal will of God ... his over-ruling providence.'[4]

Nares was to be Regius Professor of Modern History at Oxford from 1813 to 1841.

Military struggle offered drama for entire countries, with clashes re-enacted in open-air spectacles, as the tableau and the pageant became art forms, joining the panorama, such as Spring Porter's *Fall of Seringapatam* which depicted the British storming of Tipu Sultan's capital in 1799. Waterloo was celebrated accordingly including in the 1816 competition launched by the British Institution for Promoting the Fine Arts. The 360 degree panorama painting of Waterloo exhibited in 1826 in a rotunda by Henry Aston Barker made him a profit and toured throughout Britain. Philip Astley staged *The Battle of Waterloo* in his hippodrome with 144 consecutive performances on its first run in 1824, and the show was revived annually for several decades.[5]

At the same time, there was a willingness to comment critically on war. This drew on traditional religious and liberal themes that were given renewed prominence from the 1790s. Thus, Samuel Jackson Pratt, a prominent British literary figure, wrote of the Netherlands in 1795:

'With regard to the general history of this country, for many revolving ages, it resembles the general history, alas, of almost every other nation in the habitable globe; a picture of battles lost and gained, cities sacked or besieged, villages buried, burned, or desolated ... the disasters of human nature aggravated by the ambition and weakness of human creatures.'[6]

Francisco de Goya's *Disasters of War* prints (1810–20) were a more vivid account of the brutality of war, one also seen in his paintings of the unsuccessful rising of 1808 in Madrid against the recently imposed French control. As a reminder that the context and character of occupation policies could be very different, the system imposed in France in 1815 rested on force but was more benign.[7]

In China, the Manchu rulers, who ruled from 1644 to 1911, developed a new type of historical record, the *fanglue*, or campaign history, to record their various conquests. These exhaustive sources theoretically compiled all the official sources for given wars, including imperial proclamations, battlefield dispatches, reports from commanders, inter-office communications and extensive data on logistics and local conditions. That on the suppression of the nineteenth-century Muslim rebellions in northwest China runs to 30 modern bound volumes and over 16,000 pages in length. Far more detailed information on battles and campaigns is available than under previous dynasties, this providing a specific aspect of a particular Manchu culture of war in which war and martial values were made central to culture.[8]

This aspect of martial culture was embraced and extended by the Han Chinese population in the last century of Manchu rule as they increasingly became the supporters of campaigns of military expansion or recovery. This support helped generate a form of Han proto-nationalism that presaged a new multi-ethnic 'national' identity in the early republic.[9]

Separately, there could be a choice about which military history should be celebrated, and at what scale. This process was accentuated from the 1790s as ideology divided countries, notably France, from which revolutionary and radical accounts of history, recent and distant, could both be disseminated. There were also the contrasts created by the experience of conquest and occupation. These offered different possible preludes of resistance and liberation. There were variations in all the circumstances, and they helped lead to contrasting later histories of the period. Thus, for Germany, there was a Prussian-centred account of national liberation from French control in 1813, but that sat less comfortably with areas, notably Bavaria, Saxony and Württemberg, that had changed from their support for Napoleon only later in 1813. So also for differing accounts within Italy and Spain. These contrasts provided a major topic subsequently for nationalist military history, which sought not to arrive at compromise but rather to provide a clear and dominant narrative.

Drawing on a longer-established rivalry, a British colonel complained in 1807 from Ireland, which was then part of the United Kingdom of Great Britain and Ireland:

'A divided or distracted people like us are not calculated to meet such an invader as [Napoleon] Bonaparte ... the 12th of this month instead of lamenting over the fatal consequences of the battle of Friedland [Bonaparte victory over Britain's ally Russia], the Orange [Protestant] Yeomanry of this kingdom were celebrating a battle fought upwards of 100 years ago, with every mark of triumph and exultation as if Ireland had no other enemy than its Catholic inhabitants,'[10]

a reference to William III's victory over James II at the battle of the Boyne in 1690. Religious motivation remained significant, as with the role of anti-Catholicism in American attitudes during the Mexican-American War of 1846–8.[11]

And so on in the second half of the nineteenth century. 'I quote the fights historical From Marathon to Waterloo, in order categorical,' the comic 'Modern Major General Song' from Gilbert and Sullivan's *The Pirates of Penzance* (1879) was another tribute to Wellington's triumph, which was thereby presented as the culmination of military history, rather than more recent battles involving Britain that did not have such an unproblematic legacy, notably those of the Crimean War, as well as those in which Britain had not participated, especially the battles of the American Civil War and the Franco-Prussian War. The linkage of Waterloo to Marathon provided a suitable pedigree of defence of liberty and a glorious Classical echo. The song itself was a brilliant spoof either of Garnet Wolseley or of Gilbert's wife's uncle, General Henry Turner. There was also as an example of public interest a significant increase in the number of battle paintings displayed in public exhibitions: in 1876, 50,000 people came to see Lady Butler's *Balaclava* when it was displayed at the Fine Art Society; the battle had been fought in 1854.

Separately, there was a continuum between history and war news, each exciting interest in the other. Newspapers spent substantial sums on the telegraphy that brought news of conflict, but frequently unrealistically so, as noted by the historian Hans Delbrück when he served in the Franco-Prussian War of 1870–1:

'I cannot agree with Peter's conclusions on the objectivity of the war reports. We have had the same stories of bravery in our regiment, but it seems to me that some men go forward fine, whereas others have very little courage: only discipline and organisation moves the mass of men forward. I myself have seen how badly our newspapers lie, and I no longer believe them.'[12]

Very differently, histories of war extended to fiction, as with George Chesney's *The Fall of England? The Battle of Dorking: Reminiscences of a Volunteer*, an 1871 fictional account of a successful German invasion of Britain, which had a second run of 80,000 copies, and led to a tranche of such literature. Chesney, a captain in the Royal Engineers, thought Britain unprepared for war. Such invasion fears were to be expanded to include aliens with H.G. Wells' highly successful novel *The War of the Worlds* (1898). Indeed, in many respects, science fiction is a prospectus for war, one in which invention, however fantastical, draws on assessments of the nature of conflict as manifested through a reading of human psychology, society and statecraft. Given the extent to which thought draws on experience, there is necessarily an historical component to it.

A very different type of fiction ranged from the uniforms, military titles and medals of the present to the depiction of a glorious military past interpreted in terms of fortitude and heroism, whether advances under heavy fire or defences against great odds. Such accounts were staples of male literature, and not only for the young. Social identity and cohesion were part of the context of these tales of daring-do, tales that made past triumphs accessible.

Similarly, a continued role for war-leaders, monarchical gloire and dynasticism needs to be considered alongside the standard narrative of state development. They were far from incompatible. 'Bonapartism' was Karl Marx's critical response to the military adventurism of Napoleon III (r. 1852–70) and the emperor's use of war including in Crimea, Italy and Mexico, in order to acquire a prestige that would help express and sustain his domestic political position, and his role in history. Fascination with the idea of the strongman helped ensure that the anti-German general Georges Boulanger appealed in 1888–9 as a strongman who could transform France. Instead, he committed suicide at his mistress's tomb. This role of the strongman looks toward the bellicose role of some monarchs at the start of World War One.

Alongside the central part of a monarch, whether hereditary or not, it is appropriate to ask whether it became less the case in the last decades of the nineteenth century. In addition to the continued role of monarchs and dynasties, not least with the ruling houses of Prussia and Britain gaining imperial status, for Germany and India respectively (and Haiti, Brazil and Mexico doing the same), as those of France, Austria and Russia had already claimed, monarchs were increasingly absorbed within the scale and complexity of the governments and states they ruled or presided over. Moreover, dynasties had to adapt or respond to nationalism. This caused them much difficulty and created issues for empires as they strove to propagate a theme of imperial identity and therefore a supra-national, or different, nationalism.

Military history was inherently presented as a dramatic topic, as with Doyle's novel *The Sign of the Four* (1890), with its description of the Indian Mutiny of 1857–9, a conflict that is often given different names in India, including Indian Revolution and Indian War of Liberation:

> 'One month India lay as still and peaceful, to all appearance, as Surrey or Kent; the next there were two hundred thousand black devils let loose, and the country was a perfect hell ... the whole sky was alight with the burning bungalows ... Dawson's wife, all cut into ribbons ... hundreds of the black fiends ... a fight of the millions against the hundreds ... nothing but torture and murder and outrage ... fanatics and fierce devil-worshippers'.

The emphasis in Doyle's day was on the brutal treatment of British women and children, especially the massacre at Kanpur in 1857. Now the emphasis has moved, instead, to British atrocities. In *The Sign of the Four*, veterans take the Mutiny into the drama of contemporary Britain. In reality, veterans' movements were a living representation of patriotic military history. They tended to be politically conservative, which remains the case, although there have also always been veterans on the left as well. The veteran experience is a lived history of war that is frequently underplayed. In practice, this experience affects many others directly, notably family and friends, and was particularly prominent when there was/is conscription.

Doyle also offered a Social Darwinism linked to religious purpose, as in his non-Holmes *The Tragedy of the Korosko*, a serial in *The Strand Magazine* in 1897 that became a book in 1898, and, in an adaptation by Doyle, the play *Fires of Fate* (1909) which, in 1923, became a film. Set in the here-and-now of the British conflict with the Mahdists of Sudan, the latter are presented as bigoted barbarians to the civilisation of Egypt which is protected by Britain; in effect, in British eyes, adopting the burden of ancient Rome. The novel sees a fundamental debate about strategy, with Cecil Brown feeling that Britain has taken on the excessive burden of being the global policeman, only for Colonel Cochrane to argue that Brown has

> 'a very limited view of our national duties ... behind national interests and diplomacy and all that there lies a great guiding force – a Providence in fact – which is for ever getting the best out of each nation and using it for the good of the whole. When a nation ceases to respond, it is time that she went into hospital for a few centuries, like Spain or Greece – the virtue has gone out of her. A man or a nation is not placed upon the earth to do merely what is pleasant and what is profitable... That is how we rule India. We came there by a kind of natural law, like air rushing into a vacuum.'

Scarcely a modern formulation of strategy but one that is significant as an exposition that was commonplace at the time, and, moreover, can be difficult to recreate out of the standard scholarly literature. Imperial expansion served to substantiate themes of appropriate conduct and therefore legitimacy, such as Christian kingship in the case of the French invasion of Algeria in 1830. This expansionist activity and conflict also offered ways to vindicate the people through the soldiery and to link them in *gloire* to the ruling *élite*.[13]

Racism was also abundantly seen elsewhere, as in the counter-insurgency operations of the Americans in the Philippines[14] and of European powers in newly-conquered African colonies. This racism contributed directly to the high level of atrocities.

Moreover, that attitude toward war was part of a more general engagement with conflict that extended to include hunting and a willingness to fight and kill, both tendencies that look to anthropological assessments of war.

Thus, in his short story 'Black Peter,' Doyle has his heroes wait among the bushes at night to find a killer:

> 'It brought with it something of the thrill which the hunter feels when he lies beside the water-pool and waits for the coming of the thirsty beast of prey. What savage creature was it which might steal upon us out of the darkness? Was it a fierce tiger of crime, which could only be taken fighting hard with flashing fang and claw, or would it prove to be some skulking jackal ... In absolute silence we crouched amongst the bushes ... it was the darkest hour which precedes the dawn.'

The racial element was commonplace in such discussion, as in Doyle's *A Study in Scarlet* (1887): 'The savage man, and the savage beast, hunger, thirst, fatigue, and disease – every impediment which Nature could place in the way – had all been overcome with Anglo-Saxon tenacity.' Supposed ethnic characterisation thus offered a way to write about the Anglosphere and also from a perspective that drew together Britain, its empire and America.

Referring to war with Denmark in 1864, Albrecht von Stosch, a Prussian general, claimed: 'After 50 years of peace, the Prussian state needs a good baptism by fire ... much blood will be shed, but so it is with the history of man as with the land we toil over: only by our blood is it nourished.' This approach was made more acceptable by the relatively easy nature of the Prussian victory over the outnumbered Danes. Stosch, a staff officer, had not by 1864 had significant combat experience.[15]

Nationalism was strong in the present, the nineteenth century, in part due to its role in an identity grounded in past struggle, an identity that led to a new social purchase in which popular willpower was crucial. Nationalism provided a lens through which to look at past, present and future, and necessarily so given the historical character, content and purpose of nations. War was seen as a glorious means to renew people and escape decadence. Most intellectuals were convinced nationalists: internationalism was of only limited appeal. A concept of triumphant will linked the prevailing Romanticism to international relations. Millenarian theology and providentialism also contributed to a sense of the rightness of conflict. Educated élites believed in the moral value of war, and this belief illuminated the use of history.

Dynasticism, moreover, continued to be a factor, and this could lead, as before, to the representation of war in a highly misleading fashion. Thus, in his 1792 treatise, *Yuzhi shiquan ji* (*In Commemoration of the Ten Complete Military Victories*), the Qianlong emperor of China (r. 1736–96) reached ten victories by including failures that were misrepresented. In particular, he found that his major success in Xinjiang could not be repeated against Myanmar: the ecological challenge of campaigning in the latter was far greater, notably as a result of disease, but problems were also posed by the stronger coherence of Myanmar politics and governance.

The reading of war was in part a matter of rising nationalism. This was particularly apparent in republics as the dynastic element was absent there, and notably so with the development of foundation myths. Thus, in America, the wars of 1775–83 and 1812–15 against Britain were read in terms of the obtaining, securing and validation of independence, although that entailed greatly exaggerating the challenge of Britain to American independence in 1812–15. In practice, the British government, busy with war with Napoleon, had scant interest in another war that would add to its burden. This point can be overlooked, or minimised by American commentary instead keen to look at bilateral issues. Yet, far from seeking gains from America, the British wanted to end the war.

The standard American reading of conflict with Britain served also to justify particular politicians and policies, not least, in the case of the War of 1812–15 at the expense of the Federalists. The discussion of the War of Independence and the War of 1812 focused on American successes, notably in defence, such as Bunker Hill (1775), Saratoga (1777), Fort McHenry (1814) and New Orleans (1815) and not on failures, particularly to conquer Canada against whom there were unsuccessful offensives in 1775–6, 1812, 1813 and 1814. This meant that there was not a crucial debate about American capability, and thus its proper geopolitical span and meaning for strategy, not least in response to British naval power which was greater. The latter was a key factor due to America's need to trade and also to the exposure of the American coastline, which included the major cities. A failure today to assess the latter factor adequately is an aspect of histories of war written from the present position as modern America is not as Atlanticist as was then the case.

The nationalistic reading of military history could take many different forms. Thus, the militarism of Meiji Japan was linked to the development of State Shinto as an amalgam of a longstanding animist religion with a new authoritarian form of government, and this amalgam was significant in the creation of the new Japan. This was seen in 1869 with the establishment of Yasukuni as a pre-eminent shrine that was a symbol of nationalism and a site where the war dead were commemorated. Japan was far from alone. Indeed, memorials were seen more generally, and to a far greater degree than in the eighteenth century.

The challenges of change encouraged not just nationalism, for that was largely only vindicated with the many new nation states created (permanently or temporarily) in 1918–21, but also imperial loyalties and the related expansionism of national empires, such as America and France, dynastic ones, and forms and structures from the range of the British institutionalisation of empire, to, eventually, the new post-war Soviet one. Although there was internationalism and pacifism, the varied political forms encouraged a commitment to collective mission and identity that contributed to warfulness.[16]

Military success continued to be variously depicted. In Italy, success was inscribed in street names and statues after unification in 1860–70, with streets and squares named after the rulers of the House of Savoy, now kings of Italy, and after the politicians, ministers and military leaders who had furthered the *Risorgimento*, notably Mazzini, Cavour and Garibaldi. Thus, formerly a Papal town, Ancona has a *Corso Garibaldi* and a *Corso Mazzini*. Urbino, another former Papal town, gained a *Corso Garibaldi*. In Siena, the *Museo Civico* includes a *Sala del Risorgimento* offering the standard frescoes of the period that depicted the narrative of the *Risorgimento*. In Massa Marittima, the *Piazza Duomo* became the *Piazza Garibaldi*. Pride in Italian military achievement, however, led to a downplaying of the very important earlier Italian role in other armies, notably those of the Austrian and Spanish Habsburgs, because this did not correspond with the new national myths.

The varied engagement with what was recent military history could be amply seen with the Anglo-Sudan War of 1896–9. A combatant Winston Churchill, soon after in *The River War: An Historical Account of the Reconquest of the Soudan* (1899), remarked of the Mahdists:

'They lived by the sword. Why should they not perish by the magazine rifle? A state of society which, even if it were tolerable to those whom it comprised, was an annoyance to civilised nations has been swept aside ... The Government was a cruel despotism.'

Three years later, George Alfred Henty, a war correspondent turned best-selling adventure story writer about epic conflicts, in *With Kitchener in the Soudan* (sic), presented the very recent British conquest as a 'stupendous achievement.' His preface declared:

'Thus a land that had been turned into a desert by the terrible tyranny of the Mahdi and his successor, was wrested from barbarism and restored to civilization; and the stain upon British honour, caused by the desertion of Gordon [in 1885] by the British ministry of the day was wiped out.'

Aside from Henty, who was a war correspondent, including in the 1868 British expedition to Abyssinia, the Franco-Prussian War and the Ashanti War, other 'specials' included Archibald Forbes, Melton Prior and G.W. Steevens. Also in 1902 appeared A.E.W. Mason's novel *The Four Feathers*, a presentation of British operations in Sudan as a definition of manliness and heroism. Mason was to be an MP, unlike Doyle who failed in both elections in which he stood. They included that of 1900, which, fought during the Boer War (1899–1902), demonstrated the popularity of bellicosity and the bellicosity of popularity. The Tory government won re-election in part as a result of the Liberal opposition dividing over the response to the war. At the same time, the teaching of history in British schools was not always shot through with jingoistic propaganda.[17]

Technology might well seem to trump all considerations of heroism, as with the British defeat of the Mahdists at Omdurman (1898), the writer Hilaire Belloc observing that year in *The Modern Traveller*: 'Whatever happens we have got the Maxim (machine) Gun, and they have not.' Yet, the popular perception was different. Alongside the triumph of firepower, there was close-quarter fighting against opponents, including pirates and slavers. Piracy indeed persisted in many areas, for example in

South-East Asia, but largely at the expense of indigenous shipping and coastal communities.[18]

In 'The Green Flag', a Doyle story of 1893 set in Sudan, each side benefits from artillery, which obliges the British to rely on bravery. Indeed, far from a Western triumph in and through technology, Holmes's fictional colleague John Watson is wounded by Afghans at Maiwand (1880) where he sees his 'own comrades hacked to pieces ... without losing my nerve.': 962 of the outnumbered 2,500 strong British force were killed and the colours of a regiment lost. The fighting in Afghanistan was scarcely that of the victory of technology at the tactical level. Alfred Cane writing of a sortie against the village of Deh Khoja:

'We began by shelling the place. There was no reply so 800 of our infantry advanced to the attack when at once a galling fire was opened on them from loop holes round the village. Our men rushed on and entered the village on the south side but only to find it filled with armed men firing from the windows, doors and roofs. It was a hopeless task ... had to return in hot haste under the same heavy fire.'

Far from there being any automatic triumph for technology, the reality was more complex, contextual and contingent. Thus, the Carlist Wars in Spain, the most significant of which was the first, that in 1833–40, had numerous battles that tend not to attract much attention in part due to a widespread lack of interest in nineteenth-century Spanish history and in part due to an absence of engagement with civil conflict in the 1830s and 1840s. That absence makes it harder to confront the European civil wars of 1848–9 other than in terms of a misleading apparent novelty.

Yet, these battles also deserve attention, not least as they throw light on factors crucial to success in this and other periods. In battle, morale, experience, surprise, terrain and numbers were essential, and all were as important as effective tactics, if not more so. As a caveat to much scholarly writing about war, the campaigns of this war did not leave much room for complicated operational planning, nor for sophisticated tactics by complex formations. Yet, that did not prevent success. Indeed, this is an important qualification to the paradigm power and method approach to military history.

As with other civil wars, strategy, morale and generalship in the Carlist Wars were shot through with political considerations, and the war helped in the politicisation of the army and the militarisation of politics, a process affected by the flow and fortunes of campaigning, as also seen in the American Civil War with the radicalisation of Union attitudes and policies as the war became difficult in 1862, and, again, with eventual success in 1864.[19] In a more general pattern that is neglected in much military history and histories of war, Spanish generals adopted the policy of *pronunciamientos* (declarations) in which they announced their demands. In 1836, Arthur Middleton, a perceptive American diplomat, commented: 'The capital is undoubtedly at the mercy of any of the generals who can dispose of a division of 4 to 5,000 men. So that the question seems now only to be who shall exercise the dictatorship.' Military regimes dominated Spain from 1840, with coups and attempted coups. This is a crucial aspect of the history of the military, helping to develop patterns of behaviour and causes of influence.

In neighbouring Portugal, where there was civil war from the late 1820s, the lack of the manpower, matériel and funds seen in the Peninsular War in Portugal as a result of British and French participation, did not mean that military skill was absent, as the Duke of Saldanha showed against the Miguelists in 1834. Due to civil war, there was a politicisation of the army which was the major power that could stage and/or resist coups or rebellions as was to be repeatedly shown until 1926, another one being decisive in 1974. The same pattern was present in Latin America, as with several coups in Brazil from 1889 to 1964.

Coups did not feature in most commentary on military history. Instead, the idea of a decisive battle remained central. Organisation in terms of a list of famous battles, was very much established in writings from the mid-nineteenth century. The extent to which this historical concept then affected military attitudes is unclear but clearly very important.[20] It is similarly unclear how far there were ideas of such battles earlier that did not emerge in such literary forms.

Accounts of past and present conflict were (and remain) challenged by complexity, the contextual, the contingent and not least the role of foreign support, which was not a heroic offering. The interplay of these with technology both influenced the histories of war and was affected by them in terms of creating assumptions. Indeed, the idea of anachronism, however contingent and subjective, was a prime way in which change was experienced and conceptualised. This helped develop and sustain ideas of modernisation. Yet, the issue of learning from experience was left unclear due to the question of what to focus on and which lessons to draw, as with the Franco-Prussian War of 1870–1. The resulting cult of the offensive did not in practice capture the reality of the significance of defensive firepower in many of the battles of that war, notably the decisive Prussian victory at Sedan in 1870 which led to the fall of Napoleon III's regime.

Similarly, the American Civil War (1861–5) had provided important indications of the potency of defensive firepower, but they were underplayed due to the positive image of the attack. In particular, the broader relevance of trench warfare at Petersburg in Virginia in the winter of 1864–5 became apparent only fifty years later. The impact of the war on European military thought was particularly negligible in Continental Europe where the leaders of professional armies and the officer corps wrongly saw no lessons in a war fought by mass militia armies.

So also for the (Second) Boer War of 1899–1902. All the Continental armies sent observers but, afterwards, there was considerable disagreement over whether to consider it as just another colonial war, and therefore of few lessons relevant to Europe; or, alternatively, as a conflict between two opponents of European stock, and thus more relevant. Most Continental military experts saw little in the conflict relevant to European warfare, Emperor Wilhelm II of Germany, a war leader without experience, who was committed to the attack, telling Sir Ian Hamilton, the British Adjutant General, in 1909: 'It is you who have led us all astray with your South African War experiences, experiences altogether exceptional.'[21] In practice, although the force-space ratio was very different to conflicts in Europe, the war had instructive implications including the use of indirect artillery fire, smokeless powder, long-range rifle fire and camouflage; although it did not provide an indication of the potential importance of machine guns.

The Russo-Japanese War of 1904–5, fought between two leading powers, led to more attention. Observers came away noting that frontal assaults were still feasible and the bayonet still relevant, the latest technology notwithstanding. Hamilton, who had been an observer in the war, felt, when he attended Continental manoeuvres in 1909, that he could detect an overreaction to the unsuccessful Russian defensive tactics:

> 'a false principle seemed to underlie the tactics of both commanders, the principle namely that any and every problem can be solved by the adoption of a rash and desperate offensive.'[22]

This was to be seen in the fighting in the opening campaign of World War One, that of 1914. In a pattern so often seen in the reporting on war, the focus was on the tactical level and, to a lesser extent, its operational counterpart, and not on the strategic one. Most commentators overlooked the extent to which, unlike Tsushima at sea, land battles had not been decisive militarily, but, instead, had only caused the Russians to fall back. Moreover, they ignored the extent to which the conflict so strained Japan that it could not afford to pursue the Russians deeper into Manchuria. Despite the concentration of attention on the battlefield, Japanese victory owed much to political weakness in St Petersburg, as the government had a revolution to confront in 1905, one in part fostered by Japanese military intelligence. Contemporary Western racist attitudes disparaged the Japanese and encouraged European experts to believe that their armies would be able also to win by attacking, albeit at a heavy cost.[23]

There was also a failure to appreciate the 'lessons' from the Balkan Wars of 1912–13, particularly the role of field fortifications, supported by rapid-firing artillery and machine guns, in part due to the assumption that there was little to learn from the Balkans.[24]

'Learning' throughout was a multi-stage process, with history open at different levels. Just as today references to Thucydides abound when considering relations between America and China, so, in 1798, Richard Bentley complained: 'We hear of Rome and Carthage every day and in every debate, even to puerility.'[25] The Classics went on being resonant and useful, and served for the propagation of the new nationalism, as in America. This was seen at the battlefield of Gettysburg, where, on 19 November 1863, the day of Abraham Lincoln's famous speech commemorating the victory, Edward Everett, Professor of Greek Literature at Harvard, who spoke for much longer, compared the site with that of Marathon in 490 BCE. In doing so, Everett provided an echo of the glorious defence of liberty by the Greeks against the invading Persians, an account that cast Greek civilisation as the progenitor of modern America while denying that validating role for the Confederate warriors.

Failure left a difficult legacy. Thus, Spain's major defeat by America in 1898 was called *El Desastre* and perceived as shattering national prestige. Demands for regeneration were therefore based on an account of failure, one that left far too little to the difficulties of defending island colonies, in this case Cuba, Puerto Rico and the Philippines, against a superior maritime power. That Spain had been defeated by America led to a counterpointing of that 'real nation' with Spain, a state without, to its critics, true nationhood. To some critics, this was the fault of monarchy and Catholicism, to others of a more conservative stamp of a regionalism that sapped the nation. The state could be seen as too strong or too weak, or both, but the shadow of defeat, and the differing histories offered as explanation, came first.

For contemporaries, anyway, there was and is no fixed present to historicise, but rather a range of conflicts that required and prompted longer-term explanations. The expansion of Western power in the nineteenth century encouraged a geopolitical placing of military history. Drawing on the conflation of Enlightenment ideas from the eighteenth century and of the Social Darwinism of the nineteenth, this approach presented military history in terms of grand sweeps, as by Halford Mackinder, the leading British geopolitician, in 1904:

'Europe and European history … subordinate to Asia and Asiatic history, for European civilisation is … the outcome of the secular struggle against Asiatic invasions … for a thousand years a series of horse-riding people emerged from Asia.'[26]

This was not too dissimilar to Edward Gibbon's reference at the start of book seven of his *History of the Decline and Fall of the Roman Empire* (1776–88), to the 'rapid conquests' of Mongols and Tartars in terms of 'the primitive convulsions of nature, which have agitated and altered the surface of the globe.'

Geopolitics, which was given a global historical and geographical span by Mackinder, offered a history of war that apparently covered past, present and future. It focused on technology but that of communications rather than the firepower that tended to attract military attention. The replacement of horsemen by rail was seen as providing whichever power controlled the 'pivot' of the Eurasian heartland with a strategic capability that outweighed maritime links. The interior of a continent became more potent than its exterior. In practice, as with many prospectuses, this was misleading, not least due to the friction posed by the difficulties and inflexibility of rail, as well as the costs of construction and operation. Yet, as a way of advancing geopolitics as a context for strategy, the thesis helped provide a guide to Anglo-Russian competition, and notably so in South Asia.[27]

Looked at differently, that competition provided the rationale for acceptance of the geopolitical thesis as a basis for planning. Thus, the Anglo-Japanese naval treaty of 1902 could be made to seem a prescient response to the 'heartland,' one helping each power against Russia. In historical terms, this also appeared a precursor for the current American-Japanese alignment against China and Russia. Yet, as a reminder of the potentially problematic nature of histories of war by means of analogy, an alternative parallel could be found in the German-Japanese alignment under the Anti-Comintern Pact of 1936 and the Tripartite Pact of 1940; although to underline the problem of drawing parallels, Germany in these cases could be seen as an equivalent to Britain or America.

The nature of the society in question also engaged attention. Drawing on Classical roots, but with a new force, from the eighteenth century with Gibbon praising 'the warm virtues of nature' of the 'untutored Caledonians' and noting the resilience of Arabs, Sardinians and others protected by their harsh environments, in and about the nineteenth century there was/is a linked account that presented progressive change in terms of the people-under-arms. This approach linked descriptions of Greek and Republican Roman militaries to the medieval Scots and Swiss, to later militia forces and then to the conscript-based forces of the modern age.

That account was then to be read forward to the two world wars and to the conscript forces of the Cold War, notably from the revolutionary perspective. This approach, however, has proved less certain as a result of changes over the last half-century, and this qualification has led to academic revisionism, including about revolutionary forces.[28] Nationalism is still a significant theme in public culture, for example those of China and India.

However, now the norm is for nationalism no longer to be matched by compulsory male military service.

The people under arms, a concept possibly more appropriate for the Sioux and the Zulu,[29] was a theme that worked in several directions. It could lead to a justification for conscription at a time of populations that, as a result of growth, urbanisation and literacy, were increasingly volatile. Taxation could also be explained.

At the same time as conscription saw the people under arms, there was also an engagement with popular action that was outside the authority of the state. This could be categorised from lawlessness to rebellion even civil war, and, by its supporters or outside commentators, be referred to as war. Thus, the Irish Land War of 1879–82 saw violence employed against landowners and the police. On a long pattern of commentary about 'wars' in Ireland, one that stretched to the Irish 'Troubles' of the 1960s onwards, this conflict involved not just the significance of perception, in terms of levels of violence, but also the question of the legality of conduct, from trials and imprisonment to negotiations. So also, without suggesting any equivalence with opposition in the twentieth century including in Israel and Indian Kashmir.[30]

Meanwhile, there was a different history for international conflict. In large part as a consequence of successive Prussian success, German campaigns were studied in staff colleges in America, where they influenced the extended order advocated in the Infantry Drill Regulations of 1871. In the 1880s, American army commentators employed German examples, while *Kriegspiel* (war games) were introduced at the British Royal Military College in 1871. At Oxford, the University *Kriegspiel* Club played war games on a set of Prussian official maps for the Sadowa campaign of 1866. Its President, Hereford Brooke George, was a pioneer of military history and geography at the university.[31]

In the 1860s, Jomini's influence had remained strong, as in *The Operations of War Explained and Illustrated* (1866) by Edward Hamley, the new Professor of Military History at the new British Staff College at Sandhurst. However, the prestige of German warmaking in the wake of victories in 1864–71, notably at the expense of France, subsequently led to an increase in interest in the arguments of and attributed to Carl von Clausewitz (1780–1831). This interest was important to the development of a canon of 'classic' texts in military affairs that were not simply Classical, although the contradictions in Clausewitz's *Vom Kriege (On War)*, the revised as well as the unrevised parts,[32] were not probed. A course of lectures on Clausewitz was given at the *École Supérieure de Guerre* in 1884, influencing French officers, although the majority of French strategists remained sceptical. *On War* was also translated into Japanese and was claimed to have influenced Japanese conduct in their victory over Russia in 1904–5.[33] In practice, on both land and sea, Japanese options owed much to Russian dispositions and moves.

The Russians themselves were divided over the extent to which they should look to German models. General Mikhail Dragomirov, who led the 'back to Suvorov movement', emphasised the value of morale in his pressure for a Russian model focused on the example of earlier Russian commanders: Suvorov was the key commander in the 1790s. In contrast, and, indeed, a difference frequently seen, as in Japan, General Genrykh Leer, Professor of Strategy at the Military Academy in St. Petersburg from 1865 to 1889, and the academy's head from then until 1898, was a supporter of reform. Leer saw Moltke as an exponent of the concept of the operational line, which, through manoeuvre, was to be translated into victory. To him, Moltke married the ideal and the practice of strategy, although Leer also argued that manoeuvre itself only brought time and space, and could not ensure victory.[34] This was well-observed, although drawing on a German model was unwelcome to many Russian commentators.

From battlefields to the contexts created by particular opponents, Moltke was a more accessible model than Clausewitz, but he himself warned of the hazards of extrapolating from his victories. Furthermore, the tactical lessons of the battles of the Franco-Prussian war were inadequately grasped.[35] So also with the failure to understand that German success in the frontier battles culminating at Sedan had been compromised by the refusal of France to surrender at that point. Nor had the advance on Paris brought the rapid result obtained when Prussian and British forces advanced there in 1815. The overthrow of Napoleon I in 1815 led to peace but that of Napoleon III in 1870 did not have this result. Whatever the tactical and operational skills that the Germans could deploy in 1870–1, the length of the conflict posed an unexpected burden, one very different to the Austro-Prussian War of 1866. Indeed, agency in part rested with the degree of resilience that the French could display. This proved greater than anticipated. Separately, the 1870–1 war, like that in 1815, was of only limited guidance to the world war that was to follow in 1914, as France fought alone in the two former cases.

In addition, Moltke, while arguing that it was preferable to fight on the territory of one's opponent, was increasingly skeptical about the potential of the strategic offensive, because of increases in defensive firepower and the size of armies.

Deficiencies in leadership and strategy on the part of Austria and France had played into Prussian hands in 1866 and 1870, enabling the Prussians to outmanoeuvre their opponents, prefiguring the German advantages with *blitzkrieg* in 1939–41. However, the extent to which these deficiencies could not be predicted for the future, with all the implications for the strategic offensive, was underplayed by contemporaries keen to argue that they had discovered the blueprint for success. In doing so, they concealed the unease left by the wars, not only among the defeated but also in Germany where there was concern about the prospect of repeating a victory. Indeed, the German army in the 1870s and 1880s failed to maintain the comparative advantages and relative lead it had enjoyed in the 1860s. In part, this was unsurprising as it was difficult to maintain such leads, a situation that remains the case today, not only because of the changes in the militaries of specific enemies, as with Egypt in 1973 as opposed to 1967 for Israel, but also because the enemy might change.

Only a small number of thinkers anticipated and expressed concern about the horrific casualties that developments in military methods and the expansion of army size were likely to produce in any future major war. The Marxist Frederick Engels argued that the American Civil War indicated the likely massive destructiveness of future intra-European conflict, and, prefiguring what was to occur in 1917–18 but not, outside China and Eastern Europe, 1939–45, he thought that this destructiveness would undermine existing state and class hegemonies and make revolution possible. In his *War of the Future in its Technical, Economic and Political Aspects* (1897), part of which was published in English as *Is War Now Impossible?* (1899)[36], the Polish financier Jan G. Bloch suggested that the combination of modern military technology and industrial strength had made great power European warfare too destructive to be feasible, and that, if it occurred, it would resemble a giant siege and that this attritional conflict would only be won when one of the combatants succumbed to famine and revolution. Bloch argued that the stalemate on the battlefield that came from defensive firepower would translate eventually into collapse on the Home Front.[37]

There is a tendency, not least when citing Bloch, to echo the pessimism of Moltke's later years and to look towards World War One. This is part of the compartmentalisation and labelling of military history, with 1871–1914 treated as lying between the Franco-Prussian War and World War One. The conflicts of the period are then seen as important in so far as they could serve as predictors for the latter, while the ability of contemporaries to make such predictions becomes a key subject for comment. Moreover, there is a sense of a slow-moving car crash, with commanders planning for what would become disaster, unmindful both of the flaws in their plans and of the lethality of modern weaponry.

This history is not without value but it faces several problems. One of the most serious is the foreshortening of what occurred over four decades, so that the entire period is seen as a unit defined by preparation for World War One. This approach is misleading, even though the creation of alliance systems, notably joining France to Russia, made it more likely that the next war would not be restricted to two powers, as the Franco-Prussian War had been, and that it would therefore be more difficult to achieve a rapid victory. As a reminder, however, of the complex legacy from mid-century conflicts, the Crimean War and, to a lesser extent, the Austro-Prussian War had each involved several states,[38] and yet both had been limited wars.

Moreover, it was not till the Russo-Japanese War of 1904–5 indicated the lethal character of the combination of sustained attack with new weaponry that the likely shape of the conflict in a great-power clash in Europe appeared to be clear. Prior to that, there was considerable uncertainty, and even that war suggested that the attacking power would win, and would do so relatively speedily, albeit with heavy casualties, while, at sea, such a victory appeared likely without heavy casualties for the victor.

Speculation about these and other outcomes was more common in print due to the expansion of publication, itself a matter of steam-driven production technology, consumption-linked increases in readership, entrepreneurial and organisational intermediary activities, the professionalisation of the military, and the rise of higher-level practical literacy. All of these were combined with rapid technological change in weaponry and war as a whole, as well as a large number of conflicts that required discussion. At the same time, there was variety in the conflicts, such that commentators could address a range of experiences and problems. Thus, Charles Callwell, the British author of *Small Wars: Their Principles and Practice* (1896), was to serve in World War One in the Directorate of Military Operations, but the experience reflected in his book drew on his role in India and then the First Boer War (1881), as well as drawing on French, Russian and American examples. This was very different to the trajectory of Schlieffen.[39]

Hitherto, this chapter has been somewhat conventional in focusing on nationalism, technology and learning or not learning lessons prior to World War One, while the major non-Western state discussed, Japan, has been presented as deserving of attention because it became, as it were, such a state. The conspicuous omission in this chapter, other than in terms of a misplaced claim to success, has been China. Indeed, although the specialist literature is increasingly presenting China in the last century of the imperial era that ended in 1912 as developing during that period, this has not had a comparable impact on the usual treatment of China in general histories of war. This failure to address the significance of China in such works is flawed, both because of China's relative position at the time and its current strength now. The latter encourages a scrutiny of China's past position.

Improvement in the Chinese military was underappreciated, and this remains the case in general works, because of a narrative of weakness and failure, notably after the Sino-Japanese War of 1894–5. This narrative attracted Western and Japanese commentators on the one hand and Chinese republican ones on the other.[40] The latter had an interest in providing a critical account of the imperial era. This approach, that essentially of relationship with the West, provides one opportunity to reconsider China, not least by seeking to re-examine the standard narrative.

There is also, however, as still today, the tendency to downplay the significance of relative Chinese capability as shown both in terms of domestic military tasks and with reference to competition and conflict on inner-Asian frontiers. In the Communist era, that competition has included conflict with India and Vietnam, as well as the suppression of a reform movement in 1989.

In the century ending in 1912, the tasks were far greater in both respects, and this throws critical light on the notion that competition with the West/Japan should obviously have been foremost both in Chinese military capability and in assessing its effectiveness. Indeed, there is a parallel here with the emphasis on the British challenge in eighteenth-century India and the downplaying accordingly of the Persian and later Afghan invasions.

In terms of scale, the Taiping revolution in mid-nineteenth century China was greater than any since the mid-seventeenth. Yet, it remains poorly integrated into the general history of mid-nineteenth century civil wars, of nineteenth century warfare and, even, of Chinese military history. In part, this is because the Taiping revolution was a failure (although that does not prevent attention to the American Confederacy), but also as a result of the unwillingness of Chinese regimes from 1912 to claim ownership of the suppression of the revolution. Having been positively written up under the victorious Manchu, this suppression was denigrated and forgotten after the Manchu dynasty fell.[41] Such a process can now be more readily understood in the specific terms of the period, but what it entails for the present requires consideration.

Drawing attention to both Japan and China serves as a reminder about the problems of focusing on Western narratives. Even though these narratives include non-Western states, they do so in terms of their determination and success in adopting Western weaponry, as well as their more general response to Western power. This approach, however, is insufficient, not least because it underplays the understanding and usage of weaponry, but also because there is a failure to devote adequate attention to other elements, both of conflict and contextual. The standard history therefore requires more attention not only to the variety of the Western model which should, for example, give due weight to developments in Latin America, but also to the autonomy of non-Western powers.

The choices made by the latter should not be evaluated solely in terms of success in maintaining independence. For much of the non-West, and notably China, however, this pre-war period is treated as less important than that prior to the outbreak of World War Two, however the latter is dated. This relative significance can then affect the consideration of the decades prior to 1914, at least in so far as popular history is concerned. Moreover, as the emphasis in attention now focuses on World War Two, rather than One, so it is the pre-war of the latter that appears even less important.

Another aspect of the present that remains pertinent to strategy is the questioning of the integration of issues on different frontiers. This is notably so for China.[42] This is an issue for the past as well as the present, and for all contemporary and past major powers. Thus, the relationship between fronts, and debates over strategy in each world war can be fitted into the pattern. In this respect there are major questions, for all powers, of information search, acquisition, classification, interpretation and application, all of which affect strategic effectiveness. There is also discussion of the relevant changes that occurred in weapons technology and the resulting potential impact on operational possibilities. In the case of China, the judgment of Chinese strategic potential and modernisation was affected by the degree to which change too was affected by a failure of wider perception that reflected a focus on particular defeats in the 1890s and 1900s rather than on longer-term possibilities.

Chapter 9

Writing the World Wars

In Billie Houston's novel *Twice Round the Clock* (1935), Horace Manning, the noted but sinister scientist, is working on a particularly dangerous gas. He remarks to his guests:

> 'you have probably read many a time the widely-held opinion that gas is the weapon which will decide future conflicts. The country which possesses the most deadly gas will rule the world ... delayed action ... my gas in its first form is liquid ... you can imagine, for instance, the effect upon London, say, if a fleet of aeroplanes controlled by wireless, and laden with this liquid, were to be shot down over the city? Or imagine the ease with which enemy agents could deposit quantities of it almost anywhere.'[1]

This sense of an imminent future of a very different form of conflict was hardwired into the discussion of warfare from before World War One (1914–18), notably due to the development first of submarines and then of manned-powered flight (as opposed to unmechanised balloons). Conflict on land appeared to offer less radical prospect, notably due to the continuity in weaponry and tactics prior to World War One. However, the failure of the initial campaigning to deliver a decisive result, with operational and strategic deficiencies combining to sustain this failure, led to the development of large-scale trench warfare, and overcoming that problem for the offensive came to offer a radical prospect.

Change helped accentuate the problems of presenting war, while, in turn, the conflicts of the period have produced lasting debates. Thus, the contentious nature of the depiction of war was abundantly demonstrated in 2023. Ironically, this was not only a case of the wars then in bloody process, notably in Ukraine and, attracting less attention, Myanmar and Sudan, but, rather, World War One. The award of numerous BAFTAs to the new film of the novel *All Quiet on the Western Front* led to a storm of criticism in the German press, both because the character of the original had been lost and due to what was held to be an excessive focus on the mass attack.

In terms of words to the fore, whether on the page or on the screen, the world wars, especially World War Two (conventionally 1939–45, but beginning in East Asia in 1937), still dominate the coverage of conflict, and notably so in the West. This is instructive in its own right and also important for the impact on military history as a whole, indeed its very character. Personal testimony is particularly prominent and emphasises the grisly experience of campaigning as well as the mundane character but significance of food, dirt, health, smell and sound.[2]

The origins of subsequent coverage came from the discussion at the time, discussion that saw a careful cultivation of a range of patriotic positions,[3] as well as the resonance of political divisions. So also, but without the same coverage, with later controversies.

In Arthur Conan Doyle's 'His Last Bow: The War Service of Sherlock Holmes,' published in *The Strand Magazine* in September 1917, the cover declares 'You can send this Magazine Post Free to the Troops,' Baron von Herling, the fictional Chief Secretary of the German Embassy in 1914, suggests that Britain may leave France and Belgium to German conquest: 'we live in a utilitarian age. Honour is a medieval conception.' The baron's view of humanity is presented by Doyle, however, as crass, in what to him is an existential struggle. Indeed, the religious context had not passed. In that short story, there is reference to 'God's own wind ... and a cleaner, better, stronger land will lie in the sunshine when the storm has cleared.' This was very much a providential view. Such a providential and redemptive theme was highly significant in World War One,[4] and remained important in its successor.

Already, in December 1914, in *The German War*, Doyle had written 'The day of God's testing has come.' He added, in his 'Afterthought' to this volume, a reflection on the essential grounding of military success in character, which to contemporaries was a national, indeed racial theme, combined with a sense that military history spoke to the trust between the generations. Having reiterated his confidence in a 'virile nation,' a view that reflected the desideratum of contemporary Social Darwinians, Doyle added:

> 'Already those Territorials [volunteers] who were so ignorantly and ungenerously criticised in times of peace are, after nearly three months of camp-life, hardening into soldiers who may safely be trusted in the field. Behind them the greater part of a million men are formed who will also become soldiers in a record time if a desperate earnestness can make them so. It is a glorious spectacle which makes a man thankful that he has been spared to see it. One is more hopeful of our Britain and more proud of her, now that the German guns can be heard from her eastern shore,[5] than ever in the long monotony of her undisturbed prosperity. Our grandchildren will thrill as they read of the days that we endure.'

The last was not the case, not least due to the subsequent prominence of World War Two. Indeed, when Purnell followed its successful serial History of the Second World War (1966) by another on World War One (1969), the latter proved much less successful.

Doyle wrote six volumes of a factual account of World War One, beginning with *The British Campaign in France and Flanders 1914*, which appeared first as illustrated articles published in the bestselling *The Strand Magazine*. He had been one of 25 writers at a meeting called on 2 September 1914 by a government minister heading a newly-established secret war propaganda bureau that also encouraged the publication of John Buchan's *Nelson's History of the War*. This was part of an engagement with propaganda[6] different to that in Britain's recent wars, notably the Crimean War with Russia of 1854–6, and even the far more threatening French Revolutionary and Napoleonic Wars of 1793–1815.

Yet, the 'modernity' on offer with World War One, whether with weaponry or with propaganda, helped underline the ambiguity of the concept. It is easier to assert that a practice, for example, propaganda, is an aspect of 'modernity,' than to demonstrate the point, not least in the context of past comparisons, as, indeed, was the case with propaganda.

This was also the case with the commemoration at the time and subsequently. There was a major emphasis, which was to be strengthened with time, on the fate of individual soldiers, the rank and file as well as the officers, although that was less novel and complete than sometimes argued. This interest in individuals resonated in the question of how best to bury and memorialise the dead, not least the contrast between the American preference for the repatriation of bodies and the general practice of burying them in the campaign zone. There was also the question of the burial of unknown warriors, with Australia doing so for its unknown warrior from World War One only in 1993. This emphasis on individuals has become even more prominent as a result of the recent and still-strong interest in ancestors: many grandfathers took part in the war and that offered a form of graspable memory.

So also with the possibilities for approaching the conflict provided by photography and film. The latter was largely new, but many of the issues were similar to those with longer-established forms of propaganda. To a degree, there was misrepresentation of the fighting in the form of composite images.

The varied response to this indicated how histories of war were contentious not only in their content but also in their methods. Thus, while some commentators, such as the Australian official historian, C.E.W. Bean, rejected the practice of composite images, it was seen by others as a necessary response to the problems of filming and one that was essentially truthful. A more traditional form of commemoration was that of the display of captured German equipment which proved a demonstration of success, one that was to lead into postwar museums. So also with the display of Allied equipment, notably tanks which were shown on fundraising campaigns.[7]

There was a sense of history as present and striking, part indeed of a continuum that extended to the future. Thus, in July 1914, Doyle published 'Danger!' in *The Strand Magazine*, an article followed in that issue by 'What Naval Experts Think.' It was republished in 1918 when Doyle pronounced: 'It is a matter of history how fully this warning has been justified and how, even down to the smallest details, the prediction had been fulfilled.' In 'Danger!,' eight submarines attack British steamers, hitting hard the food supplies for Britain, and raising the price of food such that Britain had to negotiate. In general, Doyle was strongly thanked for his warning, but, as Admiral Sir Compton Domvile correctly pointed out, he exaggerated the length of time a submarine could stay at sea without supplies. Doyle replied that the story dealt with the submarine of the immediate future, but was wrong in that and also neglected the limited amount of torpedoes that they could carry.

In practice, the submarine still faced serious deficiencies as a weapons system, deficiencies Doyle did not address. To move submerged, submarines was dependent on battery motors that had to be recharged on the surface where submarines were highly vulnerable to attack. This vulnerability was increased by the development of air power, which was a classic instance of how one weaponry system could be made vulnerable to developments in another. In addition, submarines were slow, which lessened their chance of maintaining contact and of hitting a warship moving under full steam. Furthermore, the low silhouette of a submarine limited its surveillance potential.

Doyle can be praised for seeing into the future, notably the serious challenge German submarines were to pose, especially in early 1917 when unrestricted submarine warfare was introduced for the second time. Nevertheless, prior to World War One, the emphasis understandably still rested on battleships, which, indeed, with their gunnery, had played the decisive role in the Russo-Japanese naval battles of 1904–5, notably the crushing Japanese victory at Tsushima (1905). This result had helped spur the battleship races prior to World War One, especially between Britain and Germany. This result encouraged substantial investment in battleships over the following decade, with the famous naval race between Britain and Germany, the world's two leading naval powers, matched by smaller-scale competitive building, for example between France and Italy. This was an instance of current history, in the shape of Tsushima, refreshing older history in that of Trafalgar, a century earlier. This history might appear to have been of limited relevance due to the impact of submarines during World War One and the extent to which the major battle, Jutland (1916), was no Tsushima. However, the impact of battleship strength was still highly significant in the conflict, notably in terms of the British ability to bottle up German fleet strength in the North Sea, and thus support the Allied naval blockade.

Although this was not the predominant impression of the naval and air aspects, the popular image of World War One remains that of total futility and mindless slaughter. Furthermore, this image is more generally significant for military history as a whole because it reflects what has been since the 1960s a widespread disenchantment with war understood both as pursuit of state interest and as fighting. However, the scholarly focus in the analysis of that war, and notably recently, has instead been on the flexibility shown by the militaries, on the willingness to search for and adopt new practices and on the development of new fighting techniques in the war, techniques reflecting an ability to take ideas from allies, opponents, other services, junior ranks and civilians. Moreover, this willingness followed from the situation over the previous seventy years, one in which there had been adaptation to new weapons, new fighting methods and a range of tasks and possible tasks, not least the preparations and supposed intentions of other powers.[8] For example, there has been an emphasis on the development of successful new offensive tactics in 1916–18, especially by the Germans, as well as on the success of the British army in overcoming earlier limitations in order to produce a war-winning operational doctrine, tactical means and artillery-strong force structure, later in 1918.[9] As a reminder of the role of fashion in analysis, this emphasis on artillery replaced the earlier stress on tanks. The explanation of victory leads to a stress on the ability to deliver a verdict.

There has also been greater engagement with the global nature of war, including conflict outside Europe.[10] Linked to this, there is much interest in the role of non-European/American forces both outside Europe and within it. Indeed, the world has very much been put into World War One. This goal and process affects not only the operational understanding of the conflict, but also the tactical variety, strategic range, political complexity and number of 'wars,' that had to be justified and vindicated in national accounts.[11] The apparent contrast with World War Two that emerges from the emphasis on the Western Front was thereby lessened, although the global dimension of the latter continues to be a significant theme, and one that has been expanded in recent work.[12]

After World War One, the influential German military historian Hans Delbrück who, by December 1914, had concluded that a political solution to the war should be sought, waged a bitter controversy with the military over German policy in the conflict. In response, Erich Ludendorff, the key military policymaker in 1916–18, and his supporters condemned Delbrück, a civilian, as a journalist and an armchair strategist who lacked the intuitive understanding of war that allegedly came from technical training and practical military experience. In turn, Delbrück charged the military leadership with disastrous ambition.[13]

They were certainly extraordinarily incompetent, and notably so in strategic and operational terms, including the bungling of the opportunities offered by taking the initiative and launching the attack on the Western Front in 1914.[14] So also with the failure to derive operational mastery from taking the initiative anew in 1918.[15] More generally, German strategy was repeatedly based on the idea that they could operationalise strategy by ensuring a victory in the field that would lead their opponents to surrender. This was certainly possible as German defeats of France in 1870 and 1940 demonstrated, but not necessarily so, as indeed the defeats of Russia in 1914–15 showed.

Failure more generally caused a writing of military history in terms of a search for causes, both during and before the war. In the case of Russia, there was a tension between explanations in terms of political radicalism or alternatively, of incompetent aristocratic officers opposed to meritocracy especially within the army, with the 'army of honour' linked to Tsar Nicholas II opposed to the meritocratic 'army of virtue,' and the 'army of honour' unable to engage positively with the rank and file. These 'army of honour' officers linked to the Tsar, proved adept at shifting the blame, and enjoyed visibility as many became émigrés.[16]

There were also major differences between accounts of success on the part of the victors,[17] including in ascribing relative success to particular combatants as in how much weight to place on the presence and prospect of American troops and specific services. Thus, there was the view that British naval mastery and the maritime blockade were key enablers, as opposed to the army emphasis on victory on the Western Front. This was true of strategy and operations on the Western Front, and also of the respective role of that Front and other land commitments. Moreover, there was debate over the role of new technology in the shape, in particular, of tanks, which were greatly praised by some British commentators, notably J.F.C. Fuller. That of aircraft was much more influenced by a context of strong public interest as part of an international air-mindedness in which technological capacity and military prospects were to the fore.[18]

Aside from issues of military proficiency, there was separately to be controversy over the treatment of civilians. Beginning with wartime atrocity claims and propaganda by opponents, notably over German conduct in invading Belgium in 1914, and moving on to controversy over German submarine warfare, Allied blockade, German air attacks and the German and then Allied use of gas, among other issues, there was subsequent postwar controversy.

This controversy has extended to the present. Thus, recent scholarly work on German army atrocities in World War One (as in World War Two)[19] has been attacked from the German Right, notably by Gunter Spraul.[20] Although there are major differences in content, goal and tone, such work is an aspect of a more general nationalist reading of the war, one that not only emphasises the role of particular combatants, but also frequently argues that it has been deliberately concealed,[21] which is far less easy to substantiate. Moreover, blaming allies has been all-too-easy. To a degree, this approach is a variant on the stab-in-the-back thesis seen for example in German and Russian blame on domestic radicals and in the Turkish treatment of Arab subjects of the Ottoman Empire and the view of the German Right on Socialism.

John Buchan, Lord Tweedsmuir, was clear in 1937, when speaking as the Governor General of Canada to the Canadian Institute of International Affairs:

> 'The day has gone when foreign policy can be the preserve of a group of officials at the Foreign Office, or a small social class, or a narrow clique of statesmen from whom the rest of the nation obediently takes its cue. The foreign policy of a democracy must be the cumulative views of individual citizens, and if these views are to be sound they must in turn be the consequence of a widely diffused knowledge.'

A major adventure novelist, who had played an important role in the successful British World War One propaganda effort, Buchan captured the degree, in the aftermath of that war, to which resilience on the 'Home Front' was now regarded as a key element. This was an element seen across society, not least in including influencing children,[22] who became the warriors of that or the next generation.

In wartime, part of this resilience was historical, with, in World War Two, war films accordingly, such as the British *Henry V* (1944) and the German *Kolberg* (1945), while Stalin supported reference to Aleksandr Nevskii, an opponent of German invasion in the thirteenth century, although scarcely one from the proletariat. Film was not alone. Building on long term right-wing accounts, the Vichy regime in France turned to Joan of Arc (*c*.1412–31), a national heroine canonised in 1920, who had an appropriate anti-English pedigree. She had led a French army to victory over the English at Orléans in 1429, a victory that proved a turning point in the Hundred Years' War between the two. In Inner Mongolia, part of China, much of which it occupied, Japan encouraged the building of a large temple to Chinggis Khan (d. 1227) in Ulanhot, while the Chinese in turn sought to conjure up the Khan's martial example. In 1945, Goebbels gave Hitler a biography of Frederick the Great (r. 1740–86) in order to encourage the idea that fighting on resolutely would be rewarded with a sudden change of circumstances as had happened for Frederick when Russia changed policy in 1762.

Most analysis for the war was in practice very short term, notably an analysis of recent conflicts in order to attempt to understand the capabilities of possible opponents and of current weapon systems. Thus, the Germans analysed the poor Soviet performance in the Winter War with Finland of 1939–40, which encouraged them to plan their attack on the Soviet Union in 1941. However, as yet another instance of the tendency of theory and analysis to confirm bias, they underplayed the key point of eventual Soviet victory in the Winter War.

Such military analysis was prone to support convenience and apt to assert and confirm institutional, national and social bias and existing capabilities. Thus, the American Air Corps analysts, assessing the failure of the German *Luftwaffe* in the air offensive on Britain in 1940, attributed it to a lack of strategic bombers, rather than to the overall deficiencies of the *Luftwaffe* and the role of Britain's integrated air defence system which included radar. In July 1941, partly in response, the American Air War Plans Division No. 1 offered a comprehensive plan for defeating Germany by means of air power, which was an instance of the right opponent, in this case Germany, helping to push forward both the doctrine and the crucial support. This planning was greatly to influence post-war American and

British doctrine and strategy during the Cold War with the Soviet Union. Had war only come for America with Japan in 1941, then there would have had to be a very different basis for the use of American air power, one that would for long have been dependent on carriers.

So also with the emphasis by foreign commentators on the role of air power and equipment as a whole in the Spanish Civil War (1936–9), whereas, in practice, a range of factors played a role including logistics, cohesion and strategy. Moreover, reading between conflicts to create a general rule proved misleading. In contrast to the Russian Civil War of 1919–22, the side in the Spanish Civil War that held the central position, the Republicans, lost, while that which benefited from most external support and military experience, the Nationalists, won, as the Whites had so conspicuously failed to do during the Russian Civil War. This contrast underlines the need for caution in the assertion of reasons for victory.

As World War Two neared, began, developed and spread, the lack of certainty about the content of policy and timing of moves arose for all powers from this shared characteristic.[23] Indeed, this translates into different names and dates for the war, not least when to begin it in East Asia, whether 1931 or 1937. If the former, with the Manchuria Crisis, it is not immediately clear how to differentiate that from earlier Japanese-Chinese hostilities from 1894–5 on. Indeed, that of 1894–5 was more serious than the crisis of 1931–2.

Explanations of actions open up debates about politics then and later. Hitler's decision-making in late 1941 owed much to the changing course of conflict on the Eastern Front and the developing confrontation in the Atlantic between German submarines and American warships, with particular relevance to German consideration of Lend-Lease Aid and its potential relationship to Soviet persistence against German attack, including the links between this factor and the naval situation, with supplies to the Soviets moving by sea. In this context, the timings of when Hitler received information were more significant than the actual sequence of events. It was only on 14 December 1941, in other words after his declaration of war on America on the 11th, that Hitler began to understand that several factors had come together to create a crisis that surpassed anything witnessed thus far on the Eastern Front, and even then he did not adopt a sensible response of more manageable objectives.

The Soviet resilience already shown by December and the American counterpart that was in prospect ensured that the long-term German commitment to 'short-war' strategic thought was no longer valid. Indeed, the ability of Britain to resist German attack, and the strategic depth that it possessed as a result of naval strength and its empire, had already led to a thwarting of German plans.

While well-established, the thesis of 'short-war' strategic thought deserves, in this and other instances, a degree of scrutiny. In particular, 'short-war' thinking is in part an operationalisation of strategy that can rest on a fundamental failure to understand the contrast between the two. Whatever rationality is ascribed to Hitler, this point very much undermined the processes of his thought, let alone the notion that he had what might be presented as strategic instinct. Indeed, the role of prejudice in Hitler's consideration of other powers was neither context nor add-on, but hardwired into his thought. Yet, how that played through in the decision-making is necessarily a matter at least in part of speculation, and that helps explain why claims for definitive status for any particular interpretation are foolish.

For Hitler, relations with both America and Japan were problematic. The 1941 non-aggression pact between Japan and the Soviet Union of 13 April 1941 had woeful strategic and operational consequences for Germany, and it was necessary for Hitler to avoid a wider crisis as a result. Thus, for Japan to attack America and Britain was important to Germany, and indeed threatened by Japanese-American negotiations in late 1941. Hitler sought in December 1941 to link Japan to his policies. In the event, the German declaration of war on America after Pearl Harbor did not lead to any concerted attempt at grand strategy. The two powers fought what in effect were separate wars, which was an aspect of a more general failure of Hitler's alliance strategy.

Moreover, there was a significant gap between Hitler's determination to impose his will on events and thus mould the context of developments, and, in contrast, the multiple pressures of reality. This gap extended to a failure to assess the likely trajectory of war between Japan and America. Hitler's use of his ideological suppositions when considering his opponents was scarcely unique, but to regard America as weakened by deracination, democracy and consumerism and as lacking in martial spirit, was seriously mistaken. Any emphasis on pragmatic considerations in Hitler's thought and strategy is a sharp contrast to the previous stress on ideological prejudices. This approach is only so useful as Hitler's outlook clearly framed how he processed information.[24]

World War Two both involved an unprecedented range of powers[25] and circumstances, and was also seen as the basis for the modern age, the latter a classification that had a variety of meanings, and a changing one, but an assessment that continues. In addition, its usage to comment on the now has continued to the present, and will doubtless go on doing so. Thus, a lengthy review by Dov Zakheim, an Under Secretary of Defense from 2001 to 2004, of Paul Kennedy's *Victory at Sea: Naval Power and the Transformation of the Global Order in World War Two* (2022) drew, as is generally the case, the conclusion that the reviewer sought, in this case against China and Russia:

> 'Kennedy goes to great lengths to demonstrate that America was the arsenal of democracy because it was willing to spend whatever it took, and to produce whatever it took, to enable the Navy and its sister services to operate effectively against the Axis powers ... American could once again serve as the arsenal of democracy; but to do so, it needs to support a very different sort of arsenal, not only with resources, but with innovation, flexibility and imagination.'[26]

At the same time, modernity as a concept has to be handled with care. Thus, the long-lasting impact of religious considerations was far from being redundant, and it is unclear that secularism was necessarily a condition of modernity. This impact was seen anew in World War Two, with Nazism treated in the Anglosphere as godless and anti-Christian, and Japanese Shintoism also as anti-Christian.[27] In turn, Christianity served as an important theme in pro-German polities such as Vichy France and the collaboratist regimes in Croatia, Hungary, Slovakia and elsewhere, although not in Germany.

The commemoration of the war varied and varies greatly by combatant, not least by goal and with reference to what was to be remembered and what overlooked.[28] There can also be contention within combatants. Thus, the exhibition planned for 1995 by the Smithsonian Institution's National

Air and Space Museum on the fiftieth anniversary of the end of the war was designed to centre on the *Enola Gay*, the aircraft that dropped the atomic bomb on Hiroshima, but excited fierce controversy over the exhibit narrative and the issue of culpability for the atomic bombings.[29]

The changing frame of reference was brought out by occasion and commentators. Thus, in 2023, President Biden made clear that there would be no apologies when the G7 Summit was held in Hiroshima. In practice, there was neither expectation nor pressure to do so, but for Biden his stance was necessary in the politics of America as well as capturing the vast breadth of majority American opinion. The nuclear significance of Hiroshima in 2023 rested not so much on the event in 1945 as of the prospect that Putin might launch a nuclear attack if threatened with defeat in Ukraine. Other references drew directly on Hiroshima, President Zelensky of Ukraine saying at the G7 Summit in Hiroshima on 21 May: 'The photos of Hiroshima remind me of Bakhmut. There is absolutely nothing alive, all the buildings are destroyed. Absolute total destruction. There is nothing. There are no people.'

Other references were also instructive. Thus, on 20 May, the *Sunday Times* contrasted the isolationism over Ukraine of many Republicans with Ronald Reagan declaring on 6 June 1984 at Normandy on the 40th anniversary of D-Day that America had learned a 'bitter lesson' from that war:

'It is better to be here ready to protect the peace than to take blind shelter across the sea, rushing to respond only after freedom is lost. We've learnt that isolationism never was and never will be an acceptable response to tyrannical governments with an expansionist intent.'

The journalist, and others making that particular comparison, did not note that Hitler had declared war on America, unlike Putin, but the use of history rarely stops for the qualifications of contexts. At the same time, there has been a significant shift toward isolationism among Republicans, and the historical reference captured the difference.

Often overlapping with political accounts, the strategic and command issues of the day were refought, and within states as well as alliances. So also with reasons for success and failure, and with the significance of each.[30] Methodological approaches that had a political dimension played a significant role. In part, the historicising of accounts in a memory that could be reconfirmed through oral history and presented in visual media, was designed to validate ordinary troops and, as a linked process, the national account.

As a result, there was a marked tendency to downplay the role of allies, for example, in American presentations of D-Day, those of the British and Canadian forces. The British and Canadian accounts, in contrast, were more positive about the American role. Study of D-Day's remembrance has suggested that the American accounts owed much to the politics of the era, notably the degree to which there was confidence in the American present. This could help in honouring the past, but the latter was also a response to uncertainties about the present.[31]

The Americans' general focus on their own role was matched by the British, as with the attention devoted to fighting in Egypt and Libya in 1940–2 against Italian and German forces. However, the Americans tended to be more at fault, not least in dramatically underplaying the Chinese, British, Australian and, finally, Soviet contributions to the exhaustion and/or outfighting of Japan on land. The Americans were also apt to downplay the role of Soviet forces in providing the major commitment for the German army from 1941 to 1945. Indeed, both Mussolini and the Japanese government unsuccessfully pressed Hitler in 1943 to make peace with the Soviet Union so that Germany could concentrate its resources against Britain and America.

Furthermore, the American reading of a World War Two that was emotionally charged by Pearl Harbor had only a limited traction elsewhere.[32] This was matched, at the strategic level, by an American tendency to treat the wars with Germany and Japan as equivalents. While Japan had certainly conquered more territory and taken control over more people in 1931–42 than Germany in 1938–42, it did not pose a comparable threat to the centres of power of its opponents, and did not prove able to ground its success in popular consent among the conquered. Moreover, unlike for the Germans, the articulation of the Japanese imperial system depended on naval power in which it proved vulnerable to the American navy, and fatally so in 1944–5. Yet, separately, the focus on the navy and the marines could leap to an underplaying of the role of the American army in the Pacific.

Alongside such histories of the war, there were those countries involved as subordinate parts of broader imperial structures, such as India[33] and Korea. There were also the many states in which World War Two involved a measure of civil war. In part, the latter was a matter of opposition to occupation and to those who cooperated with occupation. Such civil warfare was vindicated as resistance. Subsequently, the acknowledgement of foreign support for resistance has varied greatly in national accounts. The vindication of resistance was eased by the absence of such activity in Germany and Japan once they had surrendered. This absence was a central element in the war. There was no comparison for example to the resistance to Reconstruction in the former Confederacy in 1865–77, nor to that in Iraq after the fall of Saddam Hussein in 2003.

When there was civil war between those not involved in the occupation, indeed resisting it, as in China, Greece, Yugoslavia and Albania,[34] then the situation was different. So also when, as in Poland, where subsequent Soviet support for Communist dictatorship was accompanied by the brutal suppression of those who had resisted the Germans, as well as others. There was the counterpart in Spain, where, against the background of civil war in 1936–9 and of atrocities then by both sides,[35] there was brutal post-war repression by the victorious Nationalists, for revenge, punishment, terror and due to concern about continuing Republican activism.

These domestic conflicts were war, and, as in other instances of insurrections and counter insurgencies, the war stretched to include a full range of political, social, economic and cultural spheres and controls. Intimidation and humiliation were part of the process, each extending to how earlier warfare and the current conflict were received, marked and presented.

The Chinese trajectory in the presentation of World War Two is instructive, as well as differing greatly from the Japanese classification of the conflict. Under Mao Zedong, Chairman of the Chinese Communist Party from 1949 until 1976, indeed a reviver in a very new form of imperial Chinese rulership, the legitimacy of the Communist regime in large part rested on its opposition to the Nationalists (Kuomintang) and America. As a result, Mao was against reference to the wartime United Front against Japan with the Nationalists. Thereafter, attitudes changed. Under Xi Jinping, the present Communist Emperor, who has been General Secretary of the Chinese Communist Party and Chairman of the Central Military Commission from 2012, the commemoration of the war, a commemoration seen in museums, films, war tourism and other forms, was of a just war fought by China for the sake of the world, and thus an aspect of global leadership. At the same time, hostility to America was on view in Xi's prominent role in October 2020 when the anniversary of Chinese entry into the Korean War in 1950 was commemorated.[36]

The Soviet Union treated the Great Patriotic War with Germany of 1941–5, its term for the conflict with Germany, and not for a World War Two that included a Soviet-German alliance in 1939–41, as the vindication of Stalin, Communism and the extent of Soviet power and influence notably in Eastern Europe but also in territory gained from Japan in 1945. These approaches were linked to the theme of a wartime popular resolve that was supposed to inspire later behaviour. Thus, the traditional Victory Day parade in Moscow included the march of the Immortal Regiment, which allowed people to hold up pictures of dead Second World War relatives. In 2023, this was cancelled because of fears that the loss of relatives in the invasion of Ukraine might turn the march into an anti-war protest. In practice, the formidable Soviet achievement in World War Two was obtained at the cost of unnecessarily high losses due to poor, often extremely poor, command and doctrine.[37]

A particularly blunt form of the warfare after each world war was that of encouraging and/or forcing mass expulsions or flight. This was a process seen after World War One from Ireland to Turkey, and after World War Two from Italy to Manchuria. The human cost was immense and led to strong individual and family recollections of military history that were, and remain, very different to those of governments.[38] Due to refugees, the eventual human geography becomes a clear pointer to the consequences of war, indeed its most profound history. This is not a process restricted to the present and slavery can in part be seen as an aspect of it. That is more especially the case if state slavery is included in the discussion of slavery, the history of which is overly written in terms of Atlantic slavery.

Indeed, World War Two saw mass enslavement on a far greater scale. Without suggesting any equivalence, this was seen with the murderous German use of Jews for labour and with the far less brutal German treatment of millions of labourers from occupied Europe, notably France.

Each category was very important to the war economy, indeed central to the German military effort, for their labour permitted the focus of working-age German men on the armed forces. So also with the Soviet use of enforced labour during and after the war, a use that continued the pre-war class warfare of Stalin's Soviet Union (a class warfare that encompassed as hostile many from the working class) and extended it to include prisoners of war. So also with the Chinese use of Japanese prisoners of war, for example for repairing a rail system that was important to the Communist thesis of continuous mobilisation. The Chinese Communists also provided a new iteration of the long-standing pattern of slave soldiers, a topic that is under-reported in Western histories of war. In the Chinese case, captured Kuomintang soldiers were used as 'cannon fodder' when China intervened in the Korean War (1950–3). They were thrown to the fore in frontal attacks. Their deaths lessened the potential risk they posed within China.

Earlier, slave soldiers had been particularly significant in Islamic militaries, especially, but not only, those of Mamluk Egypt, Ottoman Turkey and Safavid Persia (Iran). There are modern counterparts, such as Eritrea, although their conscription is not referred to as slavery. This point underlines the need in military history to think of categories that are not necessarily based on modern legal definitions. Moreover, the ideology used to justify a practice such as conscription can be understood very differently by those who were affected. This is particularly but not only the case for 'marginal' groups, or subject peoples and in authoritarian societies, such as Alsace once annexed by Germany in 1940.

Problems with specificity affect other attempts to employ comparative means in order to throw light on and from World War Two, and can also be contentious. That the Holocaust was a central episode in the conflict contributes to this, while the degree to which it is unique leads to debate. Although frequently applied in other contexts, the enormity of the Holocaust does not lend itself to this process with any accuracy.

Japanese conduct in China was very brutal, while the issue of Japanese 'comfort women,' the forced prostitution for the army, as in Korea, remains highly contentious. This is also part of the broader interest in the impact of war on women and women on war.[39]

Yet, although very brutal, Japanese conduct was not comparably genocidal. Comparisons between the Holocaust and other conflicts may be illuminating for military[40] history, but, in every case, it is necessary to understand not only specific contexts but also the problems posed by comparisons.

Furthermore, far from being extraneous to the military dimension of the war, the Holocaust was central to it, both in the sense that the Holocaust was war, a totally one-sided war of extermination, in which, indeed, much of the German military was fully complicit, and because by fighting for territory and, eventually, simply fighting on, the Germans gained space, territorial and chronological, for the Holocaust. So also with being able to pressure allies into taking part in mass slaughter. Part of the contested history of the Holocaust arises from contention, notably within Germany, over the complicity of the German military, a point that has become more apparent and prominent from the early 1990s.

Compared to this, the dissension about particular campaigns and battles, although often bitterly contested in print and conversation, might appear somewhat secondary, although, for many, and notably so in America, the anti-societal aspects of the war tended to be in the shadows of the campaigning. In practice, the two were linked, even if there were significant differences in emphasis.

A key aspect of the changing literature on each world war has been the extension to consider its impact around the world, including in colonies. The colonies are therefore given a measure of agency, while the full impact of the war is brought out.[41] It included the significant weakening of the British empire in South Asia, especially India. In contrast, there was no such weakening of the Soviet empire in Central Asia.[42]

At the same time, there are other trends. One is provided by the focus today on China's rise, intentions, policies and capabilities and therefore a case of present concerns affecting military history.

The benefits derived from military service and war, or at least the formative impact of both, are a major theme in the study of some societies, for example medieval Christendom. They are also pertinent for others and for their historiographies, a situation that continues to the present. That is also very much a topic that requires attention for the world wars. The realities of conscription and struggles for survival were grim, yet also formative and transformative for countries, their governance, politics, societies, economies and cultures.

Chapter 10

Engaging with a Changing Present, 1945–2023

The use of the past was readily apparent as the Ukraine crisis was developed from 2022, although the extent to which Vladimir Putin thought as much in historical terms for his military assessment as he did for his ambitious, expansionist, political one is less clear.[1] Moreover, if so, the chronological range may have been very different, the political one going back to the ninth-century days of Kievan Rus, while the relevant history of conflict appears to have drawn on the successful 2008 Georgia and 2014 Crimea interventions. At the annual victory parade in Moscow in May 2023, Putin declared that Russia was in a civilisational war, with the parade, a Cold War practice revived by Putin, being used by him to focus an opposition to fascism that has become the ideology of the state. His views were echoed by supporters and allies. Thus, in 2022–3, in an echo often offered, Robert Fico, the pro-Russian leader of Slovakia's opposition, likened German NATO troops to Nazis.

Conversely, Western commentators in 2022–3 made frequent reference to historical instances even if there was also talk about a new age of war. In this and other instances, the future becomes the now in military affairs with the shock of attack, while the now resets the future in discussion and planning. A lack of historical awareness was seen in the transformational argument for novelty, not least with the major emphasis on drones for reconnaissance and attack. In some respects, this discussion of drones was a new iteration of the arguments advanced at the time of the Revolution of Military Affairs, not least for example, cutting the time between reconnaissance and targeting.

The reference to history in 2022–3 took a number of forms. In 2022–3, in the face of the Russian invasion of Ukraine and of Chinese military threats to Taiwan, resilience became a doctrine of great interest in Western circles. In part, this was scarcely new, as the idea of resilience to attack or threat of potent challengers had long attracted support.[2] Yet the pushing of the doctrine to the fore served to indicate the interrogation of the past in terms of contemporary terms, as in late 2022 when resilience was the theme of the annual historical conference of the Baltic Defence Council in Tartu, the location in Estonia close to the frontier testifying to the fear of imminent and dangerous Russian attack.

There was also an attempt to warn about Russian resilience by means of reference to the eventual Soviet success over Finland in 1940 in place of the usual focus on serious initial Russian defeats in 1939. This proved an opportunity to talk about the attritional capability of Russian artillery-based tactics and the extent to which this usage had countered the Finns' operational mobility. How far this provided a direct lesson for the assessment of the Russo-Ukrainian war was unclear. So also was any emphasis that should be advanced, and therefore the consequences for conclusions that should be drawn.

Yet there was also the highly traditional character of asymmetrical warfare. Thus, Ukraine versus Russia could be readily located in terms of historical continuity. However, as an instance of the difficulty of assessing relevance, and thus of the problems posed by multiple narratives, the episode could also be seen in terms of long-standing issues with Soviet/Russian doctrine and usage. In particular, a lack of flexibility, both tactically and operationally, was seen with Soviet-trained Syrian, Egyptian, Libyan and Iraqi attacks, on Israel, Chad and Iran, as well as with Soviet limitations in Afghanistan, Chechnya and Iraq. That remark can be qualified, but it underlines the extent to which there was continuity between the Soviet and Russian militaries, thus serving to question any chronological divide at the time of the close of the Cold War. Certainly, there has been a degree of continuity in geopolitical drive and regional ambitions.

These comments could be taken further with more details for what we have already covered, as well as the addition of other factors. That possibility throws light on the problems posed by the use of examples, and indeed, the very processes of constructing examples, both in this book and more generally. It is difficult to appreciate the extent to which the building blocks offered by examples are often problematic as well as unclear; and yet that is what is entailed by military history. It proceeds in large part by example, without necessarily extending this to any explicit discussion of major issues of a more conceptual character, let alone of methodological issues.

The building blocks are also provided by very differing accounts of wars as they take place, and this becomes more apparent in the present day with the extension and insistence of reporting. Thus, on 5 May 2023, the cantankerous Yevgeny Prigozhin, the ambitious and splenetic head of Russia's semi-independent Wagner Group of mercenaries, explained its failure to take the much-contested town of Bakhmut, not with reference to the determined and resilient Ukrainian resistance but, on a video published by his press service, with reference to a failure to provide ammunition which he blamed on the Defence Minister and the Chief of the General Staff: 'You think that if you have ammunition depots then you have the right to them.' Leaving aside the accuracy of the claim, it becomes one of the texts of the war, and thus part of its overall history.

In the face of such contention, which is harder to probe for conflicts further from close external scrutiny, such as the contemporaneous one in Ethiopia, it is possible to adopt a different methodology and test ideas about current (and past) conflict through war-gaming. Yet, in this instance, history, for the recent as well as the more distant past, also provides a key frame of reference and source of evidence, not least because it serves as a reminder about unpredictability in developments and results, one that cannot be programmed as a game is. To a degree, however, this reminder is another form of war-gaming.

Military history of course serves a variety of purposes, including lobbying, institutional education, academic scholarship, popular interest, commercial opportunity and collective myth-making. All and each needs to be considered when the subject is evaluated, and to judge one by the standards of another is not necessarily helpful. Indeed, it can be positively misleading. Any call to teach military history might seem to shrink the options to the educational process. That is not, however, in practice the case, for the teaching of military history, understood in the widest sense, embraces the question of the nature and sustaining of civic militarism, and also, indeed, separately, overlaps with the issue of commercial opportunity.

To approach the subject in another typology, one that draws heavily on the role and resonance of civic militarism, there is also the question of the point of reference. The question 'Why teach military history?' can be approached in the abstract, but it also depends on the country and society that is in the forefront. The issue is different, or, at least appears very different, in Sweden or Israel, Spain or Estonia, Ireland or South Korea. As a reminder of the variety of social contexts and needs, in many states, indeed, the teaching of military history is an aspect not simply of civic patriotism, a task that, in 2008, Victor Davis Hanson, from the right of the political spectrum, chided many American academics for slighting,[3] but also of a wider social engagement that owes something to conscription. This engagement is seen, for example, in Finland, Israel, Singapore, South Korea and Switzerland, and, in recent years, far from being residual, there has been a revival of the salience of military service linked to nationalism, notably in Sweden, the Baltic States, Russia and Eritrea. The Russian response to the failure of the 2022 invasion of Ukraine was to turn to more conscription and to an increasing reliance on private armies.

In such cases, as also more generally, the teaching of military history fulfils pedagogic purposes, but also helps in fostering the engagement of the civilian soldier, including the civilian reservist, a key element in conscription systems. Thus, morale, as widely conceived, not least as an aspect of civic resilience, plays a role in the reasons for teaching military history, and also in the content and tone of the teaching.

Conscription, like other aspects of a defensive military posture, can be unrelated to immediate threats, the case, for example, in Switzerland. In Bolivia, conscripts were used as labour, for example in farming and forestry.[4]

However, usually, this is not the position, and that is certainly the case for Ukraine, the Baltic States, South Korea and Israel. Debates in the last over conscription and the value of conscripts are striking, not least in terms of the contentiousness of the exemptions granted, principally to religious students, and with regard to hostility by some conscripts toward the nature of their presence on the West Bank. In the (South) Korean Military Academy, one of the standard courses is on the 1950–3 Korean War, and it is accompanied by staff rides to the battlefields. Utility is very much the theme of these courses.

Thus, the teaching of military history, whether professional, educational or civic, is an aspect of a threat environment, and the assessment of value has to take note of this context. To divorce such history from its utilitarian contexts would be a mistake. That, indeed, helps explain the potential role of military history in America's culture wars, as its lessening is associated with a downplaying of the threat environment and vice versa.

World War Two left America (and Britain) with a pro-military world of veterans and a sense of common purpose. This was very much present in film. Many directors, actors and screenwriters,[5] and much of the audience, had military experience, and a feeling of the war as a mission can be seen in films such as *The Longest Day* (1962), a heroic account of D-Day that included many of the leading American and British actors of the day.

The Vietnam War, however, accentuated the decline of deference that was a common feature of some Western societies from the mid-1960s. An anti-heroic ethos came to characterise much artistic work about war, as in the savage British film indictment of World War One, *Oh! What a Lovely War* (1969), the popular American television series *MASH* (Mobile Army Surgical Hospital) (1972–83) and the American anti-war film *Coming Home* (1978). Moreover, what had been a positive British treatment of the RAF was replaced by a more critical one, notably of the bombing of Germany.[6]

Alongside an anti-heroic ethos came a hostility to bellicosity which to some in the West became almost a pathology. This was linked to a misrepresentation of the past and notably of aboriginal people as essentially pacific. Advanced strongly in the 1960s and 1970s, this approach failed to appreciate the consequences of a lack of state authority in making the limitation of conflict difficult. It is no accident that the term 'failed states' has been employed to describe societies with a high level of civil violence, for example, over the last three decades, Sierra Leone, Liberia and Afghanistan. In a separate topic, as already noted, the role of women in conflict has attracted much attention in recent decades, and in a range of roles, including warriors and victims, notably in 'failed states'.[7]

The prominence of the threat environment is also the case with authoritarian societies, such as Eritrea, Iran, Myanmar, and North Korea. In the last, the politics of paranoia are crucial to the mobilisation of enforced consent on behalf of the government. In a different context, China has used competitive international relations as a way to recruit popular support for a regime, where there is scant Communist unity in living circumstances, with more of a rhetoric of danger, and Russia has very much readopted the Soviet stance of the need for vigilance in the face of an alleged encirclement.

Thus, the eastward expansion of NATO was presented as a geopolitical threat one that served to locate opposition to Ukrainian independence. Indeed, authoritarian governments appear especially prone to paranoia.

In some states, moreover, such as Turkey, Pakistan, Burkina Faso, Niger, Indonesia and, to a lesser extent, Brazil, the military present themselves, or have presented themselves, as crucial, in, if necessary, an active fashion, to national integrity and identity.

Yet, an aspect of the weakness or potential weakness of state authority is provided by military coups, attempted coups or political changes dictated by the military. This happened in many countries in the decade ending in 2023, including Myanmar, Pakistan and Sudan. The failed coup in 2016 helped define subsequent Turkish politics. A functional element, moreover, is provided by the role of the military in providing employment and social mobility. This includes insurgency militia such as Lebanon's Hezbollah, which, at Mleeta, has a museum of mementoes of battles with the 'Zionist occupier', as well as the militarised drug gangs of countries such as Colombia and Mexico.

Considering these and other cases serve to underline the unusual, not to say eccentric, character of Western commitment in the discussion of military history and affairs, to intellectual independence, and to academic and educational detachment from public politics and hostility to government-backed traditions of public history. Instead, on the world level, the pressure of public politics, in the shape of government dictation on education will probably become more salient as China rises in relative importance, not least as an economic-political model, and not only for parts of Asia, Africa and Latin America. China may also be chosen as the source of military doctrine as well as the equipment already present in some allies, such as Zimbabwe.

This general point underlines the need to appreciate the diversity of national cultures within which military affairs are considered, with the teaching of military history presented as an aspect of the politics of these cultures. Moreover, in both the context and the content of military history, it is appropriate to avoid the teleology of assuming the dominance of the Western model. Or, indeed, of any particular model or set of norms. In addition, while frequently associated with the West, the advancing of norms for warfare was challenged by the conduct of Western as well as other countries.[8]

Histories of war had become more possible from the nineteenth century, as sources were more plentiful, in being created, deposited, preserved and accessible, including through national archival services. At the same time, throughout, there was a range of acceptance in and about such histories, not least related to the ideologies of particular regimes. Thus, for America there was plentiful material on divisions within its military and government, as well as tensions with allies.[9] This is far less the case with authoritarian regimes, as with the Vietnam War.

The teaching of military history in America, by far the world's leading military power, is currently a matter of controversy and in the public sphere, in a way that would not be the case in China. This controversy is not least due to the widely-repeated charge that this teaching is being downplayed by or for the 'politically correct'. Indeed, it is widely argued that they are preventing the appointment of military historians in American universities and marginalising the subject as a whole. Is this true? Does it matter? Is, indeed, military history desirable?; a question that might be seen as a 'politically correct' one. From the contrasting, 'non-politically correct', dimension, and the specific perspective of military change, is military history even relevant? This question was raised from the 1990s in response to the engagement then with technological change, notably the so-called Revolution in Military Affairs, an idea strongly advanced in the 1990s, and, after that term declined in usage, the embrace of 'Transformation,' however defined. This led to the issue of whether military history had a future to match its past value.

Aside from this concern with the now in the form of the future, an alternative emphasis on social forces as the causes and agents of change, which is a dominant theme in modern historical work, can misleadingly make military history appear redundant. Alternatively, this history can be presented as essentially the expression of social developments and best understood in terms of 'war and society'. As a different matter, such an understanding can relate for some to the argument that 'peoples' warfare' was, and is, bound to prevail over regular, professional forces. In practice, this approach is of limited validity, but it was one that flourished during the period of so-called wars of national liberation, and was powerfully advanced in and about America by particular readings of the Vietnam War.[10] However, alongside conspicuous failures for counter insurgency, especially Vietnam, Algeria and, to a lesser extent, Cyprus,[11] insurrections do not necessarily succeed. The last was shown for example in post-1945 Greece,[12] the Philippines, Malaya, Kenya and Columbia; in Iraq it was shown in the late 2000s;[13] similarly, in Syria it was shown by the early 2020s with the rebellion against the Assad regime which has broken out in the early 2010s. Moreover, these struggles emphasise the unpredictability of civil wars, as well as their complexity. Thus, the Vietnam War was primarily a defeat for the regime of South Vietnam, and one that America could not overcome. In part, a strategy of Vietnamisation simply highlighted this point. This was 'war and society' in a highly political and military context.[14]

The relative diminution of military history reflects wider currents including those in both society and in historical scholarship. In the former case, it is pertinent to note the degree to which the individualism, hedonism and atomisation of society, not only in Western society, but also for example in Japan, associated with both 1960s and post-1960s values sapped general adherence to collectivist solutions and commitments. Thus, conscription, and the accompanying mental attitudes and social patterns, no longer commanded as much support as hitherto. In part, this point is also highly relevant for the context of military history, at least compared to the 1950s. Indeed, the military are driven by cultural, social and political forces and pressures even as they try to shape them. Lobbying, part of the process of trying to shape a successful environment for the military, can involve historical references. Thus, in June 2023, in a speech, General Sir Patrick Sanders, the Chief of the General Staff, made historical references in the discussion of army size, leading the *Times* on 27 June to entitle a leader 'Government complacency about defence resembles that of the 1930s' before beginning the piece with a reference to the larger size of the army in 1854, the year of Balaclava. There is indeed a debate to be had about army size, but the comparisons are pointless, not least because there was no complacency in the 1930s but, rather, a discussion about necessary force-structures and strategies in a situation made complex by possible war with Germany, Italy and Japan.

In the case of historical scholarship, it is possible, when discussing the relative decline of military history, to point, as a cause, both to the rise of social history and cultural studies, and to the influence on historical work of perspectives derived from other social sciences including anthropology and collective psychology. This process is not restricted to America, which indicates that locating the issue of the future of military history solely in terms of America's culture wars is inadequate. Instead, considering a relative decline of military history requires a broader contextualisation that is alive to the interaction of American and international developments.

Turning more specifically to the history of war, there is a tension between military history as understood by many, but by no means all, of those who are interested in the subject, and the history of war. For many, particularly, but not only, in the non-academic world, military history is the history of war, a subject that should be about fighting, about battles and campaigns, troops, uniforms and weapons. This operational dimension is indeed important, and continues to produce first-rate accounts,[15] while military history should not be demilitarised. Yet, the operational and tactical dimensions, weaponry and the experience of combat do not constitute the complete subject. Indeed, part of the tension in the discussion of military history, not least among specialists, revolves not so much around its real or supposed neglect, for which the evidence is of relative decline in academe and not absolute in society, but, instead, is in terms of how the subject is treated.

Here, it is necessary to note differences among military historians. The operational and tactical historians and those who focus on battle, sometimes unfairly, but frequently all too accurately, referred to in terms of drum and trumpet history, are indeed neglected within the academic community. In contrast, those looking at wider dimensions, such as the staples of war and society, and war and the state, are generally assured of an audience there. This situation is further the case because the 'history' in these cases is as much explored by sociologists, anthropologists and political scientists, as by those seen more conventionally as historians, although the latter tend to do so with a greater awareness of conjunctures and contexts.

A clear theme since the development of 'War and Society' courses in academe is that of the military as a society as much as an organisation. The latter approach encouraged a combat-oriented, downward-instructing system, but the military as a society looks at more complex systems of influence and initiative. These systems were scarcely democracies, yet they left initiative or 'agency' with soldiers, and indeed encouraged care in their treatment.[16] Prisoners are a different category for study, but have also come into more prominence.

In part, therefore, the discussion of military history today is a case of tensions among military historians and about the character of such history. Although Allan Mallinson, a British veteran, publicly called for the writing of military history by those who had served rather than others, this debate is not always explicit. Yet, in practice, the debate exists not simply in terms of the content of the subject, but also of the way in which topics are pursued and presented, as well as of the powerful issues of patronage, appointment and publication strategies. These latter issues are difficult to discuss, but are none the less important for that. Indeed, this importance can lend a shadow-boxing character to public debate, with vague remarks about general attitudes when, in practice, it is the views of a small number of individuals operating in particular institutions that are crucial and at issue.[17]

Those of publishers are also extremely important, because, if the major presses do not publish military history, then it seems to lack scholarly weight. This situation makes it far more difficult for academics in this field to obtain posts in leading universities; and there is no doubt that that is a factor in the politics and culture of appointments. In contrast, less prominent presses produce much military history, much of it excellent, for example both Osprey, and Pen and Sword, in Britain.

In the Anglosphere, there is not, despite bitter, often very bitter disputes, the divisiveness over World War Two seen with many other states that were involved in that conflict; indeed, in America, both the Civil War[18] and the Vietnam War attract greater debate. In Italy, in contrast, the contest over the reputation of Mussolini, and not least over the popularity of his Salò Republic in northern Italy in 1943–5, was directly linked to the legitimacy of political groupings across the spectrum from Communists to neo-Fascists. These groupings looked back to the 1940s and earlier for evidence of their probity and of the iniquity of their opponents. As a result, the reputation of Mussolini had (and has) a greater resonance in Italian politics than that of Hitler in Germany.

In Italy, the Left sought a praiseworthy origin in terms of its wartime and earlier hostility to Mussolini, but, more generally, the emphasis in Italian public culture was not in alliance with Germany in 1940–3 (no more than the Soviets focused on their support for Germany in 1939–41), but rather, very much, on opposition in 1943–5. Thus, the focus was on a war of liberation, with the Resistance (rather than the Royalists and others in the Anglo-American zone) presented in a heroic light, not least as a redemption from Fascism. This provided an appropriate lineage for the post-war democracy, and, separately, shifted attention from the Italian imperial role, both pre-war in Libya and Ethiopia, as well as in Greece and Yugoslavia in 1941–3. In all of these cases, opposition had been harshly treated, and ignoring this helped the Italians in their self-presentation as victims of the war. Indeed, Italian troops were frequently contrasted with their German allies and seen as *brava gente* (good people) who had not been involved in war crimes, and this contrast was more generally applied by Italians to wartime occupation by the two powers.

There were also competing attempts by the different political parties in Italy to annex the positive reputation of the Resistance to their benefit. Thus, on the model of Gaullists in France, the Christian Democrats challenged the Communists' effort to present the Resistance as their movement. There were parallel or stronger tensions elsewhere, not least in China, Greece and Poland.

In turn, the Italian radicals of the 1968 generation criticised the Christian Democrats' usage of the Resistance by arguing that the true radicalism of the Resistance was thus neglected. For example, the participation of the Catholic Church in the Resistance was limited, although in some areas this was not the case, such as Lucca, where many priests were shot. Radicals also claimed that the extent to which the post-war government, although dominated by the Christian Democrats, owed much to the practice of Fascist government, was downplayed, and they criticised the 'Establishment' and the Church for backing Fascism. This argument was taken to vindicate radical opposition to the existing system in the 1960s and 1970s; there was a parallel with arguments in Germany that the Nazi regime sat within a pattern of German expansionism also seen with World War One.

From another direction in Italy, from the Right, and not only the Far-Right, there was a widespread (although far from universal) positive re-evaluation of Mussolini and Fascism. He was treated as a far more benign figure than Hitler. Mussolini indeed was (and was also more benign than Stalin), but that was scarcely a comparison of which to be proud. In particular, it was claimed that, in a self-sacrificing fashion, he had agreed to head the Salò Republic in order to protect northern Italy from harsh German rule, a claim, typical of the later neo-fascist attempt to justify themselves. Research in the German archives has failed to substantiate this.

The decline in the reputation of the Italian Communists in the 1980s was a factor in the positive re-evaluation of Mussolini, and one that gathered pace following the end of the Cold War, with Italy sharing in what was a general historiographical development in Europe, one seen for example in France, Romania and Hungary, all of which had seen wartime co-operation with Germany, although in France only after it was defeated in 1940. In part as a result of this decline in the reputation of Communism, there was a reduced stress on the role of the Resistance in Italy. Moreover, the Resistance itself was called into question by some commentators in Italy and elsewhere arguing that part of it had been compromised by its Communism. Large numbers of Italians had supported the Salò Republic and fought the Resistance in a low-level counter insurgency conflict in 1943–5, and their history came to be more favourably treated by some. Already, during the Cold War, the pressures of Italian politics, and the anti-Communist position of the Italian state, had ensured a degree of acceptance by many for those termed the *bravi ragazzi di Salò* (good guys from Salò).

More generally, military themes played a declining role in the largely hedonistic and certainly not militaristic, let alone bellicose, culture of Western Europe at the close of the twentieth century and in the early twenty-first, and this had corresponding implications for its military history. In part in order to overcome past international and domestic divisions within the European Union, notably within the European Union and particularly between France and Germany, military history was downplayed. There was a general rejection of past bellicosity and partial values, and a widespread reluctance to mark battles other than in terms of sorrow over the casualties, as with the battle of Verdun (1916) which was presented as a reason for Franco-German reconciliation.

In contrast, interest in past wars revived in Eastern Europe after the end of the Cold War in 1989–91 as the states of the period struggled in the 1990s to offer a new nationalism. The attack on the Soviet and the Russian view of World War Two was very much seen from those republics that had become independent with the fall of the Soviet Union.[19] Alongside revisiting the specifics of the previous conflict, World War Two, there was a tendency to define an acceptable military past in terms of long-term opposition to Russia. This was particularly the case with Poland, the military history of which had been totally misrepresented during the Communist years.[20] So also of Poland's role in wider military history as in the Museum of the Second World War in Gdansk opened in 2017, the contents of which have become politically contentious. In part, this was due to the tension over national background and historical context, one that is more generally instructive, not least because it was public. Thus, the museum spokesman declared it:

> 'a Polish museum financed by Polish taxpayers, Polish people simply want the museum they have financed to tell their story, to refer to the Polish point of view. The museum is located in Poland and must answer to those who financed it.'

As part of the changes, the Director, Pawel Machcewicz, was dismissed, the role of Catholic Poles in saving Jewish compatriots was emphasised, while a film illustrating the long-term consequences of the war was removed, in part because it showed, in the words of Machcewicz:

> 'that the war wasn't a closed chapter, it wasn't the past. Violence, the suffering of civilians, is still going on around us. The propensity to violence is inside us; it is part of the human condition ... emphasised the universal meaning of the exhibition.'[21]

In post-Communist Russia, in a linked fashion, but one that ignored alliance with Hitler in 1939–41 and renewed expansionism from 1944, World War Two continued to serve as the focal point for Russian patriotism and martial sentiment, offering an important continuity with the Soviet years. Victory Day, celebrated on 9 May, became Russia's most important non-religious holiday in the post-Communist era, one attended in 2015 by President Xi with Chinese troops taking part in the parade. Indeed, from 2014, the Putin government was repeatedly to invoke the memory of the 'Great Patriotic War' in order to justify aggression against Ukraine. The presentation of the latter as neo-Nazi was designed to draw on Russian patriotism and military history, and to transfer the burden of aggression onto the defender. This is a frequent practice in the state discussion of international affairs, as when North Korea complains of American aggression, and Iran of its Israeli counterpart.

At the same time, alongside the continuities represented by such Russian arguments, as well as the notion of one Russian strategic culture, came the salience of a politics of different Russian military theses. The Soviet/Russian approach was for long under the shadow of Marxist-Leninism, not least because of the attention attached to the army as both the defence of the regime and the threat to it, but that shadow still offered a range of perspectives, for example the views associated with Trotsky. On top of that, aside from simply ideology, there was the determination to present success in order to vindicate governmental positions.

Once Communist rule ended, however, in 1991, it was possible to discuss or re-present doctrine in a different fashion, with peer-group competitiveness with America irrespective of ideology now a crucial driver for Russian military commentators.[22] Such variations placed a major question mark against the argument for some geopolitical constancy in Russian policy, in so far as such an abstraction might indeed be helfpul. Possibly the same may eventually be the case for China. Indeed, the present emphasis on geography as destiny risks downplaying the significant interplay of context, conjuncture and contingency, one in which individuals have agency. Furthermore, language may be reused without necessarily implying that ideas and policies are unchanged. Instead, it is precisely when language is reused and historical examples deployed that there may actually be a break from continuity.

Chronological context was more important to the analysis of military history than most liked to acknowledge. This could be seen, for example, in the 1990s. The decade was in the aftermath of the Cold War, and before the problems of the 'War on Terror,' and the revelation that counter insurgency skills had not been sustained.[23] In this apparently benign context, at least for America which was the dominant power in the coalition that heavily defeated Iraq in 1991, there was a form of 'progressivism' similar to some aspects of the assumptions of the 1950s and early 1960s, notably in America. In particular, in the 1990s, against the background of a supposed

'End of History' in the shape of the American 'hyper-power,' there was an accentuation of the tendency to treat Western warfare, more particularly as represented by America, as the triumphant form, and as if the culmination of the historical process. This approach was seen for example in the contents of *The Cambridge Illustrated History of Warfare* (1995) edited by Geoffrey Parker; *The Reader's Companion to Military History* (1996) edited by Parker and Robert Cowley; *The Cambridge Illustrated Atlas of Warfare. The Middle Ages, 768–1487* (1996); Brian Bond's *The Pursuit of Victory* (1996); and the selection of topics to cover for series such as Longman's 'Modern Wars in Perspective' and Edward Arnold's 'Modern Wars'. So also for the literature of other countries.

Similar points about a Western-centric approach can be made with compendium works such as famous battles and commanders. The selection was part of a closed circle of familiarity. It could also be highly misleading, both reflecting and contributing to attitudes accordingly. It is as if a book on the topic must include a set coverage of, and the accustomed, proportions.

Thus, the treatment of Indian military history was greatly distorted by a focus on British victories, notably by Robert Clive at Plassey (1757), as opposed to failures, for example Wadgaon at the hands of the Marathas in 1779, and several at the hands of the rulers of Mysore, notably Pollilur (1780) and Annagudi (1782). This distortion extended to a failure to give due attention to the major battles fought between Indian rulers, and also between the latter and foreign invaders other than the British: the Persians and the Afghans, notably Karnal (1739) and Third Panipat (1761) respectively. This was a matter not only of the coverage but also of the analysis, for a focus on failure at the hands of the British established the apparent issue of judging Indian powers by their ability to match British willingness, methods and proficiency, whereas the British were only one of the challenges. Indeed, the Persians, the Afghans and the Marathas were more serious problems for the Mughal emperors. So also for other states: priorities may not be dictated by the requirements of the commentator.

The issue was one of approach as well as coverage: the two were linked, particularly in general works, although not only in them. It was uncommon to approach non-Western military history, both warfare and military organisation, from a non-Western point of view, which is necessary in order to avoid employing inappropriate methods of analysis. Indeed, Western descriptive and analytical vocabularies, categorisation, methods and prioritisation helped ensure Western constructions of the military character of other cultures and societies. This poses a problem in many respects, not least in encouraging a misunderstanding of conflicts with Western powers, with a misunderstanding of their opponents and the propagation of 'false consciousness' approaches as in 'they should have done' x, x being to adopt Western norms.

Broad-brush approaches, moreover, presented cultures as if on a point-scale set by the adoption of Western technology and organisational means. However, there also came a willingness by some specialists to understand the problematics and therefore counterfactuals offered by choices and other contingent elements, each of which was present for both Western powers and their opponents. This point could be readily seen in the case of the Sudan campaign of 1896–9, which was presented at the time, by contemporaries, such as Winston Churchill who fought there, as a triumph for British firepower and logistics. This analysis was then repeated subsequently. As with all discussions of warfare, however, this approach was unhelpful as it entailed a failure to assess the degree to which these undoubted advantages became more so due to other factors that could not be fixed. Thus, in this case, the Khalifa (Mahdist leader) failed to make use of the potential of Sudan for defence, either by attacking the long British line of communications or luring them into the hinterland. Instead, he fought at Omdurman a set-piece battle to defend his capital, Khartoum, and thus relying on a strategy and tactics that played to the British advantage.[24] At the same time, Khartoum provided the Mahdists with legitimation. There was a parallel here with other failures to disperse, for example George Washington fighting position battles in unsuccessful attempts to defend New York and Philadelphia in 1776 and 1777 respectively: Long Island and Brandywine respectively.

The problem with broad-brush approaches adopting cultural fixing as a basis for analysis was more generally pertinent for the 1990s. This was not least because of the Western, principally American, belief that technology was transforming the situation further to the benefit of the West. This belief, one that minimised the value of non-Western circumstances, developments and perspectives, made military history itself appear redundant to some commentators, and also lessened the military's commitment to such education. In the event, the revenge of history was to be readily apparent in the 2000s, as was the lesson of the role of the unexpected and unpredictable.[25] Yet, at the same time, as with geography, such a phrase, while striking, has to be employed with care, not least with a sensitivity to particular contexts, conjunctures and contingencies. Historical echoes are not the same as a replay of the previous situation.

This idea of recurrence is an aspect of the presentism of history, notably military history. This presentism reflected not only military currents, but also those of general cultural concerns. This could be seen in the case of the topics covered by books, topics reflecting the choices of authors and publishers, and the interests and perceived interests of purchasers. Thus, for example, 2021 saw the publication in America both of Alexander Bielakowski's *Proud Warriors: African American Combat Units in World War II* and of Ali Ahmad Jalali's *Afghanistan: A Military History from the Ancient Empires to the Great Game*. The latter was part of a sequence of books thrown to the fore by the Afghan war, for example Kaushik Roy's *War and Society in Afghanistan from the Mughals to the Americans, 1500–2013* (New Delhi, 2015). These books, like the many produced from 2003 in response to the war in Iraq, sought to explain the failure of the earlier conviction of technologically-based American military success, and also addressed the issue of whether there was a specific 'way of war' in the country in question. The last was held to explain why Afghanistan was difficult, if not impossible, to subjugate.

The idea of specific ways of war, ways established through the weight of historical patterning and further elicited through an assessment of the past, overlaps with the idea of strategic culture(s). Like similar concepts, such as *zeitgeist* (spirit of the age), both, however, have disadvantages, as, of course, is only to be expected in a multivalent subject and also with regard to the application of theory. The case of China is a good one, not least as the theory of strategic culture arose from discussing its history. It was argued, notably from the 1970s in America, that China's strategic culture, a thesis that argues for continuity and consistency, was primarily defensive and focused on protecting its frontiers. Indeed, from 1964, Mao Zedong, concerned about the danger of war with America, sought to develop the military capacity of the Chinese interior. Deploying military history, he criticised Stalin for failing to prepare for Hitler's invasion in 1941.[26]

As a consequence of the scholarly emphasis on defensiveness in Chinese culture, following a different policy appeared as a mistake arising from a false consciousness about circumstances, as with the unsuccessful Ming advance into the steppe and resulting disaster at the hands of the Mongols in 1449.

Such advances into areas that were marginal for one of the parties, notably exposing them to attacks by more mobile opponents, whether cavalry or infantry, have been frequent enough, as for example in the Parthian victory over the Romans at Carrhae (53 BCE) or Saladin's over the Crusaders at Hattin (1187 CE), as to create a pattern. They also helped in the construction of the psychological boundaries that were important to the way in which the mental context of strategy was created. This context owed much to the experience of success or failure, as with the crushing German defeat of a Roman army in the Teutoburg Forest in 9 CE.

In the case of China, there has also been a critique of this notion of a defensive, Confucian, strategic culture as being both inaccurate and self-interested, notably in presenting China as the victim of aggression. This critique, instead, sees long-standing expansionist themes in Chinese strategic culture, especially at the expense of steppe peoples and/or to establish a hegemony based on winning allies and protégés in part by defeating possible rivals as in the early-fifteenth century.[27]

This issue is regarded by some as of considerable relevance now, although it may also be asked how far a discussion of Chinese warmaking under the Tang dynasty in the seventh century or under the Manchu in the eighteenth century, is of relevance today, in what is a very different political context, both domestic and international, as well as with regard to the nature of war. For example, there were the contrasts between early and (more defensive) late Ming warmaking, between late Ming and Manchu attitudes, between Communist China under Mao and in the last quarter of the twentieth century, and between China's maritime assertiveness under Xi and the position under his predecessors. So even more for Islamic and Arab countries or 'the West' as the basis for the discussion of an alleged strategic culture or group of cultures.

To a degree, the use of culture is an instance of a neo-Platonic essentialism which can be misleading. This use draws in part on norms in many societies including the longstanding presentation of Western and/or American exceptionalism (itself a cultural proposition), and the resulting willingness to apply this essentialist account to other societies, and, for all, to downplay divisions and differences within them. This is a thesis which also has major limitations, as does its Chinese counterpart. Cultural elements clearly are aspects of warfare, past and present, but they are also dynamic, variable and problematic, such that the idea of a particular way of war has to be handled with care. So also with the counterpart in terms of geopolitical role.

Unfortunately, a standard approach in much writing is to employ less refined concepts of culture as an overarching, one-dimensional and fixed set of objective ideas. This is a practice that has long been challenged both theoretically and empirically, but without having much of an impact. In part, this reflects the persistence of established concepts and terms, but also the difficulties encountered in advancing different ones. Both can be related to the Whiggish (progressivist) tendency in military history and to its generally under/non/limited theorised character. There is a similar flaw in the usage of geopolitical concepts as if geography was destiny, an approach that underplays human agency, not least in the response to geographical factors and in the ability to alter some of the latter, such as forest cover and time-distance factors.

For all approaches to military history, the potential for expression was definitely increased after World War Two by technological developments, notably the spread of film, including computer-generated imagery, and, separately, of 'social media.' For each, there were repeated opportunities to offer new or different views on the past. In large part, this engagement was a matter simply of providing attention. Thus, King Mohammed IV of Morocco paid sixty per cent of the budget of the film *Indigènes* (2006), which threw light on the major role of France's North African soldiers, including Moroccans, in World War Two. The film was released in Britain as *Days of Glory*.

Aside from such national perspectives, there was also, across the formats of depicting military history, a rethinking in terms of types of conflict, as with the interest in insurrections and in counter insurgency warfare, especially in the period of the 'War on Terror'. This interest led not only to publications on such conflicts in the past (as well as present), but also to a reading of earlier conflicts in part in terms of such warfare. In particular, the American Civil War in recent decades has been presented with due attention to such fighting, which represents a major shift from the standard emphasis on large-unit manoeuvres and battle.[28]

Whether that focus on insurgency and counter insurgency conflict can lead to a disproportionate emphasis on the significance of such fighting is a different matter. In the case of World War Two, for example, resistance to German occupation in Western Europe was in fact far less significant than the subsequent public account was to assert, in, most notably, France. On the other hand, resistance was definitely important in Yugoslavia, and the subsequent national account justifiably stressed the only limited role of Soviet forces in driving out the Germans in 1944.

Yet, scholarship is not the sole definer. If attention in the case of America is moved from scholarly works to more popular ones, that shift from battle is far less apparent. Moreover, in fantasy literature and film, battle remains a key process, with the combat element of battle much to the fore. Individuals fighting remains important, whether the weapons used are stand-off or contact. So also for other countries, with the main media of discussion again being popular ones.

Formats change, social media for example offering new possibilities for gossip and conversation about war. Yet, there is a continual tendency by scholars to underplay the significance of popular views on war and the extent to which they were/are shaped by particular interpretations of the past, notably responses to individual conflicts. These interpretations can be rephrased as emotions, which is a way not to belittle them, but to capture their potency. Emotions affect the conceptualisation, methodology and historiography of subjects including military history.

Yet again, we need to move from the idea that there is an inherently rational approach to military history and, indeed, measurement of it. Accuracy in analysis certainly exists in terms of a scale of criteria, including conceptional, methodological and historiographical openness, as well as an understanding of the consequences of multiple participants, the use and usage of sources and, also, the extent of scepticism about certainty. Yet, such accuracy does not define the subject in terms of its various formats, stages and settings. Assessing the situation around the world, moreover, offers scant room for optimism about the present or hope for the future if these are to be defined in terms of a progressive rationalism.[29]

Chapter 11

Confronting the Future

'You know, there is a maxim, guns versus butter. Of course, national defence is the top priority, but in resolving strategic tasks in this area, we should not repeat the mistakes of the past and should not destroy our own economy.'

In his state-of-the-nation address in February 2023, Vladimir Putin, President of a Russia then involved in an apparently intractable conflict with a Western-backed Ukraine, captured the broad-ranging nature of strategy and bellicosity, and their capacity to reach out to most aspects of the state and society. War, in short, was not a spectator sport to be followed by the public through the media. This emphasis on national mobilisation, notably of the economy, was on a long-established pattern of statecraft. It was particularly seen in Communist states. Thus, there was the major development of Chinese industrial projects in the interior from 1964 to the 1980s, as a preparation for war, a policy greatly pushed by Mao as a 'Third Front.'[1] So also with recent Chinese rail construction. For China, as for many other governments, non-military and armed struggle are part of a continuum that includes resource buildups, capability increases, domestic control and what is more generally denoted by conflict.

Writing in 2023, we are already well into the new century, indeed millennium; that is, assuming the conventional, Western-chosen calendar, which is appropriate even if the use of century units can also be misleading in narrative, analysis and suggestion. As a result of where the present now is, the practice of framing the discussion of military developments and history primarily in terms of the world wars, the Cold War, or the post-Cold War (however the last is described), appears seriously flawed. Indeed, as a qualification, there is now also a chronology and agenda dominated by the deployment of terms such as the War on Terror and, currently, the

New Cold War: the War on Terror is yesterday's news. There will be similar phrases for the future, and also in non-Western states.

These categories have merit as a basis for recent military history, but, aside from matching a Western perception, indeed agenda, they pose and face the disadvantages of looking back and in simplistic terms. Indeed, in one respect, they represent the automatic theorisation seen with immediate classification, a temptation to pigeonhole the present that has readily-apparent deficiencies. In particular, this practice entails a tendency both to simplify individual conflicts and to group them together in pursuit of a typology, as in Wars of Religion (Europe 1559–1648), Cold War conflicts, warfare in the 1990s, the War on Terror or the New Cold War. So also for past rebellions and civil wars, as in the mid-seventeenth-century crisis, or the European revolutions of 1847–9.

Military planning, weapons procurement, training, strategic practice and flexible historical assessment are all largely innocent of such a misleading process, for they look to the future, notably, but not only, the immediate future, and are very specific in their problems and context. Indeed, strategic practice, like the very conduct and experience of individual conflicts, is task-driven, not theory-provided, as so also is doctrine even if it can present an encapsulation of a recent past.

The focus on tasks helps to explain a variety of conflicts, one that is enhanced by the degree to which, compared to a century earlier, there are far more people (2 billion in 1927; 8 billion today) and countries (50 in 1920; 195 today). This means that there is an inherently unstable background to the present situation, that of acute pressure on resources in a world that is deteriorating environmentally, and one moreover that may be accentuated further by developments including changing figures for those two criteria.

The increase in both numbers leads to more settings and circumstances for civil warfare, and, in contradiction to the 2023 focus on Ukraine and Taiwan, it may therefore be assumed that strategic practice, the experience of conflict and historical assessment in the future, will perforce focus across much of the world on such wars. That, however, does not preclude international warfare, and, indeed, as during the Cold War, the two may well overlap due to the role of subversion as part of weakening opposing coalitions, let alone full-scale intervention. Hybrid warfare, a long-established practice that existed before the term, very much came to the fore from 2014 after Russia rapidly seized Crimea, in part by successful subversion. In fact, hybrid warfare has very different potential meanings in particular contexts.

As another overlapping feature, and one also linked to hybrid warfare, there is likely to be a continual decline in the practice of a rules-based system in international relations, and, instead, a process of transactional bargaining. Russian aggression and Chinese ambition represent a rejection both of such a rules-based system and of liberal internationalism. So also with other bellicose states such as Eritrea and Iran. Moreover, the outbreak of the 2022 war saw the failure of deterrence, and there is scant sign that it is possible to revive the practice, whatever the theory might suggest. This situation can be extended to include the weakness of international law in addressing the large number of states in which internal conflict, and indeed politics, are conducted without any sense of limits on violence. Indeed, as aspects of the centrality of violence in this situation, it is instructive to consider the major role, very much a hybrid role, of bodies such as Iran's Revolutionary Guards, which acts as an elite force for war and policing, as well as controlling a large section of the economy and having a significant role in policy. The Revolutionary Guards are, as it were, a case of the party as military force. They are also an instance of the continued role of religious commitment in conflict.

This role was also seen elsewhere. Thus, in May 2023, Oleksiy Danilov, the Ukrainian National Security Advisor, declared of the forthcoming offensive: 'We have to understand that that historic opportunity that is given us - by God – to our country we cannot lose, so we can truly become an independent, big European country.'

The lack of an effective rules-based system, and particularly so for states with differing, indeed hostile, systems of political culture, such as Shia theocratic Iran, makes it more likely that strategic practices and historical categories such as deterrence or graduated escalation will not work, or will not work predictably. These two outcomes may in practice amount to the same, for the risk horizon will be very short term.

Combined with the spread of nuclear weaponry and, for the major states, concentrated militaries – those with a small number of units but a high degree of lethality, this would encourage first strikes. Indeed, the failure of the Russian attack on Ukraine in 2022 may well simply encourage future aggression in which more force, and with fewer inhibitions, are deployed from the outset. The Russian failure was an aspect of inadequate planning, notably poor intelligence and logistics and an aspect of the friction of warfare, more particularly one focused by a lack of tactical competence on the part of Russian commanders.[2] At the same time, the last is scarcely value-free in the sense that it is some 'hidden hand' of history. Instead, the friction arises from the combatants' interaction, in 2022, being created in large part by Ukrainian resilience and flexibility. Yet, this failure was widespread in 2022, not least including that of Western deterrence. There was a lack of 'situational awareness' across most of the board, and that is an aspect of strategic deficiencies, although other elements contribute to the latter including confirmation bias.

Linked with the difficulties of sustaining and replenishing concentrated militaries in the face of the inexorable depletions of conflict, and notably so of ammunition, such an attack may well mean that slow-burn warfare only arises if, as in Ukraine or the Iraqi attack on Iran in 1980, it becomes impossible to deliver the desired rapid victory. However, this warfare may then fall foul of a limited capability and restricted willingness for attritional conflict, or, differently, the latter needs to be defined and prepared for accordingly.

As such, international warfare may be distinguished from civil conflict, with the latter characterised by a particular type of attrition; namely insurgency strategies of disruption combined with counter insurgency strategies of policing. Neither is new, and the extent to which relevant contextual or technological changes, notably in surveillance and food control, may arise are unclear. However, one demographic development is of major consequence: the global population is growing rapidly, most notably in India and Nigeria. The population is also becoming far more urban. As a result, the classic geographical forcing-house of insurrectionary struggles, the 'backwoods' of marginal economic zones and difficult terrain, particularly forests and mountains, has become relatively less significant. Those milieux were the basis for Maoist strategy of the 1930s, but now the bulk of the population lives in large urban areas, indeed, very heavily populated cities, such as Kinshasa in Congo and Karachi in Pakistan. Strategies for insurgency in these zones reflect the inherent difficulties faced by governments in controlling them and, therefore, the possibility, for opponents, of exploiting that lack of control.

Conversely, the counter insurgency strategy can also understand these difficulties in the sense of accepting a degree of this very lack of control. Does it ultimately 'matter' for Brazil's government if it does not control the *favelas* (slums) in its major cities? What victory means in this context is in part a matter of the struggle over the narrative. The ability of government to accept limited control varies culturally and temporally, as does the willingness of society to accept large-scale lawlessness, which, in part, is what insurgencies entail to civilians, as there can be scant difference between insurgencies and major criminal organisations. The lawlessness seen with some counter insurgency struggles comes from a different background, but it can be felt grievously by civilians. This is the case for example in Iran today, as it was in the 'Dirty War' of the Argentine junta in 1976–82 and in the comparable Chilean repression.

The lengthy struggle over cities in the Ukraine war, Maripol in 2022 and Bakhmut in 2023, led to discussion of historical parallels, notably Verdun (1916) and Stalingrad (1942).[3] In practice, the most pertinent was Grozny, the Chechen capital, in 1994–5 and 1999–2000, not least as those were destructive and lengthy assaults by the Russians. However, reference to Grozny does not have the resonance of Verdun, even if the latter is a less pertinent comparison. The city as a battlefield may well represent a convergence of conventional with insurgency warfare and contexts; and, indeed, a sponge that soaks up forces, all forces, and lessens their effectiveness. That happened to American and British units in Iraq from 2003, creating a very different situation to that in Afghanistan.

Control over greater populations may become a matter of choking their supplies, including information, but what war means in this context is unclear, notably so with domestic conflict. The number of countries, whether authoritarian, or in theory, democracies (but those in which there is no acceptance by the governing regime that power may be exchanged peacefully), is such that violence, or the threat of force, are an integral aspect of politics.

The situation in America in January 2021 offered a possible instance of that process, with the electoral transfer of power contested in what to some appeared an episode of 'grey war,' or, at least, of growing menace that culminated in a riot at the Capitol with President Trump calling for intervention that suggested to many a type of coup however much his language was democratic in the sense of allegedly opposing a fraudulent election, which, in fact, was not fraudulent. He was lending support to what was subsequently determined by the courts to be a seditious conspiracy, with the Oath Keepers militia deploying a military formation and wearing helmets and body armour, while the Proud Boys militia saw itself as 'Trump's army.' That there was no need then to deploy the army against coup-like attempts was a key element in military history, in the sense of an element that did not occur. In contrast, the Chinese Communist government used the army in 1989 against what it saw as a coup.

So much of military history is flawed because it only deals with international conflict. And yet, major developments frequently arise from the use or non-use of the military in domestic affairs. Many states experience coups, disorder or rebellions, but not external conflict. A failed military coup can be a transformative occasion, as with Turkey in 2016, and, to a degree, in the lurch toward further fanaticism, Germany in 1944. The use of the military to suppress pressure for reform was decisive in China in 1989 while the need not to turn to the army was potentially important in the shambles of a would-be coup in America in 2021.

And so to Russia and Prigozhin's advance toward Moscow in 2023. This was not the essentially unopposed return of Napoleon in 1815 (nor his initial coup of 1799), but, as with so many military disturbances, a reminder that armed forces are a coalition and that this poses issues for all states. It can be an issue for democracies as well as autocracies: the former, whether limited or extensive, are scarcely free from the challenge of military disaffection. Moreover, such a challenge as with Spain in 1936, opens up divisions within the military as well as between military and civilian authorities.

That the Russian system has only limited control over its military is scarcely news. Doubts about this, however, unrealistic and/or manipulated by foreign powers, affected Stalin in 1937. Furthermore, the very structure of force in the Soviet system and in its Russian successor was in part intended to maintain control over the military. This was the logic of espionage oversight of the military, of political commissars and of the patronage politics that were followed.

There has not been so long a war for the Soviet Union/Russia since the Afghan commitment of 1979–89 and the failure in Ukraine has put major pressures on the Russian military. Prigozhin's advance, an indicator of broader tensions, is a reminder of the problems involved in deploying a coalition of forces as part of a conflict. Putin was weakened. In analytical terms, the failure in most studies of war to devote due attention to civil conflict is very striking.

Democracies also have to be able to wield force against violent opposition that can seek to thwart or overthrow democratic and legal processes. This is difficult, as is the definition of viable goals in international war. The latter problem led from the mid-2000s to repeated criticism of mission creep, notably in the form of peacekeeping and nation-building, and of strategic failure on the part of Western powers.[4] Ironically, the major such failure was of the Soviet Union, or rather its governing system, in 1989–91. There was no comparable Chinese failure.

Violence or the threat of force are integral to many aspects of international relations, including border clashes, subversion, limited attacks, economic sanctions and other uses of force. For example, whether Iran and Israel have in effect been at war for several years is a matter for discussion and, linked to that and other examples, comes the distinction, if any, between international relations and conflict. Despite the legal situation, or, rather, in defiance of it, there is no reason to expect that the former should be peaceful.

Seeing war as a branch of international relations makes it difficult to regard strategy as primarily a military activity. Instead, it is seen as political, with the use of force simply one aspect of politics, and one that is assessed with reference to 'political' criteria, whether in terms of forcing will on opponents or with reference to maintaining domestic support. The significance of the latter for strategy, not least in the face of possible alternatives, has never been a fixed factor, and is one that writers on strategic theory can be apt to underplay. Yet, this maintenance has been of considerable importance in the past and has become more so since the nineteenth century as a greater percentage of populations have become politically aware and often active. The nature of consent and deference is different in authoritarian societies; but both are still a factor and not least under the pressure of war. What that situation means for the acceptance of state historical accounts is unclear.

Looking to the future, the emphasis tends to be on current questions. Thus, the nature of force structure is very much up for discussion. For many, whatever the technological additions, the size of the military, notably the army, remains a key criterion, but with debate over how this is to be defined. This debate was pushed to the fore anew in 2022–3, notably across Europe, in response to war in Ukraine, not least with discussion over what mass of force was therefore required and how it could best be defined. In America, there was a comparable debate, but one that was largely motivated by concern about China, and, in particular, how best to address China's naval build-up. In Britain, in contrast, historical factors were much to the fore, with critics angered by the proposal to reduce army size: in 2021 a projected cut from 82,000 to 73,000 was announced, only for generals to demand a reversal. On 25 May 2023, speaking at the London Defence conference, Sir Tony Radakin, the Chief of the Defence Staff, and an Admiral, rejected the criticism, instead emphasising investment in new technology: 'I think we're slightly stuck in some of the numbers game. The numbers are important, and I don't want to deny that, but the numbers aren't quite as totemic and as golden as people say.'

Radakin added another historical reference: 'The way that we describe mass, it's only through humans, and the UK as an armed force has rarely been a major contributor in mass. In the future our mass will be provided by technology in a much stronger way than it is now.' This was a reprise of the standard argument that the navy man's ships while the army uses technology to support manpower. This was part of a longstanding debate, although the extent to which the historical trace/trend guided present-day assumptions is a matter of opinion. In practice, the past provided a range of possible indications. Thus, during the world wars and in the Cold War, Britain had provided mass, in part due to continental commitments and the response of conscription, but after the Cold War ended, there had been a reversion to the pre-1914 norm, and an expeditionary focus on tasking and a stress on smaller but more nimble forces.

More dramatically, the process of strategic choice in the future might be affected by systems of artificial intelligence (AI), and to a degree that is unpredictable and possibly even unplanned. Such systems are present already in tactical circumstances, notably in the interaction of sensors and firers, reducing the delays posed by the command structure. However, these systems will probably spread more generally, as in the development of logistical control practices. AI has attracted attention as 'a genie out of the bottle.'

Strategy may appear far removed from this situation. Yet, there are links, not least that tactical moves related to AI, for example the shooting down of aircraft flying in a challenging manner, may well have strategic implications, and notably so if the clash is between China and America. Moreover, as AI usage increases, it will in effect play a role in the framing of strategic choices, because information will be assembled, organised and ranked by such means. So also in the consideration of options as part of the planning stage. Thus, 'war games' will be not only played on computers but also by means of their active contribution, with parallels in actual conflict. The role of AI in histories of war can then be debated. It will probably be minimised, unless possibly future methods for recording and representing war owe something to AI.

There are plentiful reasons to be concerned about conceivable doomsday scenarios involving a degree of machine takeover. Such scenarios, however, are far less likely than the use of AI by human strategists in a manner that affects strategic formulation and execution. Very differently but more active in literature, comes speculation about military confrontation with interplanetary opponents, whether this opposition is obvious and deliberate, or not.

This element is a reminder that the future is not a static military environment, a perspective that also throws light on the past, and that provides a changing context for histories of war. Even if restricting attention to the twenty-first century, there is still just over three-quarters of a century to consider and maybe another 2.5–3 billion people to add to the size of the global population. Going back over the same period from now would include such innovations as the move to atomic rivalry when the Soviet Union acquired the relevant capacity, the development of hydrogen bombs and later space-based reconnaissance and weaponry, large-scale decolonisation, the tripling of the world's population, and a host of other changes. A high rate of change can be seen, albeit with different indicators, in some earlier periods as well. It is not just a condition of the modern.

To envisage nothing comparable in terms of new developments, as well as the major transformations brought by a different quantity or rate of pre-existing circumstances, would be to assume a steady state strategic system for which there is no precedent in modern history, however defined. Such an assumption would be foolish and also an instance of a mistaken contextual analysis.

This then opens up questions about whether the future will be a matter of stages and periods of greater change that can be seen as turning points, or whether it will be more inchoate. If the latter, this very lack of clear-cut trends will in practice be the major feature of the strategic environment. That certainly appears likely. Moreover, this rate of change, as well as its simultaneity, poses issues for producing histories of war. There are no obvious priorities determining how these topics should be addressed. So also with doctrinal documents and related conceptual contexts for training, and also for strategic formulation. The future will be the subject and basis for later histories of war that, crucial to the subject of this book, will also affect the presentation of what now is the historical period.

This process can be seen with what are clearly intended, presented and sold as major works. Thus, *The Origins of Victory. How Disruptive Military Innovation Determines the Fates of Great Powers* by Andrew Krepinevich is a typical example of the magic bullet approach to military affairs, past, present and future. As such, however, it faces the standard problems with such literature. Clearly, if the fundamental assumptions are taken for granted, then Krepinevich, a well-established exponent of such work, is well able to serve up another good book, and has indeed done so. If, however, you are somewhat sceptical about the approach, and, possibly, seek more nuance, complexity, contextualisation and the cross-currents of the inherently diverse politics and economics of international relations, then this work is less happy.

For an historian, Krepinevich is overly simplistic and, for a caller upon innovation, a bit behind the times. Take the following warning in an introduction that boldly proclaims: 'History shows that a military that first masters the new form of warfare enjoys a clear and potentially decisive advantage over its rivals.' Sounds obvious? Well the second example is less happy:

'In the spring of 1940, Germany's integration of aviation, mechanisation, and wireless (radio) to create Blitzkrieg enabled it to defeat France in six weeks, something it had failed to accomplish despite four years of effort a generation before.'

A well-established view, but there are also others, and notably the recent focus on the allocation of the French reserves to the far left of the Front, and the extent to which the strategic and political responses magnified what were essentially limited German operational advantages. In short, strategic factors trumped the technology with which Krepinevich is most happy. And so throughout his book and many similar works. There is an essential failure to address issues of strategic choice and complexity adequately, and, instead, a preference for seeing victory essentially in operational terms and with the focus on battle.

Krepinevich argues that America is failing to match 'its great-power rivals, China and Russia', essentially because it lacks the necessary engagement with disruptive innovation. Leaving aside the problematic inclusion of Russia, China indeed is making impressive efforts. Krepinevich sees a foolish focus for three decades on minor wars and the War on Terror as setting America back. I agree about the problems of matching strategic prioritisation to military capabilities, in the case of America and indeed other powers. However, as in so many cases, the catch-all central thesis of this book should be replaced by a multivalent one fully open to additional and, indeed, alternative explanations and factors.

Strategic practice and the tasking it reflects and influences, as well as the preparation and presentation of histories of war, are not only ways to try to shape the challenges of risk but also means to seek to minimise and shape the inherent volatility of the changing human condition. Strategic practice in this sense is a matter not only of planning and execution as classically understood, but also of doctrine, procurement and tasking. All are key constituents of this practice, and, in turn, help frame its processes.

There is a widespread tendency to treat flaws in analysis, institutional bias and problematic histories as factors in the past, but there is no reason to believe that there are not similar problems at present, notably for weapons procurement and, separately, the 'doctrine' that reflects ideas. Moreover, the vexed and disputatious nature of strategic reviews, which are one particular type of history of war, highlights the role of choice and politics in tasking, prioritisation, procurement and doctrine. Correspondingly, there is the extent to which these and other factors have a legacy that affects not only subsequent choices but also the frameworks and career structures, within which they are posed, debated and implemented. 'Planning for the last war' is a simplistic way of phrasing this point, as such reflection and planning, indeed, is far more insistent as a process, and one that arises from, and addresses, the need to consider experience. That consideration is ultimately the theorisation of war.

Military matters are very separately advanced or rather refracted through the teaching of recruits and, separately, popular culture, with a repeated emphasis in both on individual heroism, collective bravery and the group cohesion that helps cement resolve, indeed often proving more significant in this regard than ideology. These were a powerful factor in the earliest recorded literature, and remain important in modern literature, electronic games and other media. The theory here is of the triumph of will; although there can also be a providentialism and fatalism that ensures a heroic failure, as with the Spartans at Persian hands at Thermopylae in 480 BCE, or the Texans at Mexican hands at the Alamo in 1836.

Failure itself then becomes a form of triumphant will, which is what Hitler appears to have been seeking toward his end. As a result he was totally against negotiations. Looked at differently, and as a reminder of the extent to which a number of factors played a role, such that single explanations are generally inaccurate and thus should be unacceptable, Hitler was also hopeful that 'wonder weapons' might sway the war in his favour, notably jet aircraft and new-model submarines. He also expected a breakdown in the opposing coalition, not least as a result of Roosevelt's death, but, more profoundly, due to division between the Soviet Union and the West. To emphasise one factor at the expense of the others, which is the standard approach is, however, very unhelpful. This approach becomes a way to focus attention on the loser, and can also lead to an extrapolation of this attention more generally, presenting Hitler's failure and other cases as a consequence of opposing resources, as in the 'Lost Cause' view of Confederate failure in the American Civil War.

Discussion of conflict in terms of bravery, determination and resilience attracts the most attention. This is in part due to the directness and vividness of the writing and, separately, to the overlap with the appeal of fiction and with fantasy genres. There has also been the popularity, strengthened from the 1970s, of 'face of battle' accounts, with their emphasis on the stories of individual combatants, and the related use of oral history. This approach, which was pronounced in the democratic populist West, downplays background elements of great significance, such as strategy, logistics and communications; and focuses, instead, on the tactical dimension and also on willpower. The two are linked in such factors as unit cohesion.

Modern cultures are particularly apt to respond to visual stimuli and 'lessons'. These can focus on tales of heroism, as well as the particular capabilities of weaponry, which frequently provide the visual images, as if the weapons themselves are heroic. That is an approach adopted in Britain with reference in particular to the Spitfire. In the form of illustrations of weapons, the specific medium of history provides a message, and one that, in this case, is a long way from the use of written text, which, in contrast, is more readily able to suggest ambiguity and qualifications. Visual media, moreover, are more accessible for usage across much of the world, and they capture the interactive character of much current engagement, and notably so by the young. There is a preference with illustrations for short captions which focus on description rather than evaluation. These short captions are also the easiest to translate. At the same time, short captions or their equivalents have been normal across many media in the past.

These and other visual media are also where what in effect are theories or lessons of military history, generally implicit theories or lessons, are being expressed. They offer the modern equivalents to the oral epics that were so important in the past, epics that varied and changed in the retelling. Again, that suggests links, or at least resonances, across the ages.

At the same time, the past itself is subject to churn with the priorities and views of the once potent in turn regarded as redundant. Thus, in May 2023, at the *Palau de la Generalitat* in Barcelona, the seat of Catalonia's government, removal began of the murals created in the 1920s by artists during the military dictatorship in Spain of Miguel Primo de Rivera. In 2019, a separatist regional government established a commission to report on them, and the decision was then made to 'restore' the room to the situation prior to one of the murals. The commission concluded with an attack on the murals, including one on the victory of Lepanto (1571) over the Turks, a victory in which Spanish forces played a major role:

'They exalt militaristic values, a class order opposed to parliamentarianism – the perennial and sacred monarchy and the state based on Catholicism as a social order – and the fight against Islam, as well as belligerent and imperial patriotism.'

This was somewhat ironic as Spain's major ally at Lepanto was republican Venice, and, separately, it is unclear how modern 'parliamentarism' would necessarily have helped in 1571 against Turkish forces that had just captured Cyprus.

Looking into the future, there is no reason to believe that there will be any change from the basic context and content for the political use of the 'lessons' of military history: political leaders are apt to promote and listen to those who provide the advice that they seek. While obviously true of authoritarian governments, this is not only the case with them. Initial commitments are generally made in a secret fashion, and then troops are deployed in order to support the commitment. A particularly worrying aspect is a widespread ignorance about the nature of war, with so few politicians familiar with the frictions and uncertainties of conflict. As a consequence, the problems of securing and maintaining victory are not adequately grasped, an element for example seen in the case of the Russian invasion of Ukraine in 2022.

This point, indeed, captures the significant ambivalent nature of military history. In theory, it has a very valuable role to play in order in particular to explain the need to analyse situations with careful scepticism and to understand the frictions posed by conflict, the environment and opposing moves, each of which should induce caution. Yet, military history also serves to encode and express flawed tactical, operational and strategic perceptions and arguments, as indeed with Russia in 2022.

This point was driven home in 1999, when George Robertson, the British Secretary of State for Defence, publicly scorned military historians who had warned about the difficulty of winning the Kosovo conflict by air power alone, and also about the contrast between output and outcome. Robertson's stance reflected the need to believe that victory was possible without the deployment of troops. In part, this assessment, which largely rested on hope, belief and wishful thinking, all present with the government of which he was a member, was a product of the difficulties of deploying and supporting troops there in the face of Greek reluctance to provide access. Yet, there was also a more general concern about intervention in the form of troops. This concern accorded well with ideas about the salience of air power. The subsequent Serbian withdrawal, however, revealed that Robertson, who soon after became Secretary General of NATO, was wrong and that estimates of the damage inflicted by Allied air attacks on the Serbian armour were seriously inaccurate. Yet, the general confidence in air power remained strong.

As another instance of the complexity of judgment, and need for caution, it is highly likely that histories of war, like their prospectuses, will continue to underplay the extent to which differing understandings of victory, loss and suffering are important as activators of significant asymmetries between combatants. Given the importance of these factors for the setting of realisable goals, their neglect is particularly unhelpful. Some polities and movements, for example, in recent years, Eritrea and Islamic State (principally in Iraq), are better able to enforce or encourage a willingness to take casualties. The extent to which this is a matter of political control or of cultural and ideological patterning is a matter for debate. Moreover, the timescale is such that what might begin as patterning can become a matter of coercion. This is definitely an element in attritional struggles.

In these and other respects, war, therefore, is rather a medium of questions than the message of an easy answer. The former provides a contradiction to the style and content of much military history, namely the almost machismo argument by assertion that is so frequently offered when situations are discussed and analyses are advanced. Such assertion covers both the analysis advanced and its simplification. Qualification does not come readily in such approaches to military history, which is an issue with much of the work on the subject, notably that on supposed 'military revolutions.' In practice, there is no clear hierarchy of military capabilities, but rather challenges and responses set by very different taskings and environments, both physical and human. Fitness-for-purpose is a criterion of capability and effectiveness that does not allow for glib comments on what is 'best' in a wider sense. The key divide throughout is that of wars between states and conflict within them. It is only if both the latter and also the non-West, which provides, and has always provided, the majority of the world's population, are given sufficient attention that a sounder understanding of war can develop. A discussion of military history ought to be as helpful for, and from, Madagascar and/or Paraguay, as Germany and/or America.

Yet, to do so would be to overcome the long-standing elision of much military history. Indeed, the histories of war that are on offer remain distinctly partial, and this situation may continue to be pronounced, and become even more so. A classic instance is that of insurrections. Attention today is devoted to those that conform to what are regarded as acceptable narratives, especially anti-imperial ones, but not those that do not. Alternatively, the latter are interpreted accordingly, sometimes by treating them in a historical fashion, as with the idea in the 1960s that the American Revolution had similarities with the Vietnam War, which was very much not the case, not least as America was not the legal ruler of South Vietnam, as George III was of the American colonies.

Episodes that reveal a different reality are ignored. For example, the struggle in which the Soviet and Cuban-backed Popular Movement for the Liberation of Angola (MPLA) challenged Portuguese colonial rule has received considerable attention, as has its subsequent conflict with the American and South African backed UNITA movement. Not so for the crushing in 1977 of MPLA opponents to the dictatorial rule of Agostinho Neto in which large numbers were killed. This crushing did not conform to domestic and foreign interest and was therefore ignored.[5]

Such selection is fairly typical of the nature of historical presentation, a process that is inherently political. This character is very much seen with military history, and notably so if that is understood as extending to the use of force to maintain domestic control. Thus, in China, the most important element in military history since 1949 has been the brutal suppression of the Tiananmen Square uprising in 1989, but that has been largely written out of it's history. In Cyprus, there are very different historical accounts of conflict from Greeks and Turks. So also with the situation in many countries, not least as independence myths have come under scrutiny.

The idea that war is inherently political very much extends to its history which is also contestable. That may seem a long way from the experiences of those who risked and gave their lives, but the presentation and memorialisation reflects the political legacy of the past and the nature and weight of current concerns.

The challenge of incorporating new elements in the history of war is being constantly upgraded. In part, this is particularly so of technology. Thus, in May 2023, a conference in London on 'future combat air and space capabilities' heard from Colonel Tucker Hamilton, the American air force's chief of AI testing, that an attack drone directed by AI in a simulated mission to destroy surface-to-air missiles attacked its human operators, either to kill them or to attack the communications tower forwarding their instructions, because it did not appreciate receiving new instructions. This represented a task-focus that was ready to defy the hierarchy of control.

Yet, although such technology may play a role, it does not itself answer the question of how to discuss particular conflicts, and the geopolitical and political issues that were involved. Any focus on leading powers in this context can be misleading, for much conflict will not involve them. Moreover, technology does not provide an explanation of the definitions of victory that contemporaries pursued and were willing to accept. These definitions are affected by technological capabilities, but are not defined by them. Yet, mention of AI opens up the prospect that in future this definition will not be offered by and for humans, or supposed historical and even divine processes and purposes, but can also be seen as stemming from the needs and possibilities of sentient machines able to make choices that are far more than solely automatic ones. This indeed opens up the possibility of a new age of warfare, hitherto a much overrated concept; although it is far from clear how far AI will meet its apparent potential not least in the face of the anti-tactics, operational methods and strategies that so often come into play when new advances are made. That process is a reminder of the degree to which the apparent future can be absorbed into a history that contains recurrent elements if not of sameness, then at least of continuity.

Chapter 12

Conclusions

Nagasaki provides an abrupt history of war in the shape of the absence of old buildings near the epicentre of the bomb. And then the visual strikes increase, notably the primitive air raid shelters in which so many suffered the heat storm. Of course, the layers of meaning are more complex. The Peace Park includes a disproportionate memorialisation by Cold War Communist states, including Bulgaria, China, Cuba, Czechoslovakia and the Soviet Union, several somewhat inappropriate visually. A New Zealand monument brings in those affected by British nuclear testing in the South Pacific, which certainly is not a comparable case. In short, war bears its multiple histories, the occasion being refracted through a kaleidoscopic prism of many lenses, some of which dull, brighten or otherwise change through time.

In the case of Nagasaki, the nuclear catastrophe has borne differing domestic and international messages, both during the Cold War and thereafter, and this will continue to be the case. The domestic emphasis has usually come from the Left and been on neutralisation and opposition to American bases. The relevance today at a time of North Korean nuclear threats and Chinese expansionism is less clear.

In North Korea, indeed, the war of 1950–3 is used to bolster xenophobia, specifically hatred of America and South Korea. Rallies are held annually to mark the start of the war, and this is used to criticise both powers. The state-run Korean Central News Agency explained in a statement in June 2023: 'June 25 is kept in the minds of the Korean people as the wounds of a grudge that can never be healed. The Korean nation suffered bitter pain and misfortune due to the US imperialists.' The North Koreans deny their aggression in 1950.

A different instance of change comes from Turkey where the reaffirmation in the 2023 election, dominance by Recep Tayyip Erdogan (Prime Minister

2003–14, President 2014-) and the AK Party will accentuate a rewriting of the Turkish history of war. In place of the Kemalist emphasis on success over Greece in a war of independence over a century ago has come the downplaying of this achievement by seeking an exemplary Ottoman one, of imperial dominance in the Balkans and the Middle East and notably over Greece. Political calculation plays a role in the specifics, so that the long-lasting conflicts between the Ottomans and Russia, their major opponent from 1735 to 1918, are not a matter of much discussion, not least as Erdogan and Putin, alongside differences particularly over Syria, seek to cooperate in order to lessen the role of America. However, alongside calculation in those specific terms come the more general emphasis on Turkish bellicosity, the past serving to validate and echo present-day grandstanding, as in the stress on the capture of Constantinople (Istanbul) in 1453. However, the outcry obliged Erdogan to rein back on defacing the monument at Anzac Cove in Gallipoli in 2017 with an Islamist message. Instead, it had to be renovated anew: it had borne words attributed to Ataturk (probably misleadingly), likening Australian 'Johnnies' to Turkish 'Mehmets.'

The emphasis on political contents and contexts for histories of war serves to undermine any stress on a single history of war, however constructed, whether for example in patterns based on technology, war and society or the causes of war. The net effect is to underline the degree to which the subject is shared and/or on a continuum, with those who find and express the political meanings more salient than academics and others concerned with military matters in a less politicised fashion.

Alongside these comes two other potent tendencies in histories of war: war and the family, and war and entertainment. As far as the former is concerned, this provides a looking back to three spheres of memory: personal experience/recollection; listening to previous generations; and, beyond that, accounts of forbears. These were the key histories at the individual and family levels. How far they fed into wider collective accounts is a matter for debate but there was clearly a relationship. To a degree, personal recollection, as well as family presentation can be guided by these collective accounts. As a result, a separation of the individual from the collective can be misleading. Yet, there is an energy as well as widespread diffusion in individual and family accounts that deserves attention.

The composition of these accounts can be difficult to assess, not least in authoritarian societies where there is an emphasis on a public creed. Yet, that does not mean that such accounts lack independence. Indeed, one of the most salutary historiographical developments of recent years occurred in 1989–91 when the fall of Communist regimes encouraged an expression of opinions and convictions, notably religious ones, that had not been apparent hitherto. This expression included a reassessment of recent military history. This was most clearly the case with World War Two, but was also seen in the suppression of anti-Communist and Soviet movements in the years after, as in the Baltic Republics and Ukraine, as well as the use of force to ensure Communist orthodoxy, especially in East Germany in 1953, Hungary in 1956, Czechoslovakia in 1968 and Poland in 1981. This military reassessment was closely linked to a political repositioning in the former Communist bloc, notably a recurrence of a pre-Communist nationalism that encouraged and required this reassessment.

This process can be readily seen and encourages consideration of a similar situation for other societies, past, present and future. Thus, histories of war are readily presented as the product of politics, which is unsurprising but not necessarily what military experts prefer. Moreover, this situation calls into question the accuracy of participant and observer accounts of war, as these are readily understood as also being affected by politics. So also with analysis by commentators.

That political context indeed presents an instructive way to consider histories of war. Some of the links may appear obvious, as with the tendencies in Western culture in the eighteenth, nineteenth and twentieth centuries that encouraged developmental models of change and associated ideas of the optimalisation of rationality. From the nineteenth century ideas of revolutionary change were focused by the depiction of an Industrial Revolution and its extension to military equivalents. Indeed, the history of war apparently became an account of successive military revolutions, which marched from antiquity to the contemporary. This almost formulaic process of analysis, one that is historical in its imposition of an apparently timeless model, has been strengthened in recent decades by fresh interest in new technology and related control systems, and there are more in prospect, notably with AI.

Separately, it is possible to see histories of war at the academic level as political in the widest sense. Thus, the war and society model can be related to the strength of social history tendencies in the period. Going back, it is instructive to assess the engagement with the Classical model of warfare at the time of the Renaissance in terms of the attitudes of the latter, while Protestant commentators during the Reformation looked to Old Testament models of military engagement. The shadow of Rome was also seen in many instances.

Yet, these points still leave unexamined the vast majority of examples. Thus, histories of war are often accepted without their political content, conjuncture and context being probed, whether adequately or at all. To suggest that this problematises the history of war would possibly be to push the questions of source criticism and general analysis too hard. However, the issue does require consideration. The need for additional research therefore emerges as one conclusion.

Another is provided by the emphasis on the range of formats used for histories of war. The degree to which individual formats can entail particular implications for content and for governmental direction deserve attention. Moreover, these formats can then apparently support the idea of a unified approach in a particular society to its history of conflict. This is especially true of statuary, stamps and medals. In contrast, the case with diaries is very different. Yet, as already pointed out for Eastern Europe under Communist rule, the unified approach to assessment might be more the case in terms of appearance than in underlying reality. All the statues of Soviet soldiers as liberators could not end the view of many that they depicted the 'unknown rapist,' and criticism could be more abruptly presented after Communist rule ended. Furthermore, the statues could then be removed. Present-day 'history wars' or 'culture wars' frequently relate to the presentation of conflicts.

As a related conclusion, there is also an inherent variety and integral transience in the histories of war represented in military doctrine and manifested in strategy and planning. All of these again tend in particular contexts to suggest constancy and necessity. That is part of the orderly and deliberative character of military discussion and documentation. However, yet again, there is a contingent and contextual character to such histories of war, and not least in terms of the necessity of issues, the selection of examples, and the use to which they are put. Thus, for example, for America, the shift from a concern with great-power competition in the 1980s to conflicts of choice in the 1990s, counter insurgency struggles in the 2000s, and back to great power competition from the mid-2010s. Although not always so dramatically a switch, there have been transformations for other militaries, largely due to task-based contextual changes. It is unsurprising that such a process also affects the histories of war that are offered. This will continue.

Notes

Preface
1. T. Smollett, *Roderick Random* (London, 1748), chapter 29.

Chapter 1
1. LH. Ismay 3/1/1-83, quotes pp. 55, 58.
2. S. Morillo, *What is Military History?* (3rd edn, Cambridge, 2013).
3. A. Searle, 'A very special relationship: Basil Liddell Hart, Wehrmacht generals and the debate on West German rearmament, 1945–1953,' *War in History*, (1998), pp. 327–57.
4. M. Barcia, *West African Warfare in Bahia and Cuba: Soldier Slaves in the Atlantic World, 1807–1844* (Oxford, 2014).
5. J. McQuade, *A Genealogy of Terrorism: Colonial, Law and the Origins of an Idea* (Cambridge, 2020).
6. A reference to the ancient Mesopotamian city.
7. D. Hume, *The History of England from the Invasion of Julius Caesar to the Revolution in 1688* (6 vols, London, 1778) p. 230.
8. W. Urban, *Tannenberg and After: Lithuania, Poland and the Teutonic Order in Search of Immortality* (Chicago, Ill., 2003); S. Ekdahl, 'The Battle of Tannenberg-Grunwald-Žalgiris (1410) as reflected in twentieth-century monuments,' in V. Mallia-Milanes (ed.), *The Military Orders: History and Heritage* III (Farnham, 2008) and 'Different points of view on the Battle of Grunwald/Tannenberg 1410 from Poland and Germany and their roots in handwritten and printed traditions,' *Z Badán nad Książką i Księgozbiorami Historycznymi* (2019), pp. 41–65.
9. G. Duijzings, *Religion and the Politics of Identity in Kosovo* (London, 2000); P. Cohen, *History and Popular Memory: The Power of Story in Moments of Crisis* (New York, 2014).
10. M. Gabriele, *An Empire of Memory: The Legend of Charlemagne, the Franks, and Jerusalem before the First Crusade* (Oxford, 2011).
11. J. Matthews, *Reluctant Warriors: Republican Popular Army and Nationalist Army Conscripts in the Spanish Civil War, 1936–1939* (Oxford, 2012).
12. S. Morillo, 'The Sword of Justice: War and State Formation in Comparative Perspective,' *Journal of Medieval Military History*, (2006), pp. 1–17; G. Sørensen, 'War and State-Making. Why Doesn't It Work in the Third World?', *Security Dialogue* (2001), pp. 341–54; B.D. Taylor and R. Botea, 'Tilly Tally: War-Making and State-Making in the Contemporary Third World,' *International Studies Review* (2008), pp. 27–56; L.B. Kaspersen and J. Strandsbjerg (eds), *Does War Make States? Investigations of Charles Tilly's Historical Sociology* (Cambridge, 2017).
13. C.S. Gray, *Strategy and Defence Planning. Meeting the Challenge of Uncertainty* (Oxford, 2014).
14. G. Hanlon, *Italy 1636: Cemetery of Armies* (Oxford, 2016).
15. K. Helleiner, 'The Vital Revolution Reconsidered,' *Canadian Journal of Economics and Political Science* (1957), p. 1.

16. For a critical examination of the concept of decisive battles, S. Morillo (ed.), *The Battle of Hastings. Sources and Interpretations* (Woodbridge, 1996). See also A. Querengäser, Grosse Schlachten und Belagerungen der Weltgeschichte (Berlin 2024).
17. G. Satterfield, *Princes, Posts and Partisans. The Army of Louis XIV and Partisan Warfare in the Netherlands, 1673–1678* (Leiden, 2003).
18. For a different focus, D. Armitage, *Civil War: A History in Ideas* (New York, 2016).
19. Stone to Black, email, 29 April 2015.
20. S. Morillo 'The "Age of Cavalry" Revisited,' in D. Kagay (ed.), *The Circle of War* (Woodbridge, 1999).
21. J. Browning and T. Silver, *An Environmental History of the Civil War* (Chapel Hill, NC, 2020).
22. J. Black, *War and Technology* (Bloomington, Ind., 2013).
23. Burgoyne to Earl of Shelburne, 1 Nov. 1782, BL., Shelburne papers, vol. 37.

Chapter 2
1. J.M. Black, *Clio's Battles. Historiography in Practice* (Bloomington, Ind., 2015).
2. T.J. Brown, *Civil War Monuments and the Militarization of America* (Chapel Hill, NC, 2019).
3. SLA Marshall, *Men Against Fire: The Problem of Battle Command* (Norman, Ok., 1947). For part of the broader controversy, a controversy which itself brings together many different elements in military history, K.C. Jordan, 'Right for the Wrong Reasons: SLA Marshall and the Ratio of Fire in Korea,' *Military History* (2002), pp. 135–62.
4. G. Russell, *The Theatres of War: Performance, Politics, and Society, 1793–1815* (Oxford, 1995); S. Valladares, *Staging the Peninsular War: English Theatres, 1707–1815* (Farnham, 2015).
5. V. Brown, *Tacky's Revolt. The Story of an Atlantic Slave War* (Cambridge, Mass., 2020).
6. T. Hughes, *The Scouring of the White Horse, or, The Long Vacation Ramble of a London Clerk* (London, 1859); *Historical Associations of the Westbury White Horse* (Westbury, 1871).
7. R.W. Johansen, *To the Halls of the Montezumas: The Mexican War in the American Imagination* (New York, 1985); M.A. Sandweiss et al, *Eyewitness to War: Prints and Daguerreotypes of the Mexican War, 1846–1848* (Washington, 1989); R.C. Tyler, *The Mexican War: A Lithographic Record* (Austin, Tx, 1973); G.W. Kendall, *Dispatches from the Mexican War* edited by L.D. Cress (Norman, Ok., 1999).
8. A.M. Forssberg, *The Story of War: Church and Propaganda in France and Sweden, 1610–1710* (Lund, 2016).
9. J. Adams, *The Works of John Adams*, ed. C.F. Adams (Boston, Mass., 1856) pp. 393–6; J. Boyd (ed.), *Papers of Thomas Jefferson* (Charlottesville, Va.) pp. 364–5.
10. J. Wilson, 'Tactics of Attraction: Saints, Pilgrims and Warriors in the Portuguese Reconquista,' *Portuguese Studies* (2014), pp. 204–21.
11. O. Benesch and R. Zwigenberg, *Japan's Castles: Citadels of Modernity in War and Peace* (Cambridge, 2019).
12. I Beckett, 'Military Commemoration in Britain: A Pre-History,' *Journal of the Society for Army Historical Research* (2014), pp. 147–59; D. Lloyd, *Battlefield Tourism: Pilgrimage and the Commemoration of the Great War in Britain, Australia and Canada, 1919–1939* (London, 1998).
13. C. Ryan (ed.), *Battlefield Tourism. History, Place and Interpretation* (Oxford, 2007), esp. Introduction, p. 1.
14. *Ibid.*, p. 4.
15. The *Times*, 27 June 2023.
16. E. Caudill and P. Ashdown, *Inventing Custer: The Making of an American Legend* (Lanham, MD, 2015).
17. B.J. Fischer, *Albania at War 1939–1945* (London, 1999), p. 24.
18. H. Duccini, *Faire voir, faire croire: L'Opinion publique sous Louis XIII* (Paris, 2003).

19. G. Rowlands, *Financial Decline of a Great Power: War, Influence, and Money in Louis XIV's France* (Oxford, 2012) and *Dangerous and Dishonest Men: The International Bankers of Louis XIV's France* (Basingstoke, 2015).
20. NA. SP. 84/202 fols 73, 126, 84/207 fol. 124.
21. The painting now hangs in the Musée des Beaux-Arts de Lyon.
22. See illustrations in A. Husslein-Arco (ed.), *Prince Eugene's Winter Palace* (Vienna, 2013), esp. pp. 41, 59, 77–84.
23. Leopold I.
24. BL. Stowe Mss. 447 f. 1.
25. A. Sepinwall, *Slave Revolt on Screen: The Haitian Revolution in Film and Video Games* (Jackson, Miss., 2021).
26. J. Hurl-Eamon, *Marriage and the British Army in the Long Eighteenth Century: 'The Girl I Left Behind Me'* (Oxford, 2014); T. Glymph, *The Women's Fight: The Civil War's Battles for Home, Freedom, and Nation* (Chapel Hill, NC, 2020); J. Crang, *Sisters in Arms: Women in the British Armed Forces during the Second World War* (Cambridge, 2020).
27. C. Esdaile, *Women in the Peninsular War* (Norman, Ok., 2014).
28. K.A. Hass, *Carried to the Wall: American Memory and the Vietnam Veterans Memorial* (Berkeley, Calif., 1998).
29. S. Williams, *White Malice: The CIA and the Neocolonisation of Africa* (London, 2021); N. Telepneva, *Cild War Liberation: The Soviet Union and the Collapse of the Portuguese Empire in Africa, 1961–75* (Chapel Hill, NC, 2021).

Chapter 3
1. T. Blackmore, *Gorgeous War: The Branding War between the Third Reich and the United States* (Waterloo, Canada, 2019).
2. J. Grey (ed.), *The Last Word? Essays on Official History in the United States and British Commonwealth* (Westport, Conn., 2003).
3. B. Robson, 'The Strange Case of the Missing Official History,' *Soldiers of the Queen*, 76 (1984), pp. 3–6; I. Beckett, 'The Historiography of Small Wars: Early Histories and the South African War,' *Small Wars and Insurgencies* (1991), pp. 276–98.
4. M. Seligmann, 'Sir Henry Newbolt, the Naval Staff, and the Writing of the Official History of the Origins and Inauguration of Convoy in 1917,' *JMH*, 87 (2023), pp. 125–44.
5. D. Welch, *Germany and Propaganda in World War I: Pacifism, Mobilisation and Total War* (London, 2014).
6. Recent, relatively positive, accounts, that correct earlier work, include G. Sheffield, *Forgotten Victory. The First World War: Myths and Realities* (London, 2002) and M. Seligmann, 'A Service Ready for Total War? The State of the Royal Navy in July 1914,' *EHR*, 133 (2018), pp. 98–122.
7. C. Bell, *Churchill and the Dardanelles* (Oxford, 2017).
8. P. Haun, 'Foundation Bias: The Impact of the Air Corps Tactical School on United States Air Force Doctrine,' *JMH*, 85 (2021), pp. 453–74.
9. M. Faulkner and C. Bell (eds), *Decision in the Atlantic: The Allies and the Longest Campaign of the Second World War* (Lexington, KY, 2019).
10. M. Uyar and S. Güvenç, 'One Battle and Two Accounts: The Turkish Brigade at Kunu-ri in November 1950,' *JMH*, 80 (2016), pp. 1117–47, esp. 1142–3.
11. J. Hutečka, *Men Under Fire: Motivation, Morale and Masculinity Among Czech Soldiers in the Great War, 1914–1918* (New York, 2020).

Chapter 4
1. E.A. Fraser, *Delacroix, Art, and Patrimony in Post-Revolutionary France* (Cambridge, 2004).
2. *Times*, 4 May 2023.
3. An excellent example is J. Lopez, N. Aubin, V. Bernardo and N. Guillerat, *World War Two: Infographics* (London, 2019), which is the translation of a French original.

Chapter 5
1. P.B. Ellis and P. Williams, *By Jove, Biggles!* (London, 1981).
2. S.A. Carney, *The Occupation of Mexico, 1846–1848* (Washington, 2006), p. 27.
3. Sir James Graham, First Lord of the Admiralty, to Fitzroy, Lord Raglan, commander of the British land forces sent to the Black Sea, 8 Oct., 22 Nov. 1854, BL. Add. 79696 fols 131, 135.
4. R.J.B. Knight, *Convoys: The British Struggle Against Napoleonic Europe and America* (New Haven, Conn., 2022).
5. W.J. Nutall, *Britain and the Bomb: Technology, Culture, and the Cold War* (Dunbeath, 2019).
6. Q. Zhai, '*China and the Vietnam Wars, 1950–1975* (Chapel Hill, NC, 1999); X. Li, *Building Ho's Army: Chinese Military Assistance to North Vietnam* (Lexington, KY, 2019).
7. T.S. Wolters, 'Harvey A. DeWeerd and the Dawn of Academic Military History in the United States,' *JMH*, 85 (2021), pp. 95–133.
8. M.P. Bradley and M.L. Dudziak (eds), *Making the Forever War: Marilyn B. Young on the Culture and Politics of American Militarism* (Amherst, Mass., 2021).
9. J. Grey, *The Austrian Army* (Oxford, 2001).
10. M. Thompson, *Disputed Decisions of World War II: Decision Science and Game Theory Perspectives* (Jefferson, NC, 2019).
11. A.D. Lee, *Warfare in the Roman World* (Cambridge, 2020).

Chapter 6
1. A.D. Lee, *Warfare in the Roman World* (Cambridge, 2020).
2. J. Malegam, *The Sleep of Behemoth: Disputing Peace and Violence in Medieval Europe, 1000–1200* (Ithaca, NY, 2013).
3. T. Brekke (ed.), *The Ethics of War in Asian Civilizations: A Comparative Perspective* (London, 2006); S. Morillo, 'A General Typology of Transcultural Wars: The Early Middle Ages and Beyond,' in H.H. Kortüm (ed.), *Transcultural Wars from the Middle Ages to the 21st Century* (Berlin, 2006), pp. 29–42, and 'Justifications, Theories and Customs of War,' in D. Graff et al (eds), *The Cambridge History of War* I (Cambridge, 2013), pp. 615–39; M. Adolphson, *The Teeth and Claws of the Buddha: Monastic Warriors and Sōhei in Japanese History* (Honolulu, HI, 2007).
4. See S. Melville, *The Campaigns of Sargon II, King of Assyria, 721–705 B.C.* (Norman, Ok., 2016); M. Healy, *The Ancient Assyrians: Empire and Army, 883–612 BC* (Oxford, 2023).
5. T. Wilkinson, *Ramesses the Great* (New Haven, Conn., 2023).
6. R Cox, *Origins of the Just War. Military Ethics and Culture in the Ancient Near East* (Princeton, NJ, 2023).
7. R.D. Cox, *The Religious Life of Robert E. Lee* (Grand Rapids, Mich., 2017).
8. J. Rubenstein, *Nebuchadnezzar's Dream: The Crusades, Apocalyptic Prophecy, and the End of History* (Oxford, 2019).
9. A. Wink, *The Making of the Indo-Islamic World, c. 700–1800 CE* (Cambridge, 2020).
10. M.J. Taylor, *Soldiers and Silver: Mobilising Resources in the Age of Roman Conquest* (Austin, TX, 2020).

11. J. Bellis and L. Slater (eds), *Representing War and Violence 1250–1600* (Woodbridge, 2016); C. Taylor, *Chivalry and the Ideals of Knighthood in France during the Hundred Years War* (Cambridge, 2016).
12. J. Bellis (ed.), *John Page's 'The Siege of Rouen'* (Heidelberg, 2015).
13. C. Tyerman, *How to Plan a Crusade: Reason and Religious War in the High Middle Ages* (London, 2015).
14. T. McArthur, 'Should Roman Soldiers be Called "Professional" Prior to Augustus?,' *JMH*, 85 (2021), pp. 9–26.
15. C.H. Lange and F.J. Vervaet (eds), *The Historiography of Late Republican Civil War* (Leiden, 2019).
16. D. Hoyos, *Carthage's Other Wars: Carthaginian Warfare Outside the 'Punic Wars' against Rome* (Barnsley, 2019), and J. Rop, *Greek Military Service in the Ancient Near East, 401–330 BCE* (Cambridge, 2019).
17. K.F. Jensen (ed.), *The History of the Danes: Saxo Grammaticus, Gesta Danorum* (Oxford, 2015).
18. B.S. Bachrach, *Charlemagne's Early Campaigns (768–777): A Diplomatic and Military Analysis* (Leiden, 2013); L. Petersen, *Siege Warfare and Military Organisation in the Successor States, 400–800 AD* (Leiden, 2013).
19. G. Halsall, *Warfare and Society in the Barbarian West, 450–900* (London, 2003); S. Morillo and R. Abels, 'A Lying Legacy? A Preliminary Discussion of Images of Antiquity and Altered Reality in Medieval Military History,' *Journal of Medieval Military History* (2005), pp. 1–13.
20. S. Morillo, 'Battle Seeking, 'The Contexts and Limits of Vegetian Strategy', *Journal of Medieval Military History* (2002), pp. 21–41.

Chapter 7
1. J. Black, 'Modernisation Theory and (some of) the conceptual flaws of the Early-Modern Military Revolution,' *Nuova Antologia Militare* (June 2022), pp. 3–7.
2. R.H. Jackson, *Conflict and Conversion in Sixteenth Century Central Mexico: The Augustinian War On and Beyond the Chichimeca Frontier* (Leiden, 2013).
3. A.W. Devereux, *The Other Side of Empire: Just War in the Mediterranean and the Rise of Early Modern Spain* (Ithaca, NY, 2020).
4. J.K. Thornton, *A History of West Central Africa to 1850* (Cambridge, 2020).
5. D. Grummitt, 'The Defence of Calais and the Development of Gunpowder Weaponry in England in the Late Fifteenth Century', *War in History* (2000), pp. 253–72.
6. G. Hanlon, *The Twilight of a Military Tradition: Italian Aristocrats and European Conflicts, 1560–1800* (London, 1996); W. Maltby, *Alba* (Berkeley, Calif., 1983).
7. D. and B. Bachrach, *Writing the Military History of Pre-Crusade Europe: Studies in Sources and Source Criticism* (London, 2021).
8. C. Nall, *Reading and War in Fifteenth-Century England: From Lydgate to Malory* (Woodbridge, 2012).
9. R. Appelbaum, *Terrorism Before the Letter. Mythography and Political Violence in England, Scotland, and France, 1559–1642* (Oxford, 2015).
10. G. Parker, 'The Limits of Revolutions in Military Affairs: Maurice of Nassau, the Battle of Nieuwpoort (1600), and the Legacy', *Journal of Military History* (2007), pp. 331–47.
11. T. Smollett, *Travels through France and Italy* (London, 1766), chapter 32.
12. P. Brugh, *Gunpowder, Masculinity, and Warfare in German Texts, 1400–1700* (Rochester, NY, 2019).
13. R.M. Eaton and P.B. Wagoner, 'Warfare on the Deccan Plateau, 1450–1600: A Military Revolution in Early Modern India?', *Journal of World History* (2014), p. 50.

14. B. Teschke, 'Revisiting the "War-Makes-States" Thesis: War, Taxation and Social Property Relations in Early Modern Europe', in O. Asbach and P. Schröder (eds), *War, the State and International Law in Seventeenth-Century Europe* (Farnham, 2010), p. 58.
15. D. Parrott, *Richelieu's Army: War, Government and Society in France, 1624–1642* (Cambridge, 2002); G. Rowlands, *The Dynastic State and the Army under Louis XIV: Royal Service and Private Interest, 1661–1701* (Cambridge, 2002).
16. A. Hopper, '"The Great Blow" and the Politics of Popular Royalism in Civil War Norwich,' *EHR*, 133 (2018), pp. 32–64.
17. P. Gaunt, *The English Civil War: A Military History* (London, 2014).
18. G. Rowlands, *The Financial Decline of a Great Power: War, Influence, and Money in Louis XIV's France* (Oxford, 2012).
19. J. Osman, *Citizen Soldiers and the Key to the Bastille* (Basingstoke, 2015).
20. For a typical failure to engage with this longer resonance, T. Claydon and C. Levillain (eds), *Louis XIV Outside In: Images of the Sun King Beyond France, 1661–1715* (Farnham, 2015).
21. P. McCluskey, *Absolute Monarchy on the Frontiers: Louis XIV's Military Occupations of Lorraine and Savoy* (Manchester, 2013).
22. D. Bell, *The First Total War. Napoleon's Europe and the Birth of Warfare as We Know It* (Boston, Mass., 2007). This is seriously flawed as a result of its limited engagement with earlier periods and non-Western warfare.
23. G. Baker, *Spare No One: Mass Violence in Roman Warfare* (Lanham, MD, 2021).

Chapter 8

1. T. Munck, *Conflict and Enlightenment: Print and Political Culture in Europe, 1635–1795* (Cambridge, 2019).
2. A. Lovelace, 'Meade and the Media: Civil War Journalism and the New History of War Reporting,' *Journal of Military History* (2021), pp. 907–29.
3. G. Quilley, *Empire to Nation: Art, History and the Visualisation of Maritime Britain, 1768–1829* (New Haven, Conn., 2011).
4. E. Nares, *A Sermon, Preached at the Parish Church of Shobdon ...* (no place, 1798).
5. L. Reynolds, *Who Owned Waterloo? Battle, Memory, and Myth in British History, 1815–1852* (Oxford, 2022); I. Beckett, *Military Panoramas: Battle in the Round, 1800–1914* (London, 2022).
6. S.J. Pratt, *Gleanings through Wales, Holland and Westphalia* (3 vols, London, 1795), II, 532.
7. B. de Graaf, *Fighting Terror after Napoleon: How Europe Became Secure after 1815* (Cambridge, 2020).
8. J. Waley-Cohen, *The Culture of War in China: Empire and the Military Under the Qing Dynasty* (London, 2006).
9. K. Swope, *Struggle for Empire in Nineteenth-Century China: The Battles of General Quo Zongtang* (Annapolis, MD., 2024).
10. Colonel James Hawthorne to Henry, Viscount Sidmouth, 17 July 1807, Exeter, Devon Record Office, 152 M/C 1807/018.
11. J. Pinheiro, *Missionaries of Republicanism: A Religious History of the Mexican-American War* (Oxford, 2014).
12. Delbrück to his mother, 11 Sept. 1870, in A. Bucholz (ed.), *Delbruck's Modern Military History* (Lincoln, NB, 1997), p 49.
13. J.E. Sessions, *By Sword and Plow: France and the Conquest of Algeria* (Ithaca, NY, 2011).
14. J.S. Reed, *The U.S. Volunteers in the Southern Philippines: Counterinsurgency, Pacification, and Collaboration, 1899–1901* (Lawrence, KS, 2020).
15. F. Holyday, *Bismarck's Rival: A Political Biography of General and Admiral Albrecht von Stosch* (Durham, NC., 1960).

16. L. Rosenthal and V. Rodic (eds), *The New Nationalism and the First World War* (Basingstoke, 2015).
17. P. Yeandle, *Citizenship, Nation, Empire: The Politics of History Teaching in England, 1870–1930* (Manchester, 2015).
18. S. Amirell, *Pirates of Empire: Colonisation and Maritime Violence in Southeast Asia* (Cambridge, 2019).
19. Z.A. Fry, *A Republic in the Ranks: Loyalty and Dissent in the Army of the Potomac* (Chapel Hill, NC, 2020); P.D. Escott, *The Worst Passions of Human Nature: White Supremacy in the Civil War North* (Charlottesville, Va., 2020).
20. O.B. Hemmerle, 'Learning from Decisive Battles. Prerequisites to Define and Identify Them. The legacy of Sir Edward S. Creasy for the imagination and predictions of war,' *Estonian Yearbook of Military History* (2017), pp. 60–88.
21. King's College London, Liddell Hart Archive, Hamilton papers 4/2/9, p. 10.
22. Hamilton to Richard Haldane, Secretary of State for War, 1 Sept. 1909, KCL. Hamilton 4/2/6, p. 5.
23. G.C. Cox, 'Of Aphorisms, Lessons and Paradigms: Comparing the British and German Official Histories of the Russo-Japanese War,' *JMH*, 66 (1992), pp. 389–401; S.P. Mackenzie, 'Willpower or Firepower? The Unlearned Military Lessons of the Russo-Japanese War,' in D. Wells and S. Wilson (eds), *The Russo-Japanese War in Cultural Perspective, 1904–05* (London, 1999), p. 367.
24. R. Hall, *The Balkan Wars 1912–13. Prelude to the First World War* (London, 2000), p. 134.
25. R. Bentley, *Considerations upon the State of Public Affairs* (London, 1798), p. 63.
26. H.J. Mackinder, 'The Geographical Pivot of History,' *Geographical Journal* (1904), pp. 423, 429.
27. J. Hevia, *The Imperial Security State: British Colonial Knowledge and Empire-Building in Asia* (Cambridge, 2015)
28. S.P. Mackenzie, *Revolutionary Armies in the Modern Era: A Revisionist Approach* (London, 1997).
29. I. Beckett, *Rorke's Drift and Isandlwana* (Oxford, 2019), pp. 23–4.
30. H. Cohen, *Year Zero of the Arab-Israeli Conflict: 1929* (Brandeis, Mass., 2015).
31. R.A. Butlin, 'Historical Geographies of the British Empire, *c.* 1887–1925'; M. Bell, Butlin and M. Heferman (eds), *Geography and Imperialism 1820–1940* (Manchester, 1995), pp. 169–70.
32. A.J. Echevarria, *Clausewitz and Contemporary War* (Oxford, 2007); A. Herberg-Rothe, *Clausewitz's Puzzle: The Political Theory of War* (Oxford, 2007); H. Strachan, *Clausewitz's On War: A Biography* (New York, 2007).
33. M. Howard, 'The Influence of Clausewitz', in Carl von Clausewitz, *On War*, edited by Howard and P. Paret (Princeton, NJ., 1976, London, 1993 edn), pp. 40–1; B. Heuser, *Reading Clausewitz* (London, 2002), p. 15.
34. P. von Wahlde, 'A Pioneer of Russian Strategic Thought: G.A. Leer, 1829–1904', *Military Affairs* (1971), pp. 148–151.
35. G. Wawro, *The Franco-Prussian War. The German Conquest of France in 1870–1871* (Cambridge, 2003), pp. 307–8.
36. The work was published in full in French, German, Polish and Russian.
37. M. Welch, 'The Centenary of the British Publication of Jean de Bloch's *Is War Now Impossible?*', *War in History* (2000), pp. 273–94.
38. Aside from Austria and Prussia, Austria's German allies such as Hanover.
39. D. Whittingham, *Charles E. Callwell and the British Way in Warfare* (Cambridge, 2020).
40. B.A. Elman, 'Naval Warfare and the Refraction of China's Self-Strengthening Reforms into Scientific and Technological Failure,' *Modern Asian Studies* (2004), pp. 283–326.

41. T. Meyer-Fong, *What Remains: Coming to Terms with Civil War in Nineteenth-Century China* (Stanford, Calif., 2015).
42. M. Mosca, *From Frontier Policy to Foreign Policy: The Question of India and the Transformation of Geopolitics in Qing China* (Stanford, Calif., 2013).

Chapter 9
1. B. Houston, *Twice Round the Clock* (London, 1935), pp. 78–80.
2. M.L. Roberts, *Sheer Misery: Soldiers in Battle in WWII* (Chicago, 2021).
3. D. Monger, *Patriotism and Propaganda in First World War Britain: The National War Aims Committee and Civilian Morale* (Liverpool, 2012).
4. J. Crouthamel, *Trauma, Religion, and Spirituality in Germany during the First World War* (London, 2021).
5. This was indeed the case.
6. E. Demm, *Censorship and Propaganda in World War I: A Comprehensive History* (London, 2019).
7. J. Wellington, *Exhibiting War: The Great War, Museums, and Memory in Britain, Canada, and Australia* (Cambridge, 2017).
8. A. Fox, *Learning to Fight: Military Innovation and Change in the British Army, 1914–1918* (Cambridge, 2018).
9. D. Clayton, *Decisive Victory: The Battle of the Sambre, 4 November 1918* (Wolverhampton, 2018).
10. J. Fantauzzo, *The Other Wars: The Experience and Memory of the First World War in the Middle East and Macedonia* (Cambridge, 2020).
11. D.E. Delaney and N. Gardner (eds), *Turning Point 1917: The British Empire at War* (Vancouver, 2017).
12. M.J. McConahay, *The Tango War: The Struggle for the Hearts, Minds and Riches of Latin America during World War II* (New York, 2018).
13. A. Bucholz, *Hans Delbrück and the German Military Establishment* (Lincoln, NB, 1997).
14. D. Showalter, J. Robinson and J. Robinson, *The German Failure in Belgium, August 1914* (Jefferson, NC, 2019).
15. D. Zabecki, *The German 1918 Offensives: a case study in the operational level of war* (Abingdon, 2006).
16. R. Reese, *The Imperial Russian Army in Peace, War, and Revolution, 1856–1917* (Lawrence, KS, 2019).
17. E. Greenhalgh, 'Myth and Memory: Sir Douglas Haig and the Imposition of Allied Unified Command in March 1918,' *JMH*, 68 (2004), pp. 771–820, *Victory Through Coalition: Britain and France during the First World War* (Cambridge, 2005) and *Foch in Command: The Forging of a First World War General* (Cambridge, 2014); B. Apter, '"Old Men Forget" or do they "Remember with Advantages"? The Problem of Primary Sources and Objectivity', *History in the Making* (2012), pp. 83–91.
18. J.P. Melzer, *Wings for the Rising Sun: A Transnational History of Japanese Aviation* (Cambridge, Mass., 2020).
19. J. Horne and A. Kramer, *German Atrocities 1914: A History of Denial* (New Haven, Conn., 2001).
20. G. Spraul, *Der Franktireurkrieg 1914: Untersuchungen zum Verfall einer Wissenschaft und zum Umgang mit nationalen Mythen* (Berlin, 2016).
21. G. Wawro, *Sons of Freedom: The Forgotten American Soldiers Who Defeated Germany in World War I* (New York, 2018).
22. V. Newman, *Children at War, 1914–18: 'It's My War Too!'* (Barnsley, 2019).

23. R-D. Müller, *Enemy in the East. Hitler's Secret Plans to Invade the Soviet Union* (London, 2015).
24. K.H. Schmider, *Hitler's Fatal Miscalculation. Why Germany Declared War on the United States* (Cambridge, 2021).
25. J. Gilmour and J. Stephenson (eds), *Hitler's Scandinavian Legacy* (London, 2013).
26. D. Zakheim, 'Revisiting Naval Power in World War Two,' *Orbis* (2022), p. 448.
27. M. Snape, *God and Uncle Sam: Religion and America's Armed Forces in World War II* (Woodbridge, 2015).
28. M. Brown, *Politics of Forgetting: New Zealand, Greece, and Britain at War* (Melbourne, 2019).
29. For the wider issue, S. Jaeger, *The Second World War in the Twenty-first Century Museum: From Narrative, Memory and Experience to Experientiality* (Boston, Mass., 2020).
30. S. Ball, *Alamein* (Oxford, 2016).
31. M. Dolski, *D-Day Remembered: the Normandy Landings in American Collective Memory* (Knoxville, Tenn., 2016).
32. B. Bailey and D. Farber (eds), *Beyond Pearl Harbor: A Pacific History* (Lawrence, KS, 2019).
33. Y. Khan, *India at War: The Subcontinent and the Second World War* (Oxford, 2015).
34. S. Tsoutsoumpis, *A History of the Greek Resistance in the Second World War: The People's Armies* (Manchester, 2016).
35. J. Ruiz, *The 'Red Terror' and the Spanish Civil War: Revolutionary Violence in Madrid* (Cambridge, 2014).
36. R. Mitter, *China's Good War: How World War II Is Shaping a New Nationalism* (Cambridge, Mass., 2020).
37. A. Hill, *The Red Army and the Second World War* (Cambridge, 2017).
38. G. Clark, *Everyday Violence in the Irish Civil War* (Cambridge, 2014); E. Biagini, 'The Irish Revolution, 1916–23,' *EHR*, 131 (2016), pp. 122–32.
39. J. Crang, *Sisters in Arms: Women in the British Armed Forces during the Second World War* (Cambridge, 2020).
40. E. Westermann, *Hitler's Ostkrieg and the India Wars: Comparing Genocide and Conquest* (Norman, Ok., 2016).
41. C. Korieh, *Nigeria and World War II: Colonialism, Empire and Global Conflict* (Cambridge, 2020).
42. S. Keller, *Russia and Central Asia: Coexistence, Conquest, Convergence* (Toronto, 2020).

Chapter 10
1. S. Plokhy, *The Russo-Ukrainian War* (London, 2023).
2. J. Haldon, *The Empire That Would Not Die: The Paradox of Eastern Roman Survival* (Cambridge, Mass., 2016).
3. V.D. Hanson, 'Why Study War?', *Army History* (2008), pp. 26–32.
4. Covering 1900–64, E. Shesko, *Conscript Nation: Coercion and Citizenship in the Bolivian Barracks* (Pittsburg, Penn., 2022).
5. M. Gordon, *Film is Like a Battleground: Sam Fuller's War Movies* (New York, 2017).
6. S.P. Mackenzie, *Bomber Boys on Screen: R.A.F. Bomber Command in Film and Television Drama* (London, 2019).
7. B. Cochran, J. Judge and A. Shubert (eds), *Women Warriors and National Heroes: Global Histories* (London, 2020).
8. A. Barros and M. Thomas (eds), *The Civilianization of War: The Changing Civil-Military Divide 1914–2014* (Cambridge, 2018).
9. S.C. Smith (ed.), *The Wilson-Johnson Correspondence, 1964–69* (Farnham, 2015).

10. E.R. May, *'Lessons' of the Past: The Use and Misuse of History in American Foreign Policy* (London, 1973); Y.F. Khong, *Analogies at War: Korea, Munich, Dien Bien Phu and the Vietnam Decisions of 1965* (Princeton, NJ, 1992); E. Schrecker (ed.), *Cold War Triumphalism: The Misuse of History after the Fall of Communism* (New York, 2004); D.H. Noon, 'Operation Enduring Analogy: World War II, the War on Terror, and the Uses of Historical Memory,' *Rhetoric and Public Affairs* (2004), pp. 339–66; L.C. Gardner and M.B. Young (eds), *Iraq and the Lessons of Vietnam* (New York, 2007); J.H. Willbanks, 'The Legacy of the Vietnam War for the US Army,' in A. Wiest, M.K. Barbier and G. Robins (eds), *America and the Vietnam War: Re-examining the Culture and History of a Generation* (New York, 2010), pp. 271–88.
11. EOKA wanted union with Greece, not independence and partition. D. French, *Fighting EOKA: The British Counter-Insurgency Campaign on Cyprus, 1955–1959* (Oxford, 2015).
12. S. Plakoudas, *The Greek Civil War. Strategy, Counterinsurgency, and the Monarchy* (London, 2017).
13. F. Finchelstein, *The Ideological Origins of the Dirty War: Fascism, Populism and Dictatorship in Twentieth Century Argentina* (Oxford, 2014).
14. D.L. Anderson, *Vietnamization: Politics, Strategy, Legacy* (Lanham, MD, 2019).
15. E.S. Rafuse, *From Mountains to the Bay: The War in Virginia, January-May 1862* (Lawrence, KS, 2023).
16. C.J. Tyerman, 'Commoners on Crusade: The Creation of Political Space?,' *EHR*, 136 (2021), pp. 245–75.
17. For an analogous discussion of political history, K. Kowol, 'His(Tory): why British History needs Conservatives,' *Political Quarterly*, 94 (2023), pp. 265–71.
18. For example, for criticisms of Grant for misrepresentation of Union generalship, F.P. Varney, *General Grant and the Rewriting of History* (El Dorado Hills, Calif., 2013) and *General Grant and the Verdict of History. Memoir, Memory, and the Civil War* (El Dorado Hills, Calif., 2023).
19. A. Laaneots, 'Two Histories of World War II,' *Estonian Yearbook of Military History* (2014), pp. 263–94.
20. D.A. Messenger, *War and Public Memory: Case Studies in Twentieth-Century Europe* (Tuscaloosa, Al., 2020).
21. J. Michalska, 'Outcry over Polish government's changes to Second World War museum,' *The Art Newspaper*, 21 Dec. 2017.
22. O. Jonsson, *The Russian Understanding of War: Blurring the Lines between War and Peace* (Washington, 2019).
23. D. Fitzgerald, *Learning to Forget: U.S. Army Counterinsurgency Doctrine from Vietnam to Iraq* (Stanford, Calif., 2013).
24. E.M. Spiers, *Wars of Intervention: A Case-Study – The Reconquest of the Sudan 1896–1899* (Camberley, 1998), pp. 46–7.
25. N.J. Schlosser, 'The Iraq War. Twenty Years Later,' *Army History* (winter 2023), p. 22.
26. C.F. Meyskens, *Mao's Third Front: The Militarization of Cold War China* (Cambridge, 2020).
27. D. Robinson, *Ming China and Its Allies: Imperial Rule in Eurasia* (Cambridge, 2020).
28. M. Stith, *Extreme Civil War: Guerrilla Warfare, Environment, and Race on the Trans-Mississippi Frontier* (Baton Rouge, LA, 2016).
29. See also J. Black, *A Brief History of History* (Bloomington, Ind, 2023).

Chapter 11
1. C. Meyskens, *Mao's Third Front: The Militarization of Cold War China* (CUP, 2020).
2. S. Plokhy, *The Russo-Ukrainian War* (London, 2023), p. 161.
3. 'Charlemagne' [Anon.], 'Bakhmut and the Spirit of Verdun,' *The Economist*, vol. 447, no. 9349 (June 2023), p. 30.

4. D. Stoker, *Why America Loses Wars: Limited War and US Strategy from the Korean War to the Present* (Cambridge, 2019); J. Black, *Military Strategy: A Global History* (New Haven, Conn., 2020).
5. L. Pawson, *In the Name of the People: Angola's Forgotten Massacre* (London, 2014).

Index

Abbasid rulers, 85
Abyssinia
   British expedition, 122
Achilles, Trojan War, 10, 70
Actium (31 BCE), 100
Adams, John, 34
Aelianus Tacticus, 97
Aelan, 98
Afghanistan, 5, 65 –7, 123, 178, 179
Africa, 90, 108
Age of Cavalry, 21
Albigensians, heresy and Cathars, 72, 104
Alberti, Leon Battista, *De Re Aedificatoria*, 97
Algeria, Algiers, 90, 118, 160
Ain Jalut (1260), 85
Air-photography depicting war, 30–1
Ajax armoured vehicle programme, 53
Alcobaça (UNESCO Heritage Site, 29
Alexander the Great, 10–11, 39, 82
Alfonso IV, 29
Alfred, the Great, 31, 77
Alien, *The Tactics of Alien or the Art of Embattling an Army after the Grecian Method* (London 1616), 98
All Quiet on the Western Front, 137
Alma, 33
America, 59, 66, 145, 120, 128
   Iraq, Vietnam and Afghanistan, 5
   Soviet Union, 5
   air power, 22
   nuclear power, 22
   submarine warfare, 51
   First World War, 61–2
   Canada, attempts to conquer, 120
   Vietnam War, 160
   military history, 160
   Japan and great power competition, 195
American Air Corps, 144 1941
   see also Pearl Harbor
American war of Independence (1775–83), 31
American 'history of wars', 58–9

American Wars against Britain (1775–83) and (1812–15 and 1812–15), 120
American Air War Plans Division 1, 144–5
   see also Luftwaffe
American reading of Second World War, 149
American Civil War (1861–5), 12, 16, 26–7, 34, 36, 49, 61, 120, 124, 172–3
   statues, 26–7
   'Lost Cause', 185
   see also Lee, Robert E. Lee
Andalusia, 81
Anglosphere, 119
Anglo-Sudan War (1896–90), 112–3
Angola, 65, 87, 90
Ankara (1402), 85
Annagudi (1782), 168
Anti-Comintern Pact (1936), 128
Antietam (1662), 36
Antioch, 35
Antiochus (Seleucid King r.192–187 BCE), 82
Argentina, 84
   and 'dirty war' (1976–82), 178
Arteaga, Sebastion Lopez de (1610–52), 71
artificial intelligence (AI)
   strategy, 181–2, 190
   and military revolution, 193
Asanti War, 122
Ashurbanpal (Assyria), 73–4
Ashurbanipal, King and Susa capture (653 BCE), 73
Astley, Philip, *The Battle of Waterloo*, 113
Aurangzeb, Mughal Emperor, 7
Auschwitz, 35
   see also Holocaust
Austerlitz, 53
Austria, 108
Austro-Prussian war (1866), 130

Badar (siege 1646), 41
Babar (r.1526–30), 11
Baghdad, 85

Balaclava (1854), 115
Baltic States, 157
Balkan Wars (1912–13), 126
Baltic Defence Council, 155
Baltic Republics, 193
Bank Hill (1775), 120
Banks, *Compendious History of the House of Austria and German Empire*, 106–7
Baptista della Vallie, (*Libro Continente Appertinentie à Capitani, Ritenere e Fortificare una Citta con Bastionni*) 97–8
Barker, Henry Aston
  and Waterloo (1815), 113
Barrès, 35
Basra, 67
Bastille Day, 71
Battle of the Atlantic, 16
battlefields as history, 34–5
Bean, C E W, 139
BEF (British Expeditionary Force), 49
Beja, 82
Belgium, 62
  invasion (1914), 143
Beloc, Hilaire
  and *The Modern Traveller*, 122–3
Benkos Bioho, Slave rebellion, 30
Bentley, Richard, 126
Bialaszewski, Alexander, Proud Warriors :African American Combat Units in World War II 170
Bible, the
  divine intervention, 70
Biden, President Joe, 148
  Hiroshima and nuclear power, 148
Biggles (1932–68), 61
  see Children's war stories
  see Johns, William
Billie Houston, *Twice Round the Clock*, 136
Black Sea, 171
Blenheim (1704), 107
Blenheim Column of Victory (1730), 107
blitzkrieg, 3
Bloch, Jan G, 131–2
Bodkin, Mathias McDonnell and 'Murder by Proxy' (1897), 111
Boer War (1899–1902), 50, 111, 122, 125, 173–5
Bolingbroke, Viscount Henry, 107–08
  see also Craftsman, the
  see also Marlborough, John, 1st Duke
Bolivia, 157
Bond, Brian, 168
Boris III (1918–436), 54

Bosch, Heteronymous, 29
Boulanger, Georges, 116
Borneo 'Confrontation', 152
Boyne (1690), 115
BJP (Bharatiya Janata Party 57
  see Modi, Narendra
'Black Lives Matter', 28
'Black Peter', 119
  see Arthur Conan Doyle
Black Sea, 171
Bolivia, 157
Bond, Brian *see* End of History
Boyne (1690), 115
Brahmaputra, 92
Brandywine, (1777), 169
Brazil, 117, 159
  and *Favelas*, 178
Breda, siege (1625), 39
Brigadier Gerard, 109
  see Doyle, Arthur Conan
Brigs, Andy, 4
Britain, 45–6, 65–6, 91, 114–5, 117, 118
  history, xx
  and Russian intervention in Central and Western Europe, 27
British Army Museum, 55
British Empire and Soviet Empire, 153
British Expeditionary Force, *see* BEF
British Institution for Promoting the Fine Arts
  and Waterloo (1815), 113
British Somaliland, 1–2
  air attacks on Mullah's base, 1
  Italy, conquered by, 1940, 1
  neglect by Britain, 1
British 'Ultra' System, 50
Brown, Cecil, 118
  see also Doyle, Arthur Conan
Brun, Charles Le, *The Second Conquest of Franche-Comté 1628)*, 39
Bucha
  massacre and rapes, 30
  see also Ukraine
Buchan, John, Lord Tweedsmuir
  and foreign policy of a democrat, 143
  and *Nelson's History of the War*, 138
Buckingham, George, Duke of, 40
Buda (siege 1646), 41
Bulgaria, 53–54, 191
  see also Peace Park
Buller, Sir Redvers, 28
Bundeswehr, 27
Burgoyne, Major General, John, 23

Butler, Lady and *Balaclava* (1876, 115
  see also Balaclava (1854)
Byron, Lord, 34–5
Byzantium, 84, 99

Cahn, Mirriam, 29–30
Calabria, 63
Campbell, John, *Military History of the late Prince Eugene of Savoy and the late Duke of Marlborough* (1736), 106
Canadian Institute of International Affairs, 143
Canae (216 BCE), 8
Canevari, Colonel Emilio, 37
Cane, Alfred, 123
Cantabrian Mountain range, refuge 84
Carlist Wars (1833–40), 123–4
Carthage (and Rome), 81
Carrhae (53 BCE), 171
castles in war, 35–6
casualties
  see also Engels, Frederick, 131
Catholic Church
  and fascism, 164
  and Resistance, 164
Catalan (rising 1640), 38
Cavour, Camillo, 121
Ceausescu regime, 27 (cedilla on s)
Central African Republic, 45
Ceylon (Sri Lanka), 13
Chad, 155
Charlamagne, (Charles the Great), 11
Charles III, 46
Charles V Emperor (r.1519–56), 92, 107
Charles VIII, 40
Charles I 40
Charles II, 34
Charles XII, 18
Charles VIII, 40
Charles X (overthrow 1830), 58
Chesney, George, *The Fall of England?* (1871), 116
Chechnya, 155
Chichimec (demonic agents), 89
  see also New Spain, 89
children's novels and war, 61
Chile, 108, 164
China, 10, 11, 22, 46, 55, 59, 64, 66, 75, 92, 93, 100, 114, 128, 134–5, 150–1, 157–8, 160, 169, 184, 191
  dynasties, 11, 77–8
  tat ung (great harmony)19
  scientific and technical development, 22

Hann, 24, 114
Opium War, 62
contentious issues and history, 65–8
'Ora, god of fertility and war, 75
rules–based international relations, 112
Manchu rule, 114
Muslim rebellion, 114
military capacity, 133–5
American Confederacy, 134
Taiping rebellion, 134
Japan, 145, 152
Communist Party, 150–1
political model, 159
strategic culture, 170
Confucian culture, 171
and war–making, 171
mercantile expansion, 173, 177
preparation for war, 174
artificial intelligence (AI), 182
  see also Peace Park
  see also Mao Zedong
  see also Ming
  see also Tang
  see also Xi Jinping
Chinese–Vietnam War (1979), 65
Chinggis Khan (d.1227), 11, 144
Chivalry, 94
Christian Democrats
  and Resistance, 164
Christian Military Orders, 101
Christianity as peaceful theme, 147–8
chronology control, 167–171
Churchill, (Sir) Winston, 51–2, 121–2
  and *The River War and the Reconquest of the Soudan* (1899).
  and Omdurman, 169
  see also Anglo–Sudan War (1896–9)
  see also Dardanelles
City as battlefield, 187
civil wars, 16
  American Civil War (1861–5)
  English Civil War (1642–6, 1648)
  Spanish Civil, War (1936–9)
Clausewitz, Carl von (1780–1831), *On War (Von Krieg)*, 2–3, 9–10, 27, 62, 110, 129–130
Cochrane, Colonel, 118
  see also Doyle, Arthur Conan
Colantonio, Marzio di, *Alexander the Great and the Conquest of Asia* (1620), 11
Cold War, (1989–94) 27–8, 43, 50, 104, 128, 154–5, 167, 174–5, 181, 191
  American and British strategy, 145

Coleman, George, the Younger, *The Battle of Hexham* (1789) and *The Surrender of Calais* (1791), 112
Colombia, 161
Column of Victory, 107
　see also John, 1st Duke of Marlborough
Coming Home (1978), 158
Constantinople (capture 1453), 91
contemporary reporting and historians, 23–4
Coral Sea (1942), 16
Corso, Mazzini, 121
　see also Risorgimento
Corso Garibaldi, 121
　see also Risorgimento
Corunna, 110
　see also Dunkirk (1940)
　see also Moore, Sir John
Cossacks, 116
　see also Chyhyryn (Chigirin) (1677)
counterfactualism, 23
counterinsurgency, 52, 66, 178
coups and military history, 124
Courtrai (1302), 81
Coysevox, Antoine *Salon de la Guerre* (1686), 39–40
Counterstrike (video game), 59
Cowley, Robert, see End of History
Craftsman, the, and standing army, 103, 107
Crécy (1346), 69
creation accounts, *passim*
Crimea, 116, 176, 184
　Russian seizure, (2014), 56
　see also Putin, Vladimir
　see also Crimean War
Crimean War (1854–6), 30, 32, 111, 132, 138
Croatia, 147
Cromwell, Oliver, 34, 106
Crusade of 1444, 53–4
Coysevox, Antoine, *Salon de la Guerre*, 40
Cuba, 10, 127
　and Peace Park, 106, 191
Custer, George, 36
Culloden (1746), 38
Cumberland, Richard
　and *The Battle of Hastings* (1778), 112
cyber warfare, 56
Cyprus
　capture by Turkish forces, 187
　Greek and Turkish conflict, 189
Czechoslovakia, 54
　Peace Park, 191
　Communism, 193

Dalrymple, William (*The Anarchy*), 42
'Danger' in submarine warfare, 139–40
　see also Doyle, Arthur Conan
Danilov, Oleksiy, 176
　see also Ukraine
Danorum, 81
Danube, 92
Dardanelles campaign, 51–2
　see also Churchill, Sir Winston S
Days of Glory (film), 172
D–Day, 35, 148, 158
　and Ronald Reagan, 148
　and role of Allies, 149
David, Jaques–Louis
　Bonaparte Crossing the Great St Bernard Pass (1800), *The Distribution of the Eagle Standards* (1810), 110
de Rivera, Miguel Primo, 186
Delbrück, Hans, 115–6, 141–2
Delacroix, Eugène, (*The Death of Sardanapalus*), 58
Denmark, 119
desecration of defeated, 75
Dettingen, (1743), x, 38
digital photography, 32
different forms of warfare, 136–7
'Dirty War' (1976–82), 176
　see Argentina
divisions in the military, 47–9
Domville, Admiral Sir Compton, 139–40
Donkin, Major Robert, (*Military Collections and Remarks* (1777), 99
Doyle, Arthur Conan
　Brigadier Gerard, 109
　Rodney Stone (1896), 109
　Sherlock Holmes, 110
　Social Darwinism, 110, 118
　'Resident Patient', 111
　'The Blanched Soldier', 111
　'Murder by Proxy, 111
　The Sign of the Four (1890), 117
　The Tragedy of Korosoko, (1897) and *Fires of Fate* (1909) and film 1923, 118
　'Black Peter', 119
　A Study in Scarlet (1887), 119
　'The Green Flag#, 123
　'His Last Bow', The War Service of Sherlock Holmes' and existential struggle, *Strand Magazine*, and *The German War (*1914), 137–8
　'Danger', 'What the Experts Think' *Strand Magazine*, 137–9

The British Campaign in France and Flanders 1914, 139–40
and 'Danger' submarine warfare, 139–40
Dragomirov, Mikhail, General, 130, 137–8
Drake, Sir Francis, 110
drum and trumpet history, 162
Dunkirk (1940), 110
Dürer, Albrecht and Apocalypse, (1497–8), 86
Dyungars and Jao do 1696), 93

Eastern Roman Empire, 84, 99
East Africa, 2
East Germany, and Communist orthodoxy 1953, 193
East India Company, (EIC) 42, 91–2
Ecole Superieure de Guerre (acute on E), 130
see also Clausewitz, Carl von
Edgehill (1642), 34
Edward III (and Calais), 112
Egypt, 11, 45, 64, 118, 153
El Alamein (1942), 15–16
El Cid, 28
Edward the Black Prince, 77
El Desastre (1818) 127
Elizabeth II, 46
'End of History', 167–8
English Civil War (142–6, 1648), 16, 34
see also Civil Wars
environmental factors, 2–8
Ethandun (878), 31
Ethiopia, 39, 65, 156, 164
see also Mussolini
Erdogan, Recep Tayyip, 57, 92
Hagia Sophia, 86
military history
re-writing Turkish history, 191–2
see also Turkey
Eritrea, (and casualties), 152, 188
Estonia, 157
Eucherius Silber, 97
Eugene of Savoy (1663–36), 40–1
European transoceanic expansion, 89–90
European Union (EU), and Military history 165
European Wars of Religion (1559–1648), 57, 100
Everett, Edward, 126–7

'face of battle' approach, 88
failure and legacy in war, 127
Falklands War (1982), 105

Ferdinand of Aragon, 90
Fico, Robert, 154
fiction, film and war history, 116–18
Fielding, Henry, 106
film, social and war, 172
Finland, 155
Findlater, Piper George VC, and Expedition Force (1897–8), 36–7
firepower, defensive, 125–8
First Crusade (1097–9), 35, 75–6
and local populations, 85
First World War (1914–18), 1, 8, 15, 36, 44, 48, 50–1, 61, 63–4, 116, 126, 128, 132–3, 136–41, 143, 158, 164
Battle-field sites, 36
Allied blockade, 48
German defeat, 48
Nazi account, 49
preparedness, 51–2
fighting the last war, *passim*
battleships, 140
image of, 140
new offensive tactics, 141
propaganda, 143
Flavius, Vegetius (c.96–175), *De Re Militari*, 97
Flodden (1513), 93
Fontenoy (1745), 38
Forbes, Archibald, 122
see also Prior, Melton
see also Steevens, G W
Fornovo (1495), 3
Fort Mchenry (1814), 120
Foyles War (TV), (2020–5), 55
France, 90, 108, 142, 147
Resistance, 164
cooperation with Germany, 165
Vichy France, 147, 165, 173
Francesco Gonzaga, 93
Francis I, 93
Franco-Prussian War (1870–1), 122, 125
Francesco II, Gonzaga, 93
Franco-Prussian War (1870–1), 115–6, 125, 130, 132
Frederich, John, Elector of Saxony, 92
Frederick II the Great of Prussia, (r.1740–86), 38, 104, 106
French, Lieutenant General, Sir John, 174
French *Philosophes*, 18
French Revolutionary Wars (1793–1815), 37, 138
Frondes (civil war 1648–53), 39

Fuller, J F C, 3, 142
  and tanks, 142–3
  see also strategy

Gallipoli Association, 55
Galvao, Duart, *Chronicle of El–Rei D Alfonso Henriques*, 77
Garfield, James A, President (1831–1881), 61
Gas, 136
  Allied use of, 143
  see also Housten, Billie
Gaskell, Elizabeth, *Cranfield*, 61
geopolitics, 127–8
  see also Mackinder, Halford
George, Hereford Brooke
  and *Kriegspiel*, 129
George II, 38
George III, 34, 25, 37, 189
  see also American War of Independence (1775–83)
George IV, 37
Georgia, 154
  see also Putin, Vladimir
Gerald the Fearless, 28
Germany, 61–2, 114, 129–30, 183, 189
  and 'shortwar', 146
  Strategy, 1941–3 and 1917–18, 61
  see also *Blitzkrieg*
  see also First World War
  see also Second World War
Ghent siege (1678), 39
Gibbs, Robert, 30
Gibbon, Edward, 104–5, 127–8
Gibraltar, 84
Gilbert and Sullivan, *The Pirates of Penzance* and *The Modern Major General*, 115
Gimlet (1943–54), 61
Global South
  rise of, 43
global warfare, 141
gods, deities and intervention, 69–70
Goebbels, Joseph, 144
  rise of, 43
Gordon, General Sir Charles, 36, 110–11
Goya, Francisco de, *Disaster of War* (1810–20), 113–14
Goya, Louis de *Treatise of the Arms and Engineering and War Both Ancient and Modern* (1689), 100
Great Patriotic War, 144, 151, 166–7
  see also Putin, Vladimir
Grant, President, 61

Greece, 118, 150, 154, 160–1, 164
  see also Mussolini
Gregory of Tours (r.538–94), 23
'grey war', 178
Glieg, George, 111
Grozny, 178
Gulf War (1991), 105
Guillaume Du Chol, 97
gunpowder
  and armour, 87
  and weaponry, 87. 90
  and impact, 100
  see also China
  see also Islamic world
  see also Japan
Gustavus Adolphus King of Sweden (r.1611–32), 14, 92
  see also Thirty Years War

Hagia Sophia as mosque, 86
Hamilton, Adjutant General, Sir Ian, 125
  see also (Second) Boer War
Hamilton, Colonel Tucker, 190
  see also AI
Han dynasty, 77
Han Kuang–wuti (r. 25–57), 77
Hanley, Edward, 129–30
  see also British Staff College Sandhurst
  see also Clausewitz, Carl von
Hanson, Victor Davis, and civic preparation, 157
Hannabal, 8, 39, 43, 75
  and Second Punic War, 15
  and Scipio, 11
Harris, Robert, 55
Harrison, President, 61
Hart, Basil Liddell, 3
  see also theory and theorists
  see also strategy
Hašek, Jaroslav, *The Good Soldier Svejk* (1921–2), 54
Hattin (1187 CE), 171
Hayes, President, 61
Henry IV (1589–1610, 39
Henry V, 77
Henry V film, (1944), 144
Henry VIII, 93
Herodatus, 79
heroism in war, 109–10
  and in defeat, 58
Henty, George, Henry, *With Kitchener in the Soudan*, 122
  and Mahadi, 122

Herling, Baron von, 137
Hezbollah, 159
history of war, *passim*
  multiple forms, 194–5
  periodisation, 21
  sceptical introduction, 24
Hitler, Adolf, 47– 9, 144–7, 149, 163–4
  crisis of 1941, 15
  prejudice in strategy, 16
  and Armenian massacres, 26
  and defeat in First World War, 48
  propaganda, 49
  decision–making, 145
  war on America (1941), 145, 146
  short war strategy, 146
  Soviet Union, 146, 180
  imposition of will, 146
  and Mussolini, 164
  and Japan, 176
Hittite culture, 174
Holocaust, the, 152
  central to Second World War 153–4
Homer
  Trojan War, 69–70
  Odessey, 77, 81
Hospitallers, 11
  see also Christian Military Orders
Hume, David, 6–7
  see also theory and theorists
Hundred Years War, 144
Hungary, 41, 54, 193
Hussites and heresy, 72, 104
hybrid warfare, 175–6

Iberia, 82
  and Moors, 83
India, 55, 59, 70, 76, 128, 133
  North–West Frontier, 1, 36
  Purusha Suk the Hymn and Primevalman, 69
  Mutiny (1857–9), Indian Revolution, Indian War of Independence, 117
  see also Brown, Cecil, 118
  see also Doyle, Arthur Conan
Indian Ocean, 2
Industrial Revolution and military, 193
Inner Mongolia, 144
Iraq, 5, 67, 155, 161
  and American invasion, 5, 95, 178
Iran, 23, 73, 155, 158, 167, 180
  and religious war, 56–7
Israel, 3, 157, 180
  and children of, 70

Ireland, 115
  and Napoleon, 115
  see also 'Irish Troubles'
Irish Land War (1879–82), 129
Irish 'Troubles', 129
Islamic world, 108
Italian East Africa, 1
Italo-British War, 2
Italy, 2, 62, 121, 151
  Italian Wars, 87
  and Communism, 165
  and the Left, 121, 163–4
  and imperial rule, 164
  and Resistance, 164
Ivan IV the Terrible (d.1584), 9

Jacobi, Johann, 98
James II, 115
James IV (Scotland), 93
Jan Maudijn and *Temptation of St Anthony*, 29
Jao Modo (1696), 93
Japan, 130, 161
  past leaders, 11–12
  technology, 11–12
  castles, 35–6
  intervention in Korea, 93
  rulers as gods, 71
  Anglo–Japanese Naval Treaty, 128
  Japan and Russia War (1904–5, 130
  non–aggression pact with Soviet Union (1941), 146
  Shintoism, 147
  and Hitler, 149
  Korea and brutal conduct, 152
  and Holocaust, 152–3
  and enslavement, 152–3
  see also Hiroshima
  see also Pearl Harbor
Jefferson, Thomas, President 1801–9
  and English Civil Wars (1642–6 and 1648), 32
  militia forces, 103
Jena (battle), 33
Jesuits, 100–03
Jewish culture, 74
Jin, Emperor, 77
Joan of Arc (c. 141–31) and film, 144
  see also Hundred Years War
Johns, William Earl, 61
  see also children's fiction
Jomini, see also Hamley, Edward, The Th Operations of War Explained and Illustrated (1866), 129

Julus Caesar
    Hispania, 82–3
    Pax Julia, 82–3
    Iberia campaign, (45 BCE), 83
    Commentaries, 98
Just war and religion, 75
Jutland (1916), 63, 140

Kadesh (1274 BCE), 74
Kangxi, Emperor of China, 44
    see also China
Kanpur (1857), 17
    see also Indian Mutiny
Kao–tsung (c.1127–62), 77–8
Kapur, Siddharth Roy, 42
Kazan, 99, 100
    see also 'Eurasian Heartland'
Kennedy, John Fitzgerald, President 37
Kenya, 161
Kerr, Philip, 55
Kingsley, Charles (1819–75) historian and historic novels, *Westward Ho* (1855) and *Hereward the Wake* (1866), 31–2
Kolberg (1945) film, 144
Korea, 64, 93, 150
    see also Japan
    see also Korean War
Korean War (1950–3), 53, 151–2
Krepinevich, Andrew, *The Origins of Victory. How Disruptive Military Innovation Determines the Fate of Great Powers*, 183–4
Kuomintang, 150
Kurk (1943), 15

Latin America, 159
Lediard, Thomas, *Naval History of England* (1735), *Marlborough*, and *The Lives of the Admirals and Other Eminent British Seamen* (1742–4), 106
Lee, Robert E, 27–8
    American Civil War (1861–5)
Lepanto (1571), 92, 188
Liddell Hart, Basil, 3
    and *blitzkrieg* (1939–41)
    and Israel 1956, 1967
    see also strategy and theorists
Lincoln, Abraham, 126–7
Louis XI, 104
Louis XIII (r.1610–43), 38
Louis XIV (r.1643–1715), 38, 104
Louis XV, 38
Louis XVI (r.1774–92), 38

Ludendorff, Erich, 141
Lützen (1632), 14

Mackinder, Halford, 127–8
    Enlightenment 127
    'pivot' and Eurasia, 129
    see also Social Darwinism
Madagascar, 90, 189
Mallison, Alan, 163
Maltiempo (1895), 33
    (1644–1911), 114
    see also campaigns and culture of war
Manchuria, 126
Mao Zedong, 144, 150, 171
    'Third Front', 174
    1930s strategy, 177
    see also China
Maurice, John Frederick, *A Popular History of the Ashanti Campaign*, 112
Maurice of Nassau, 98
MacArthur, General Douglas, 50
MacCarthy, Captain, James, *Recollections of the Storming of the Castle of Badajos* (1836), and *Recollections of Rifleman Harris* (1861), 111
Macheewicz, Pawel, 166
Maclise, Daniel, and *Wellington and Blucher at Waterloo (1861), Death of Nelson* (1866), *Alfred the Great in Tent of Guthruyn (1852)*, 31
McKinley, President, 61
Mahdists, 118
    see also Omdurman
Maiwand (1880), 123
Malaga, 161
male bellicosity and battle, 13
Malta, Turkish invasion (1565), 86
Mamluks and Egypt, 14, 78, 152
Manley, 136
    see also Billie Houston
Mantegra, Andria, *Madonna della Vittoria* and *Triumph of Caesar*, 91
Marathon (490 BCE), 34, 126
Marie, de Medici, 39
Marlborough, 1st Duke, 106, 107
    and Column of Victory, 107
    see also Blenheim
MASH (Mobile Army Surgical Hospital), TV series 1972–83, 158
Mason, A E W, *The Four Feathers*, 122
mass enslavement, 151–2
mass expulsions, 151
May Day, 28

Mamluk Sultanate of Egypt, 35
Manchu, 171
Marx, Karl, 116
Maxwell, Robert, 142
Mediums, *passim*
Mehmed II, 85–6
   see also Lepanto (1571)
   see also Malta
Mecca, 78
Medina, 78
Mediums and military history, 25–43 *passim*
Melton, Prior, 122
memorialisation of war dead, 139
Mexican–American War (1846–8), 32, 49, 62
Mexico, 70, 117, 159
   and popular views, 2–3, 10
   military history and war, 47, 162
   see also New Spain (Mexico)
Middle East, 2
Midway (1942), 16
military heroes, 116
   and in print media, 111–12
military and policing, 7
military history, practical and popular, 2
'military revolution', 88–9
military–run states, 45
military service benefits, 153
military theory and revolutionary states, 10
Ming, 171
Minho, river, 82
mission creep, 180
Miriam Calin, 29–30
   see also rape as weapon of war
Mirren, Helen, *Eye in the Sky* (film 2015) and drone warfare, 43
Mhodi, Narendra, 57 check
MOD (Ministry of Defence), 53
Modestus, 97
modern industrial society and war, 22
Moltke von, 110, 130–1
Mong Khan (r. 2250–9), 73, 75
Monitor, the, and Punic Wars and Seven Years War (1756–63), 99
Mongols, 85
Moors
   and Spain and Portugal, 28–9
   defeat at Tours (1732 or 1733), 34
   Manuel I (r.1495–1521), 77
   and Iberia, 84
   Christain populations, 84–5
   Pad do Salado, 29
   see also Alfonso IV

Moore, Sir John, 110
   see also Corunna
Mons, siege, (1691), 39
Mons (1914), 35
Montgomery, Field Marshall, 3
morale and honour, 101
Morocco, 65, 74, 143
   and La Mamora, 74
   and Spanish alignment. 89–91
   and defeat at Tours, (732–3), 84
Monitor
   and Punic Wars, 99
Moyer, Mark, *Triumph Forsaken: The Vietnam War: 1956–1963*, 65
Mozambique, 90
Mughal Emperors, and Empire, 11, 57, 168
   and India, 93
   see also Afghans
   see also Marathas
   see also Persians
Muhammad II
   fall of Constantinople (1453), 85–6
multi–sphere activity, 91
Museum of the Second World War (Gdansk), 166
music celebratory, 32–3
Muslim expansion, 83–4
Musketeers, 87
Mussolini, Benito, 39, 149
   and fascism, 164–5
   and Communists, 165
   and re–valuation, 165
   and reputation, 165
Mughals, 103–104
Myanmar (Burma), 45, 90, 120, 136
   and military coups, 159

Nadir Shahar (Persia), 41
Nagasaki, 192
Namur (seige 1692), 39
Napier, William, 33, 62
   and *History of the War in the Peninsula* (1840), 111
   Observations of Illuminating Sir John Moore's Campaign (1832), 111
   The Conquest of Scinde (1844–6), 111
   History of Sir Charles Napier's Administration (1851), 111
Napoleonic Wars (1792–1815), 37, 62–3, 106, 111
Napoleon I (Bonaparte), 39, 62, 160, 120, 130–1
   and Egypt, 11

Napoleon III, 125, 130–1
Naras, Edward, and naval victories, 112–13
Nasser, Gamel Abdul, 26
   see also Six Days War (1967)
nationalism, 119, 1289
NATO, 2, 59, 154
   see also Ukraine
Nelson Horatio, 63, 110
Netherlands, the 113
Neto, Augustino, 189
Nevskii, Aleksandr, 144
Newbolt, Sir Henry, and *Admirals All (1897)* and *'Vitae Lampada'*, 50–1
New Cold War, 53, 175
New Guinea, 71 89
New Spain (Mexico), 189
Newtonian physics, *19*
Niger, 45
Nimitz, 50
Norse sagas, 81
Normandy (1944), 16
   see also D-Day
Nordlingen (1634), 39
non–Western cultures, 74
North Korea, 158, 167, 191
North Vietnam, 66
North Xiorgna, 55
   see also China

'Oh! What a Lovely War' (1969), 158
Official Histories, *passim*
Omdurman (1898), 122
   see also Kitchener
Operation Goodwood, 15
Ostrogoths, 59
Ottoman Empire, 24, 143
   and Mamluks, 14
Ottoman Turks, 85, 90–1, 152
   and Algiers, 90
   and Morocco, 90
Ourigue (1147), 77

Pacific War (1941–5)
   and army, navy and marines tensions, 53
Parker, Geoffrey, 168
   see also Ending of History
   see also 'Military Revolution
Palau de la Generalitat, 186
Panini, Giovani
   Alexander the Great at the Tomb of Achilles (c.1712–19), 10
Pakistan, 177
   and military identity, 159

periodisation, 20–1
Peter the Great (r.1697–1725), x
   Western methods, 18
   and critical view of the *Craftsman*, 104–5
   see also Banks, John
   see also Putin, Vladimir
Philadelphia, (battle 1776), 169
Philippines, 161
Philip II of Spain, 2
   and Spain's military history, 92–3
Philippines
   and insurrection, 161
pillaging the dead
   Waterloo (1815), 60
   see also Ukraine
'planning the last war;, 184–5
Plassey (1757), 168
Platonic essentialism, 171–2
Plain Dealer (1724), the, 105
Pollihur (1780), 168
Poltava (1709), 18
poplar buzz, *passim*
Popular Movement for the Liberation of Angola (PMLA), 189
Porter, Spring, *Fall of Seringapatam*, 113
Portugal, Portuguese, 83
   in Morocco, 89
   Spain and invasion, 92
Prigozhin, Yevgeny, 156
   see also Ukraine
   see also Wagner Group
Prokofiev, and *War and Peace*, 33
Provisional IRA, 4
Prussia, 91
   see also Delbruck, Hans, 115–6
   and Frederick II, the Great, 91
   and Seven Years War (1756–63), 13
Purusha, Sukta, *Hymn to Universal Man*, 69
Putin, Vladimir x, 166–7, 191
   and neo–Nazis, 8
   and Ukraine, 8
   and Wagner Group 8
   'Putin's children' 59
   mis–reading military history, 59
   Ukraine invasion (2022), defence, 59
   and 'Great Patriotic War', 166–7
   use of past from 2022, 154–6
   and 'civilisation' war, 154
   see also Ivan IV, the Terrible (d.1584)
   see also Peter the Great

Quianlong, Emperor of China (r.1736–96), 120

Radakin, Admiral Sir Tony, and new technology, 181
Radetsky, Major General (1756–1858), 62
Raglan, Lord, 63
  see also Crimean War
  see also Wellington, Arthur, Duke of
Rameses II, 73
rape as war crime, 30
  see also Ukraine and Buca
Reconquista, 35, 95
  see also Spain
Re-fighting the last war, 60–8
Reformation, the, and Old Testament models of war, 194
Reiters (armoured cavalry, 96
religious war as normative, 72–86
Renaissance and Classical warfare, 104
Revolution in military affairs, 154, 160
Resistance, 164
  see also Catholic Church, China, France, Greece, Poland
Revolutionary Guards, 176
  see also Iran
Rhine as contested crossing (1672), 39
Richards Jacob, and conflict reporting, 41
Richelieu, Cardinal, 39
Rituals of war, 71–6
Risorgimento, 122
  see also Italy
Robens, Peter Paul, *The Triumph of Henry IV* (1630), 39
Robertson, George and Kosova conflict, 187–8
  see also Kosova
  see also NATO
Robertson, William and *History of the Reign of Emperor Charles V with a View of the Progress of Society in Europe from the Subversion of the Roman Empire to the Beginning of the Sixteenth Century* (1769), 87
Roderic, Visigoth, 83–4
Roman Empire, 24
  Expansion, 81–4
Rouen siege (1418–19), 77
  see also Henry V
Royal Canadian Mounted Police, 169
Royal Commision 1916–17, 51–2
  see also Churchill, Winston S
  see also Dardanelles
Royal Engineers, 116
rulers as war leaders, 4–6, 37–41
Russia, 61–2, 64, 1–5, 117, 128, 179, 184

Russian National Party, 30
Russo–Japanese War (104–05), 125–6
Russian Civil War (1919–22), 140, 143
  see also Soviet Union, USSR
Russo–Polish conflict (1654–7) 116
  see also Poland
Russell, Howard, 30
  see also Crimean War (1854–6)

Sadam Hussein, 150
Sadowa, (1866), 129
Safavid Persia (Iran), 152
Saint Andrew, 35
Saint Denis (battle 1567), 97
Saint George, 35
Saint James 'Moor-Slayer', 35
Salamis (480 BCE), 86
Saldanha, Duke of, 124
Salò Republic, 165
Sanders, General Sir Patrick, and Defence Academy, 163
Sarah, Duchess of Marlborough, 107
  see also, Marlborough, John 1st Duke
Saratoga, (1777), 120
Saxo Grammatcus, *Gesta Danorum*, 81
Second Afghan War, (1878–80), 50
Second Punic War, (1218–201 BCE), 81
Second World War (1939–45), *passim*
  geopolitics, 50, 61, 67
  American reading of Allies' war, 49–50
  gods, 71
  German strategy failure 1941–3, 61
  Cold War, 145
  Christain religion, 147
  Egypt and Libya, 149
  German–Soviet alliance, 151
  China, 150–1
  civil war, counterinsurgency and Resistance, 150, 172
  American reading of Allies' war, 49–50
  mass enslavement, 151–2
  film and social media, 172
Schlieffen, Alfred von, 8
Schlüter, Andreas, 40 (umlout on u)
Scott, Winfield, 49
seiges, significance of, 39–40
Serbia, Serbs, 9
Seven Years War (1756–63), 100, 103–4
shadow of war, 61
Shakespeare, William, and *Hamlet* as war commander, 38
Shelley, Percy Bysshe, *Ozymandias* (1818), critic of war history, 73

Sheridan, Richard, 'The Critic' 1779), 112
Sikh cavalry, 165
Sioux, 129
Six Days War (1967), 26
Skipio Africanus, 11
Slovakia, 147
Smithsonian National Air ad Space Museum
   and atomic bombing, 146
Smolensk (siege 1654), 38
Smollett, Tobias
   Roderick Random (1748), ix
   and naval strategy, ix, 100
   see also Actium (31BCE)
   see also Dettingen (1743)
Social Darwinism, 116
Solferino, (battle), 73
Solomon Islands, 71
Somme (1916), 15–16
South-East Asia, 123
South Vietnam, 65
Soult (1769–1851), 62
Soviet Empire and Central Asia, 153
   see also USSR
Soviet–German Alliance (1939–41), 151
Spain, 4, 67, 81, 84, 95, 118, 123, 127, 150, 157, 186
   and Napoleon, 63
   and Roman conquest, 83
   and Ottoman Empire, 95
Spanish–American War, 61
Spanish Civil War (1936–9), 12, 36, 62, 145
Spanish Habsburgs, 121
Spitfire, 186
Spraul, Gunter, 143
staff rides, 22–3
St Denis (battle 1676), 40
Stone, Norman, 17
Stalin, Josef, 61, 164
Stalingrad (1942), 67, 178
   and forced labour, 151
   and control of military, 179
statue memorials, 27–9
Stevens, G W, 122
Steeley, (1936–9) and children's novels, 61
Stosch, Albrecht, von, 119
South Korea, 157
   and Military Academy, 157
Soviet Union (USSR), 5, 10, 66, 91, 149, 151, 180
   and Japan, 146
   and Peace Park, 191
   and bloc, 28
   see also Stalin Joseph

strategy, 2–3
   see also Clausewitz, Carl, von
   see also Fuller, J F C
   see also Liddell Hart, Basil
Sudan, 145, 136
   and Military *coups*, 159
   and Mahdists, 118
   see also Churchill, Winston S
Suleiman, the Magnificent (r.1520–66), 92
Susa (capture 653 BCE), 73
Sweden, 157
Switzerland, 157
   see also Conscription
Syria, 155
   and Assad regime, 161

Tagus river, 82
Taiwan, 33, 154, 175
Tamu (1449), 87
Tang, 171
Tangier, 91
Tannenberg (1914), 8
Taylor, Zachary, 49
Technology and transformation, 21–2
   see also America
Tell Kushaf (750), 60
Templers, 101
   see also Christian Military Orders
Temple of Mars Ultov, (2 BCE), 11
Texas, 164
Thailand, 90
The Thin Red Line (1881), 30
   see also Gibbs, Robert
Thermopylae (480 BCE), 35, 185
Third Punic War (149–146 BCE), 82
Thirty Years War (1618–48), 14, 117–18, 121
Thucydides, *History of Peloponnesian War (*1460–1425 BCE*)*, 79–81, 126
Tiananmen Square rising (1989), 189
Tilly, Charles, 12
Timur, (d.1405), 10–11
Timbuktu, 91
Timur, 85, 106
Tirah Expedition Force, 36
Tolbiac (446), 31
Tolkien, J R R, *The Lord of the Rings* (1954–5), 191
Tolstoy. Leo and *War and Peace* (1865–9), 60–1
Trafalgar (1805), 109
   and Trafalgar Square, 33
Tsar Nicholas II, 'army of honour' 142
Trajan Emperor, 11

Trincomalee (port Ceylon/Sri Lanka), 23
Tripartite, Pact (1940), 128
Trooping the Colour, 46
Trotsky, Leon, 167
Truman, President, Harry, 37
Trump, President, 4, 71
   and capital riot, 178–9
Tsar Alexis, 38
Tsushima (1905), 140
Tuoba (clan), 55
   see also China
Turkey, Turks, 9, 54, 151
   and military *coup*, 179
   see also Ottomans and Ottoman Empire
Turin (1706), 40
Turner, General Sir Henry, 115
Turnhout, (1597), 98

Uffington White Horse, 31
Ukraine war (2022), 23, 37, 41–2, 59, 136, 148, 154, 175
   combatant views, 26
   Bucha (2022), 30
   photographs and film, 37
   Russian reporting, 41–2
   NATO, 59
   video games, 59
   miss–reading of military history, 59, 154
   initial Russian failure, 67
   technology, tanks and drones, 67
   heavy losses, 95
   debates and media, 136–52
   and Bakht (2023), 138
   isolation and Reagan, Ronald, 148
   Russo–Ukraine War, 155
   invasion, 151, 157
   Bakhmut, 156
   historical terms, (Putin, Vladimir), 154
   Western backing, 174
   Olesiy, Danilov, and Ukraine independence, 176
   'hidden hand of history, 177
   Russian failure, 177
   failure of Russian attack, 176–7
   Marpol (2022), 178
   Russian invasion, 187
   Communism, 193
   see also Putin, Vladimir
   see also Wagner group
UNITA, National Union for the Total Independence of Angola, 89
   see also Angola

United Provinces, 98
   see also the Netherlands
Umayyads, 2

Varangian Guard, 67
Verdun (1916), 15–16, 178
Victor, Amadeus III (r.1675–1730), 40
   see also Turin (1706)
Vichy France, 147
video games, 59
Vietcong, 66
Viriathus (147–139 BCE), 82
Vietnam war, 5, 24, 65, 66, 163, 170–1
   and deference decline, 158
Visigoths, 83
visual images, 33
Voina (Slavic city), 59

Wagner group, 8, 156
   see also Prigozin, Yevgeny
Wagram (battle) 33
Walpole, Sir Robert, 107, 108
war and media, 137–44
War and Society, in academe, 162–3
War theory and history, 2–24
   see also Clausewitz, Carl von
   see also Fuller, J F C
   see also Hart, Basil Liddell
   see also Hume, David
War of the Austrian Succession, (1740–8), 106–7
War of the Pacific (1870–83), 164
War of the Spanish Succession, (1702–13), 106–7
'War on Terror', 53, 175, 184
warfare on stage and screen, 137–40
   see also Doyle, Arthur Conan
Wars and environment, 53
Wars of Religion (1559–1648), 175
Wars and society, 'Cultural Turn', 16–17
Waterloo (1815), 33, 63, 113. 115
Washington, George, 37
Watson, John, 123
   see also Maiwand (1880)
Wehrmacht, 47
Wei dynasty (439–534), 55
   see also China
Wellington, Arthur, Duke of, 62, 111–13
   Waterloo (film 1970)), 33
   Wellington's victory (Beethoven), 33
Waterloo (1815), 63
   legacy, 63
Wells, H G and *War of the Worlds* (1898), 116

Wen-ti (r. 180–157 BCE), 78
West, Benjamin, 30–1, 37
Westbury White Horse, 31
Western capitalism and conflict, 74–5
Westminster Jornal, 106–7
Westphalia, Peace of (1648), 104
Westward Ho, Charles Kingsley, 32
Winter War (1939–40), 144
Willam III of Orange, conquest of England, (1679), 40, 41, 104, 106, 115
   see also Boyne (1690)
Wilhelm II Emperor, 125
William, Duke of Cumberland, 38
Wolfe, Charles 110
   see also Moore, Sir John
Wolseley, Major General Sir Garnet, 112
   see also Ashanti campaign
women in war, and treatment, 43, 152
   see also Mirren, Helen
world wars reporting, 137–40
   see also Doyle, Arthur Conan
Württemberg, 114

Xenophon, 80
Xinjiang, 120

Yugoslavia, 150, 164
   see also Mussolini

Zama (202 BCE), 15
Zeitgeist and War history, 47
Zelensky, President
   at G7 summit and Hiroshima and Bakhmut, 148
   see also Ukraine
Zenobia (Queen), 58
Zhu Hai, 31
Zi Jinping, and global leadership, 150–1, 171
Zumalacárregui, Tomás, 62

Dear Reader,

We hope you have enjoyed this book, but why not share your views on social media? You can also follow our pages to see more about our other products: facebook.com/penandswordbooks or follow us on Twitter @penswordbooks

You can also view our products at www.pen-and-sword.co.uk (UK and ROW) or www.penandswordbooks.com (North America).

To keep up to date with our latest releases and online catalogues, please sign up to our newsletter at: www.pen-and-sword.co.uk/newsletter

If you would like a printed catalogue with our latest books, then please email: enquiries@pen-and-sword.co.uk or telephone: 01226 734555 (UK and ROW) or email: uspen-and-sword@casematepublishers.com or telephone: (610) 853-9131 (North America).

We respect your privacy and we will only use personal information to send you information about our products.

Thank you!